14.95

W9-BSX-940

ETHICS
AND
LIBERATION

ETHICS
AND
LIBERATION

An Introduction

Charles L. Kammer III

ORBIS BOOKS

Maryknoll, New York 10545

The Catholic Foreign Mission Society of America (Maryknoll) recruits and trains people for overseas missionary service. Through Orbis Books Maryknoll aims to foster the international dialogue that is essential to mission. The books published, however, reflect the opinions of their authors and are not meant to represent the official position of the society.

Bible quotations are from the *Revised Standard Version*. Some quotations have been adapted using inclusive language by the author.

Manuscript editor and indexer: William E. Jerman

LIBRARY OF CONGRESS
Library of Congress Cataloging-in-Publication Data

Kammer, Charles L.
    Ethics and liberation: an introduction / Charles L. Kammer III.
      p. cm.
    Bibliography: p.
    Includes index.
    ISBN 0-88344-608-1 (pbk.)
    1. Christian ethics.   2. Liberation theology.   I. Title.
BJ1251.K247   1988
241—dc19   87-34889
                                       CIP

To my children,
Nicole, Alec, Mark, and Carly,
and to all who work for justice
with a child's faith

CONTENTS

ACKNOWLEDGMENTS

Every book is a conversation, a product of many persons and of many human interactions. In this work I have tried to give voice to the concerns and experiences of the many persons who have enriched my life. Some of these conversations extend far into the past and include members of the Edgemont Community in Durham, North Carolina, and members of Trinity Lutheran Church, McKean, Pennsylvania. They also include the students who for years have continued to challenge my perspectives and have kept me from becoming complacent. This book also evidences a series of ongoing academic conversations with persons who are recognized throughout these pages.

In addition, I want to thank several persons who provided professional help and support for the project. These include Beverly Harrison, Susan Lindley, and Karen Warren, all of whom read early forms of the manuscript and made suggestions. My thanks also go to Dorothy Bolton, Kennedy Lemke, and Al Heigl, who helped with manuscript preparation, and William Jerman whose work as copy editor improved the stylistic quality of the manuscript. Special thanks as well to Charles Martin and the rest of the Orbis community whose style of work and communication exhibit the deep commitments and sensitivity that have become the hallmarks of Orbis Books. I want to acknowledge as well Kim Aakre and Andy Kelley, whose friendship and support have been invaluable to both myself and my family; and my parents, Charles and Pearl Kammer who, early on, provided me with an environment in which to grow and develop.

Finally, a word of thanks and love to my wife, Linda, who has been a partner in all that I do. Through her eyes she has helped me to see the beauty and magic in life's small gifts. This vision has been sustaining in a world where there is often too little beauty and little reason for hope.

INTRODUCTION

This work is a product of ten years of teaching ethics to undergraduates and of a much longer attempt to relate Christian ethics to the sensibilities and problems of our age. As such, the work shows a number of influences and concerns. At one level, it is an attempt to produce a didactic text that reflects my inability to discover an introductory text for Christian ethics that meets my needs. There are a number of excellent works that relate Christian ethics to particular contemporary issues. There are also good specialized works and short essays that deal with the task and distinctiveness of Christian ethics. What I have been unable to find is a suitable text that deals with the task of ethics and the distinctive elements of Christian ethics in an introductory fashion. This work attempts to do both. Chapter 1 is an attempt to present the task of ethics; chapters 2 and 3 present the distinctive characteristics of Christian ethics.

The introductory nature of the work means that I have consciously tried to avoid, where possible, technical language and have often, for purposes of clarity, oversimplified some important issues and debates. I have tried to compensate somewhat for this shortcoming by providing extensive footnoting to indicate sources the reader might use to get a fuller discussion of the point in question. It also allows the reader to identify the sources that have informed my own views and positions.

Even a cursory reading of the work will make it clear that it is not intended to be either a history of Christian ethics (although it does make use of historical materials) or a typology of Christian ethics (although it does present many "types" of Christian ethics). The work has a very distinct point of view and this has been consciously developed. In working with students, one of the most frequently asked questions is, "How does someone do Christian ethics?" The question usually represents a search by students to find models for their own lives. I have tried here to present a model, not in the belief that it is the only, or necessarily the best model, but in the belief that we often discover what we believe in the encounter with others' thoughts and ideas. I have tried to use a style of writing that indicates that the model is my own and is the product of my own struggle to live responsibly. At the same time, it should become clear that there are many who share a model similar to my own. I hope this style will encourage others to develop their own models of Christian responsibility.

The point of view represented in the work reflects my conviction that socially and religiously we are at a critical juncture. A host of new, and newly discovered, issues and problems, coupled with a radically altered modern consciousness, have called into question many traditional Christian beliefs and responses. For many of my students, and for myself, many of the traditional answers and approaches are no longer compelling. Yet, there is still something powerful and profound about the Christian tradition, which provides important resources in responding to the modern world and consciousness. It is a world in crisis, a world that demands immediate change and reformation if we are to end the unbearable suffering of the majority of humankind and assure our own survival.

As a response to our current situation, the various liberation theologies, I am convinced, have raised important questions concerning our traditional ways of doing Christian ethics and offer some helpful responses. The issues raised involve the style, theological presuppositions, and methodology of traditional Christian ethics.

This work, then, is an introduction to Christian ethics that attempts to show how we might understand it if we take seriously the concerns raised by liberation theologies. This concern is most evident in chapter 6 where I take seriously liberationist criticisms of traditional models of moral development, and in chapter 8 where I present a liberationist response to the limits of Christian realism. This viewpoint, however, informs the whole of this book in many ways. It is already evident in the first chapter, in the definition of the task of ethics as our attempt to discover what we should be and become both as individuals and societies. The influence remains present throughout the work. It determines my use of nonsexist and nonracist language and images, for most traditional texts use language and symbols that are, in themselves, oppressive.

A liberationist perspective is also apparent in the issues I have chosen to illustrate ideas and concepts in my work. Most traditional texts use examples drawn from sexuality and personal life, or more recently from bioethics or business. All of these are important issues and need to be addressed. However, the usual absence of examples drawn from the experiences of racial, sexual, and economic oppression leave the suggestion that these are less important issues. I have tried to use such examples throughout even though it gives the work a much more controversial tone.

Liberation theology has also shaped many of the theological presumptions of this work. This should be evident throughout. God is presented as historically active and as being especially concerned for the poor and oppressed. God is also viewed as being fundamentally concerned with the transformation of social structures. Similarly, an emphasis is placed on the historical Jesus and the radical nature of the kingdom he proclaims. I have directly addressed the way in which traditional images of Jesus reinforce racist and sexist ideologies, and why we need new (rediscovered) images. Finally, despite the inescapably sinful aspects of human nature, an emphasis is placed on human freedom and our role in creating and transforming history. Consistent with the views of liberation theology, persons are understood as fundamentally social beings inescapably shaped by their communities but ultimately finding their fulfillment in the creation of the good society.[1]

Lastly, the concerns of liberation theology have helped to shape the ethical methodology of this work in a number of ways. First, as Beverly Harrison has shown, liberation theology transcends the debate between proponents of deontological and teleological forms of ethics.[2] A liberationist perspective also allows one to take seriously the concerns of an "ethics of character" and yet escape its massive shortcomings. As chapters 4 and 5 illustrate, the most responsible ethic combines elements from all these approaches and tries to maintain a creative tension among the various concerns each expresses. Each can check the excesses and limitations of the other. A second methodological influence is shown in the heavy reliance on experience and not simply on abstract reason. This is consistent with the liberationist emphasis on "praxis," and honestly acknowledges the embodied nature of our ideas and existence. We are shaped by our experiences and emotions, and both bring moral insights that are often hidden from abstract reason. Again, a creative tension between reason and experience seems the best guarantor of moral responsibility.

Other obvious influences from liberation theology include a heavy use of the social sciences and the attempt to describe various "historical projects."[3] Responsible action requires a clear understanding of the social forces that shape us and a careful projection of the consequences of alternative courses of action. Neither is possible without the use of social sciences. On the other hand, inasmuch as the task of ethics includes personal and social transformation, an important task for ethics is the sketching of tentative visions of the good person and the good society (historical projects). All our actions presume some vision of an end. Ethics must be concerned with providing appropriate, responsible visions of those ends, but must do so in open, nonideological ways. Most important, as the above indicates, the final concerns of ethics are not a clear description of the good or of appropriate principles of human action. The goal is human action, the motivation of persons to transform themselves and their societies in accordance with those visions and principles.

Despite the dependence on liberationist thought, my work draws heavily on the work of many others as well. Liberation theology is clearly a development of the Christian tradition and has deep roots in it. Its newness is more a matter of the insights it chooses to emphasize. This dependence on a host of others should be evident in the heavy use of historical and biblical materials. It is perhaps most clear in the extensive use of the work and ideas of Paul Tillich and H. Richard Niebuhr. Both of them struggled in their timeframe with many of the concerns that now occupy liberation theologians. This is especially true in their struggle to acknowledge and represent the historical, social nature of our existence and yet provide a stable framework for ethical reflection and moral action. Liberation theologians have sometimes been limited, for good and obvious reasons, in the issues to which they address themselves. The possibilities of nuclear war or concern for the environment have sometimes been overlooked.[4] Both issues are critical, however, and both raise serious questions about traditional forms and styles of Christian ethics. Concerns about both issues have shaped this work and, as the work shows, both can be addressed creatively from a liberationist perspective.

A last concern of the work is to be responsive to the pluralistic nature of the world in which we live. There are hundreds of moral frameworks that a person might adopt. What we can no longer claim is the absolute superiority of any one of these positions. Certainly we can and must conclude, given what we know about ourselves and our current situation, that some frameworks are better than others; some may be completely unacceptable. Still, we do not have the wisdom to proclaim the absolute superiority of any particular view. Additionally, the world can no longer afford the intolerance, bigotry, and often persecution that such a claim so regularly creates. Rather, we must recognize that we are involved in a corporate undertaking, sharing alternative visions of what we should be and become. We must learn to talk to one another and to share our insights. We must work toward a common future that provides us with the possibility of respecting each other's humanity while preserving the possibility of difference and disagreement. Liberation theology should be open to such a stance: it proclaims the relative, socially conditioned nature of all thought and action. Likewise, the traditional Christian emphasis on human finitude and human sinfulness should allow us to recognize the partial nature of our claims. Similarly, the Christian recognition of the fundamental worth of all persons should make us reluctant to lightly dismiss the possible wisdom that others might bring. If nothing else, the practical observation that Christian nations, institutions, and persons have often been guilty of the most brutal acts and that non-Christians have often proved to be very loving and humane, should remind us that no person or group has a monopoly on either sinfulness or virtue.

This work, then, attempts to reflect the belief that Christianity has much to offer us as individuals and societies as we seek to act responsibly in a pain-filled, threatened world. At the same time, we, as Christians, can learn much from the experiences, wisdom, and struggles of others who are also trying to create a powerful, compelling vision of a shared world and act together to help create it.

1

ETHICS AS A
HUMAN ENTERPRISE

To say that we are moral beings is to say that we are human—for it is precisely the fact that we are moral beings that defines our "humanness." As William E. May observes: "A human being is an animal, but an animal 'with a difference.' This difference can be explained in different ways, but one major and critically important way of putting this difference is to say that man, and man alone of all animals, is a moral being."[1] Unlike other beings with which we are acquainted, we are fundamentally incomplete. We lack many of the instinctive responses of other beings and so, rather than simply adapting ourselves to the existing environment, we have the power to modify both the environment and ourselves in significant ways. In the words of Peter Berger:

> By contrast [to animals], man's instinctual structure at birth is both underspecialized and undirected towards a species-specific environment. There is no man-world in the above sense. Man's world is imperfectly programmed by his own constitution. It is an open world. That is, it is a world that must be fashioned by man's own activity.[2]

But in fashioning our world, we also fashion our own personhood. The institutions and ideologies we form return to shape us. Unlike other beings, we have an important role in determining our own nature. Granted, the biological, psychological, spiritual, and historical contexts within which we operate place important constraints upon the ability of individuals to determine their own character. Nevertheless, we create ourselves and our world in a way that no other known being does.

This self-creation, then, is the essence of morality. We can make decisions about our own nature, what we are and what we will become. Morality is thus the embodying of particular values and options in ourselves and in our communities. Granted, not all our values and options are directly moral (e.g., health, wealth, beauty, control of the environment); still all these values and options, to the extent that they determine the shape of our humanity, have moral effects. Daniel Maguire offers the following helpful definition of moral values and their relationship to other values:

> Moral values are more basic than all other values, because moral values touch, not just on what we do or experience or have, but on what we "are." It is admittedly unfortunate if a person is not gifted with the values of wealth, gracefulness, beauty, education, and aesthetic sophistication. But it is a qualitative leap beyond the merely unfortunate if a person is a murderer, a liar, or a thief. Here the failure is at the level of what a person is and has to be as a person.[3]

According to the above understanding of morality, we are all, inescapably, moral persons. We must all choose, and choose continually, what we are and what we will do. Collectively as well, we choose what we will be as societies and communities, and how we will respond and act as groups of actors. We are the ongoing embodiment of our choices and values. It is interesting, however, as Smith and Hodges note, that, "in practice most of us are not aware of our choice to turn here or there, but the choice is presupposed by and reflected in every decision we make."[4]

We are, in effect, unaware of most of what we value and of the consequences of our decisions for our individual and collective personhood. Society, family, friends, social organizations, schools, have all provided us with images of what we should be and how we should act. As such, the moral environment in which we operate is often as invisible as the air we breathe. This fact means that a distinction between personal and social morality is not very helpful and is, in fact, misleading. The seemingly most private and personal acts are greatly influenced by social training and norms. We tend to respect monogamy, hard work, and obedience to laws because we have been socialized to see such activities as virtuous. Likewise our attitudes toward permissible premarital sexual activity, the use of alcohol and drugs, and the value of education are products of social training.

In addition, the seemingly most private acts affect the shape of the society in which we live. Hundreds of thousands of affluent white parents decided, individually, to move to the suburbs or to place their children in exclusive private schools in order to assure a better education for them. The cumulative effect of these "private" acts was to create schools that were racially and economically segregated, and to divert a source of tax revenues away from inner-city public schools, with the result that education declined there.

Our moral lives, then, are all of a piece. Although there are some areas of our lives where we have more freedom to act unilaterally than in others, still, all morality is social morality, largely determined by the communities of which we are a part, and all our acts are social acts affecting the communities to which we belong. That social influences on our behavior obscure the fact that we choose to be what we are does not mean that we have ceased to be moral beings. Simply to conform to society's standards, to learn what others would have us learn, to value what society would have us value, is de facto to choose to be a particular person, and to support a particular community. There is no way to escape choosing. Even in acquiescing we bear the responsibility for our character and the nature of our communities.

To reiterate, to be human is to be moral. It is impossible to be fundamentally amoral, uncommitted. With each action, we form our own personhood; and in the communities we support and create, the institutions we form and the cultures we develop, we help to determine the personhood of others; and vice versa.

By now it should be clear that the question of morals and morality concerns much more than simply what I should do in a particular circumstance or in relation to a particular context. Each individual response is related to the broader process of self- and community-formation. The fundamental moral questions are the questions of what we ought to be as persons and what we ought to be as communities. The specific questions of how to respond to particular issues are always asked in the context of these two broader questions.

As we have also seen, the two fundamental moral questions about the shape of our personhood and the shape of our communities cannot be separated. The question of what I ought to be cannot be separated from the question of what kind of communities I want to live in and support, because our communities will largely determine the shape of our personhood. I may decide that I ought to be a loving, peaceful, just person who does not impose unnecessary burdens upon others, but discover that to be a member of my society requires payment of taxes used to build military weaponry and support military repression in other countries; that my daily work fosters an economic system that leaves many unnecessarily impoverished. I sit down to eat and discover that the meat and vegetables on my table have been imported from a Third World nation where malnutrition is rampant, but the structure of the international capitalist economy makes it more profitable to export food to the affluent, already overweight peoples of the First World, rather than to use the food to feed the hungry of a Third World nation. At another level, I discover that, try as I might, I cannot escape my society's competitiveness, the drive for success, its sexist, racist, class-biased attitudes. I discover that I cannot become what I know I ought to be without fundamentally transforming the society in which I live.

Although it is impossible to be fundamentally amoral, it is possible to be immoral. But what does it mean to say something or someone is immoral? All too often it simply means that a person does not live according to our standards or that an action does not jibe with our conception of how a person or group should have acted. "Communism is immoral" usually means that it does not conform to our idea of what an economic system should be. "Abortion is wrong" often means that it is something I would not do. In a more fundamental sense, however, the word "immoral" has to do with the improper shaping of our humanity. The immoral is that which "does not befit persons as persons."[5] This, of course, assumes that we have some notion of what befits persons as persons. But how do we decide what befits persons? How do we free ourselves from our entrapment in socially imposed norms and standards? How do we decide what is moral and what is not? These are the tasks of ethics.

Before beginning a discussion of ethics, however, I want to reemphasize several elements from the discussion of morality, for these elements will shape much of the discussion that follows. First, morality is not so much a matter of what we do but rather of what we are. As Richard McCormick recognizes, "moral theology concerns itself with both character formation and decision-making. Perhaps attention has fallen somewhat one-sidedly on the latter to the neglect of the former."[6] These two aspects of morality are, of course, dialectically related. What we do both reflects and influences who we are. Secondly, morality is not just a question of what persons do and are; it is also a matter of what communities do and are, for communities are the matrix in which persons are formed. Again, however, the relationship is dialectical: persons are both formed by and form their communities. Thirdly, although we cannot separate persons from the communities in which they are formed, nevertheless the plurality of communities to which persons now belong gives them a degree of independence over against any particular community. This means that morality is more a matter of community formation than of discovering proper rules and moral guidelines.

Stanley Hauerwas offers a good summary statement of the conception of morality that I have been trying to portray when he states:[7]

> Communities teach us what kind of intentions are appropriate if we are to be the kind of person appropriate to living among these people. Thus questions of what we ought to be are necessary background for questions of what we ought to do. The concentration on obligations and rules as morally primary ignores the fact that action descriptions gain their intelligibility from the role they play in a community's history and therefore for individuals in that community.[8]

Finally, our morality is both cognitive (rational) and emotive (emotional). It is a matter of moral feelings and intuitions as well as rational standards, a matter of personal experience as well as reasonable reflection.

THE TASK OF ETHICS

Arthur J. Dyck offers the following helpful definition of ethics: "In a very general way, ethics can be defined as systematic reflection upon human actions, institutions, and character."[9] Here Dyck points to the three central ethical questions that I isolated in the first section. The three questions emerge as: (1) What should I (we) do in particular circumstances? (2) How should we shape our communities (institutions)? (3) What should we be as persons (character)? As Dyck indicates, ethics is systematic reflection upon these questions. It is the attempt to be self-conscious, aware, of what we are about and what we value. Ethics also includes the self-reflection that allows us to recognize and evaluate the forces that have led us to answer moral questions as we do. In most traditional understandings of ethics, such reflection is concerned primarily with identifying the norms and values that should inform our answers to moral questions and so control our behavior. Such a task, as Dyck himself realizes, is only part of the task of ethics. Self-conscious reflection is much broader than this traditional understanding would allow. As I view ethics, such reflection has multiple tasks and moves through stages, stages that may occur simultaneously or even in reverse order, but nevertheless are distinct stages, and so distinct functions, of ethical reflection.

First, ethics has a descriptive function. It provides, as nearly as possible, an objective cataloguing of personal and social behavior. If morality concerns who we are, we need first to get reasonable descriptions of the "who" that "we are." Interestingly, we are often unaware of this basic dimension of ourselves. We do not easily recognize the competitive, self-centered, destructive aspects of ourselves. We easily rationalize our own behavior by making it seem much more altruistic than it really is. Nevertheless, self-conscious reflection upon our de facto behavior may allow us to break through such rationalization. The 1960s in the United States were disturbing years for many persons who reflected upon our corporate actions.[10] We discovered that our social policies did not reflect a real belief in the equality of persons. In Vietnam we discovered that the motives of our foreign policy were often base and self-interested.[11] The discovery of the "other America"[12] of the poor showed that we were a hardhearted, vindictive people. Such insights are painful; such self-scrutiny is difficult. It is little wonder that many in our society turned their backs on these basic insights about our corporate personhood. Nevertheless, no change is possible, no further ethical reflection is useful, if we refuse to engage in the descriptive aspect of ethical reflection.

Secondly, ethics has a critical function. At this level it judges our behavior according to some set of pronounced norms and values and also begins to investigate the consistency and adequacy of the set of norms and values we are employing. So, we might begin by declaring that racial segregation is immoral because it conflicts with our constitutional belief that all persons are equal. The failure of husbands to regularly cook dinner, do dishes and laundry, change diapers, and assume an equal share of child care, is seen as inconsistent with the claim that marriage is a partnership of equals. Initially, then, ethics serves as a prod to get us to conform our behavior to the norms and standards we profess.

However, because we as persons and societies value many things, ethics must go on to reflect upon the consistency in the multiplicity of values we hold and norms we profess. Here we may discover that certain values and norms are simply inconsistent with other norms and values. To choose one set is to choose against another set. We believe in the absolute right of private property, which allows persons to do whatever they wish with what they own. On the other hand, we believe in the equality of all persons. Can a person who owns a restaurant, a motel, a private school, refuse service to others because of their race, sex, or religion? Ethics thus tries to probe the compatibility of various norms and values. It tries to provide a personal and social consistency so that we do not work at cross-purposes with ourselves and one another. We value wealth, power, prestige, but we also want to be kind, loving, just persons. Are these values even remotely compatible? If so, how? As a nation we are concerned about increasing our own GNP and standard of living, but also claim to be concerned about respecting the human rights of others. Can the two concerns be combined? At this level, however, ethical reflection still does not free us from our socially acquired morality. It only provides us with insights into our behavior and tries to sort out inconsistencies in our socially derived morality.

Ethics must perform at least one more critical function if it is to free us from our socially derived morality and give us the freedom to determine for ourselves what kind of persons we would like to be and the kinds of communities in which we want to live. Ethics must reflect upon the adequacy of the values we hold as persons and communities. It may do this in several ways. One way is to compare our actual norms and values with some alternative set of norms and values. We can compare our norms with a set of religious or classic norms. In this way we can better see that there are various options and so be free to choose standards other than those that have been socially imposed. Such a choice, of course, is a choice to be something other than what our society claims we should be, and is to make a statement that it is our intention to make our society into something different from what it currently is. Anthropology and comparative ethics have been very helpful in disclosing the arbitrary nature of many of our values, and also in demonstrating the wide-ranging options that exist for the construction of our societies and personhood.

A second, and more traditional, way of deciding upon the adequacy of existing norms and values is to compare them to some standard perceived as being absolute. For many religious traditions, this standard is perceived to be God's revealed moral standards or, as in the case of Christianity, God's revealed "word." Anything that conforms to this standard is adequate; anything that does not conform needs to be discarded. Another absolute standard used by both theologians and philosophers is that of natural law. The claim is made that human reason is capable of discovering absolute, universal moral laws. Once such laws are discovered, existing norms need only be compared to the absolute standard in order to determine their adequacy.

In retrospect, the inability of persons in religious traditions to agree upon what constitutes the word of God, and the inability of philosophers to agree upon the absolutes found in natural law, suggests the inadequacy of both approaches. It becomes more and more apparent that such "absolute" standards are strongly conditioned by the social setting of those who claim the absoluteness of particular understandings of the word of God or of natural law.[13]

Yet another way to measure the adequacy of existing norms and values used by philosophers and theologians is by appeal to an instinctual morality or sense of fairness. Such an approach is commonly stated in the Kantian maxim, "Act only on that maxim whereby thou canst at the same time will that it should become a universal law."[14] A similar claim is made by the Jewish-Christian aphorism, "So whatever you wish that men would do to you, do so to them."[15] This approach is given a sophisticated elaboration in John Rawls's *A Theory of Justice* where Rawls suggests that our innate sense of justice will guide us in making social decisions.

We can encounter this innate sense of justice by engaging in a simple philosophical exercise. We are to imagine that we are about to construct a society and that we may construct it however we please. The only thing we do not know is what position we will occupy in the society we are creating. We do not know our sex, race, age, IQ, economic status, or abilities. Lacking this knowledge, What kind of society will we construct? What conception will we have of a just society? Rawls believes that our innate sense of justice will lead us to construct laws and policies that will assure the maximum degree of freedom for all persons and a distribution of goods and privileges that will contribute to the well-being of all persons, but especially the least well-off.[16] This appeal to an innate sense of morality can provide important insights into the adequacy of our existing morality and social policies.

It seems clear that we can never completely escape the effects of social conditioning on our morality, and it seems that none of the above approaches gives us a conclusive answer about the adequacy of our values, but nevertheless, used in combination, they free us to take a more critical look at what we are and aspire to be. They allow us a degree of personal liberation and provide us the possibility of heightened self-awareness. For Thomas Merton is quite right: "We cannot begin to know ourselves until we can see the real reasons why we do the things we do, and we cannot be ourselves until our actions correspond to our intentions, and our intentions are appropriate to our own situation."[17]

It should be clear by now that ethics is more than the attempt to decide what to do in particular circumstances, though that too, as we shall see, is an important function of ethics. Ethics also does not provide us with absolute, infallible guidelines for our behavior. Rather, as a colleague of mine suggests, ethics is more like turning on a light in a dark room. It provides us with clearer information about the predicament in which we find ourselves and so provides us some guidance for responding to this context.[18] Arthur J. Dyck makes a similar point when he states:

I would appeal to the reader's own conception of what it means to live a dignified, human life and ask whether it is not the case that one requisite of rationality is to be conscientious in trying to avoid tragedy. . . . A moral tragedy occurs when, after you have acted in a certain way and reflected on how you have acted, you come to the conclusion that, upon reflection, had you thought about it before you acted, you would have acted differently.[19]

DESCRIBING THE MORALSCAPE

The last section, despite some claims to the contrary, may have left the impression that morality and ethics deal largely with norms and values. Both terms were used often and both, purposefully, were left vague and undefined with the hope that they would be understood in their broadest, most commonsense meaning.[20] The two terms were used in order to refer to two related, but distinct, human moral responses. Values refer to that which we value, that for which we care or to which we aspire. In this sense, who we are is greatly influenced by what we desire, what we want, what we would like to become. Morality has a very strong affective component. Many of our moral sentiments are nonrational (as opposed to irrational).

On the other hand, we also develop norms (rules, guidelines) that help us determine how to embody our values in our lives and relationships. We can say that we value life, but in order to value it we must develop rules and guidelines that embody that respect in our behavior and social structures. We develop laws prohibiting murder, wanton destruction of the environment, protection of endangered species in order to live out this value. In this respect, our rationality is placed at the service of our affections. As both Augustine and Luther were aware, our rationality is a slave to that which we love.[21]

Nevertheless, as I will show in this section, values and norms are themselves only one of the factors that determine our moral existence. Rather, our moral existence is governed by a comprehensive set of beliefs, feelings, and attitudes, some elements of which are quite distinct and observable, but others are vague and largely hidden from view. The factors that determine our moral lives are perhaps best compared to a landscape. Some features are dominant and set a tone for that particular landscape, yet the landscape is actually composed of elements too numerous to list, and they blend together with the dominant ones into a discernible whole. Similarly, our attempt to view the elements that determine our moral existence is like our attempt to view a landscape. We can note the dominant features, perhaps even prepare a topographical map of the terrain, yet still we must experience the landscape, "feel" it, as much as "know" it. In discussion of our individual and social moral existence, then, it is perhaps useful to talk about the existing "moralscape." In this way we indicate that, although we may be able to define dominant features of it, in some other sense, the totality of it escapes the possibility of complete description and definition, and so of complete predictability.[22]

Having made the above statement, it is still helpful and useful to attempt to describe the dominant elements in the moralscape, just as describing such features in the landscape helps us to identify a particular geographical area and so allows us to navigate in that particular location. It also allows us to distinguish one geographical area from another. In this regard, Ralph B. Potter, in his book *War and Moral Discourse,* offers a very useful typology for identifying the dominant elements of particular moralscapes.[23] In discussing the formation of public policy, Potter states: "Every statement which proposes a policy by specifying a responsible agent, a goal, and an appropriate means for its realization is derived through a complex reasoning pattern which may be analyzed into four elements."[24] Potter then goes on to describe the four elements:

(1) . . . an empirical definition of the situation, a series of judgments concerning . . . facts and potentially falsifiable predictions concerning the outcomes of alternative courses of action.

(2) Affirmation of loyalty. . . . Consciously or unconsciously, [persons] make decisions regarding what shall be taken as their primary object of concern. They create expressive symbols which represent a center of value, locus of commitment, a source of identity.

(3) . . . mode of ethical reasoning. . . . What constitutes a good reason for choosing one course or another? What factors are to be taken into consideration? What priority and weight is to be given each?

(4) . . . quasi theological beliefs concerning God, man, and human destiny. Anthropological assumptions concerning the range of human freedom and man's power to predict and control historical events have particular importance.[25]

These influences upon policy decisions and upon our moral existence are not absolutely distinct from each other. In fact, they flow into each other and mutually determine one another. Despite all our attempts to be objective, our assessment of empirical data will be weighted by our view of the world and our loyalties. Likewise, our presumptions about the nature of God or persons may determine our mode of decision-making. On the other hand, an empirical happening, the death of a loved one, the Holocaust,[26] may alter our entire worldview. Still, the attempt to isolate some distinct areas of moral influence is helpful in allowing us to see the complexity of moral existence and ethical reflection, and also helps in allowing us to engage more fruitfully in ethical discourse with others, because we are more clearly able to isolate areas of agreement and disagreement.[27]

In developing the rest of this section, I want to use a modified form of Potter's typology. I will list the areas of influence on our moral life, beginning with what I consider to be the most comprehensive and influential areas, and ending with those that are more restricted in scope and influence. Nevertheless, it must be remembered that the less comprehensive levels have the potential for altering the more comprehensive levels. In addition, I will slightly alter the labels and definitions of some of the areas, add to others, and finally separate out a fifth category, which I feel is distinct enough to deserve concentrated attention. I am claiming, then, that we can focus more clearly on the complexity of moral existence, and get a better sense of our moralscape, by isolating the following components: (1) worldview; (2) loyalties; (3) norms and values; (4) experiential and empirical elements; (5) mode of decision-making. In the rest of this section we will look at the significance of each of these components for our moral life.

It is important to remember that each of these components refers to the moral life both of the individual and of communities and societies. As we look at each of these areas, the profound influence of society on the moral life of the individual should be apparent. Society is the source of our worldviews, makes claims upon our loyalties, provides us with rules for living together, and makes claims about what we should value. Society is also largely responsible for determining what empirical information is available to us and how we will interpret it.[28] Our social setting will also determine the experiences we have that shape our personhood. It also seems likely that particular societies favor certain modes of decision-making (e.g., pragmatism in most modern Western societies). With this reminder I now begin a more detailed look at each of the above elements of the moralscape.

Worldview

As I have already indicated, we are deficient, when compared with other animals, in instinctive responses. Rather, our actions and reactions involve a very complex process of analysis and interpretation. We must first interpret what has occurred and then act appropriately. A wrong interpretation will mean an inappropriate response. In describing human action, H. Richard Niebuhr gives the following account: "But more complexly, we interpret the things that force themselves upon us as parts of wholes, as related to and symbolic of larger meanings. And these large patterns of interpretation we employ seem to determine—though in no mechanical way—our responses to action upon us."[29] Again, it should be noted that we are often not conscious of the interpretive process. Most of our frameworks are so familiar, most interpretations so routine, that interpretations and responses seem almost automatic. In the moral realm, they have become moral habits.

However, at times we are quite aware of our frameworks and the interpretive process. This occurs particularly when something happens that is new and unfamiliar, or when something simply does not fit the normal pattern. At the personal level, someone we thought was angry with us does something kind for us. We are uncertain how to respond. Is this some form of deception or have that person's feelings toward us changed? At the social level, as Thomas

Kuhn has shown, anomalies may build to such levels that our entire framework may shift. So, we come to discover that our observations of the movement of planetary bodies do not fit the Ptolemaic framework. We must find a new one.[30]

Likewise, in the moral realm, both Carol Gilligan and Lawrence Kohlberg have shown that moral shifts occur when we are confronted with a situation that our existing interpretive framework cannot handle.[31] We believe that it is always right to follow society's laws and then discover that our society denies, by law, equal rights to blacks. Or our society requires us, by law, to participate in a war that we believe to be immoral. Suddenly our moral framework no longer fits.

Obviously we have a number of frameworks that come into play in various areas of our lives. When in the science laboratory, we may have one framework. When we are on the golf course, we have another. We do not hit the ball in order to study the effects of physical forces on its flight. Other frameworks may govern our political life, our family life. But finally there is a comprehensive framework to which the other frameworks relate; it gives a general coherence to our lives as actors. This broadest framework I am labeling our "worldview." I have dropped Potter's term "quasi theological," in order to indicate that our worldview may exclude any conception of God. Included in our worldview, however, is some general presumption about the final principles and powers that underlie the existence of both natural and human history. Likewise included are presumptions about human nature, the nature of the world in which we live, and human society. Such worldviews are largely products of the societies and communities in which we live and we are socialized into their views.

It is clear, however, that we do have freedom to transcend a particular worldview and adopt another. Such "conversion" is usually the product of experiences that call into question our existing views, or is the result of reflection that shows the inadequacy or inconsistency of the original worldview. What we cannot do, though, is live without some framework, for to be alive is to act. And we cannot act without first ascertaining the framework within which we are acting.

One final point is that our worldview contains elements of very different types, the mix varying from individual to individual. We may develop a portion of our worldview in a very rational, systematic form, stating coherently all the constituent parts, as is done in systematic theology or philosophy. Such formulations of our worldview are enriched, however, through stories and narratives, and through personal and cultural experiences that enlarge upon the rationally stated elements of a worldview. In this respect, some aspects of a worldview may be more felt, more affective, than rationally known.[32] All worldviews are varying mixtures of materials of both types.

At this point, a few examples might be helpful in showing how our worldview affects our decisions about what we should be and, correspondingly, how we should act. If our worldview includes a conception of an all-powerful God who will save us or destroy us, depending upon whether or not we do God's bidding, we will likely decide that we should become obedient citizens of God's rule. On the other hand, if our worldview presumes that there is no ultimate ordering principle, that existence is a matter of chance events, we may decide with Nietzsche that the most powerful should impose some coherent moral order upon human existence. Alternatively, we may decide that the best course is simply to enjoy ourselves as much as possible: "to eat, drink, and be merry."[33]

At the level of activity, we may decide that active voluntary suicide (killing ourselves rather than suffering the effects of a terminal illness) is unacceptable because our life belongs to God and we have no right to take it ourselves. Or we may decide that, because life has no purpose, suicide in such circumstances makes considerably more sense than does suffering the debilitating effects of an illness. At the social level, the debate about nuclear deterrence is profoundly affected by our worldviews. Those who view the world as a place of perpetual struggle between forces of good and evil, who see the world as geographically divided into such spheres of good and evil, will find nuclear arms buildup absolutely essential. Because we can never trust the evil side to honestly disarm, to abide by treaties and guidelines, we have no option but to continue the escalating balance of terror. Others, who view all persons as having the capacity for both humanitarian and misanthropic responses, will favor reduction of nuclear arsenals as a way of reducing world tensions and creating an environment in which the humanitarian aspects of all nations will have greater opportunity to flourish.

As a final comment on the concept of worldview, I want to note that ultimately the truth or falsity of a particular worldview cannot be definitively stated. We can assess the adequacy of a particular worldview only by referring it to yet another worldview (for all thought must have a framework from which to work),[34] by testing its parts for internal consistency, or by seeing whether it provides an adequate description of our experience. Nevertheless, we are not absolved of the responsibility to consciously reflect upon our worldview. Such reflection involves assessing its adequacy for our experiences and its implications if consistently applied. For example, if we believe that the world is divided into good nations and evil nations and are certain that the United States is one of the good nations, how can we account for our nation's theft of land and resources from Amerindians and our policy of genocide in their regard? How do we explain the enslavement of blacks and the brutal treatment of blacks in our country, which continues to this very moment? How do we explain our actions in Vietnam or the fact that we are the only nation ever to use nuclear weapons on other human beings and that we used them not on soldiers, but on civilians, women, children, the sick, the elderly? Such experiences radically challenge the adequacy of a worldview that sees our nation as aligned with the forces of good.

On the other hand, if we believe in a God who stands at the end of history, whose kingdom will be established no matter what we do, does human history have any meaning? If we can be saved if we just "believe that Jesus is Lord" irrespective of the lives we live and the structures we support, why should we take the needs of others seriously? Does it really matter if we act to establish human rights in society, or try to prevent a nuclear holocaust? Does it matter that we support structures that impoverish and dehumanize others? The implication is, of course, that it really does not matter.[35] The sorrowful history of the church shows the way in which human concerns have been perceived as unimportant as long as doctrinal and liturgical orthodoxy is preserved. Churches have permitted and supported slavery, apartheid, and genocide by teaching that slave masters, apartheid rulers, and genocidal executioners can all be saved as long as they have a "right relation with God." Issues such as slavery, poverty, and oppression should be kept out of the church pulpits because politics and things of the world have no place in church. Likewise, the sorry history of Christian missionaries who have served as collaborators in the enslavement and oppression of Third World peoples demonstrates the way in which a worldview can be a brutal support for the historical suffering of peoples.

Finally, the adoption of a worldview is an act of faith, and this is true whether it is a theistic or atheistic worldview. It can even be an act of blind faith. In scrutinizing our worldview we must realize that we risk our own lives and those of others in committing ourselves to a particular worldview. The worldview to which we commit ourselves will help determine the persons we will become and the way in which we will use our life. What a tragedy to come to the end of our life and discover that we have used it on something inane, unimportant, or even destructive. Ethical reflection requires that we scrutinize our worldview and decide whether it is something to which we want to commit ourselves. Again, ethics provides no absolute answers about what constitutes a good or bad worldview, but ethical reflection can help us avoid a moral tragedy, discovering later that had we but reflected a bit more, we would have committed our lives to something else, to a different worldview.

Loyalties

Whereas worldview emphasizes cognitive influences on the moral life, loyalties emphasize affective influences. As we have seen, Augustine and Luther, along with many other theological figures, consider this element to be the most important influence on morality. Augustine went so far as to divide humanity into two large groups, which he described as residents of two cities, cities defined by their differing loyalties. "We see that the two cities were created by two kinds of love: the earthly city was created by self-love reaching the point of contempt for God, the Heavenly City by love of God carried as far as contempt of self."[36] Augustine even suggests that if we have the proper loyalty, all other aspects of our moral existence will fall into place: "Love God, and do what you want."[37]

This focus on loyalties is important, for it reminds us that we are not only rational, contemplative beings; we are also loving, wanting, desiring beings. Our morality cannot be freed from our particular, embodied existence.

Still there is an important sense in which our loyalties are connected to our worldview: our worldview provides information on what are proper loyalties. A worldview that includes the first of the Ten Commandments reminds us that God should receive our primary loyalty. A worldview that strongly identifies with the values of classic capitalism informs us that we and our own self-interest should be the primary focus of our loyalties. Of course, our worldview may be an attempt to rationalize our loyalties. Our love of money, power, and self may lead us to construct a worldview that fosters selfishness.

In reality we all have multiple loyalties and usually they function together rather smoothly. Normally there are few conflicts in our being loyal to our own interests, those of our family, employer, community, nation, and, for some, God. In fact, we discover that our loyalties have an important function. We are finite beings with finite resources of time, talent, energy, and wealth. Although we may in some sense be concerned about all humankind, we cannot directly and simultaneously act to support and help all persons. We must decide where to commit our resources, and our loyalties help us to make such decisions. We can commit ourselves to the well-being of our family and community, and be reasonably sure that, because of their loyalties, others are doing the same for their families and communities. In this way, all persons have resources for the support and aid they need. Such loyalties assure the commitment of resources and talents needed by persons and communities if they are to survive and thrive.

There are occasions, though, when our loyalties collide. Suppose our job demands that we spend extra time that should be spent with the family? Suppose our nation requires us to participate in a war that we feel God has proscribed? There is also the problem of whether proper loyalties may be made improper by overcommitment to them. If the benefit of loyalties is that in a world of finite persons, it helps to ensure that all persons have their needs met, what about situations where some persons' overcommitment to their loyalties leads to the suffering of others? At what point does my expenditure of resources on my family begin to reduce the overall well-being of the community and of others who live in the community? Does concern for my children's education, which leads me to enroll them in private schools and so weakens public education, step beyond the bounds of a healthy loyalty? Does buying yet another car or television, constructing a private swimming pool, moving to a more expensive, larger home, violate a responsibility I have to others in the community who are hungry or homeless?

The issue that arises, then, is how my various loyalties relate to each other. How do I resolve conflicts between loyalties? We do this both consciously and unconsciously by developing a hierarchy of loyalties: job comes ahead of family, family ahead of strangers. In this way a single loyalty or several dominant loyalties, will set the basic shape of our lives and societies. So the businessman[38] is primarily a businessman. He has a family, belongs to a church, is part of a nation, but his business loyalties shape his life. Family is not permitted to interfere with work; the church is analyzed as a business so that the good church is one that is large, growing, and financially sound; and, of course, "what is good for General Motors is good for the country." As far as our society is concerned, Karl Marx observed that in capitalist societies everything, including the human person, is reduced to its monetary value.[39] We decide whether to have children on the basis of whether we can afford it; decide whether all persons should receive adequate food and health care on the basis of the costs of the services; decide environmental and work safety regulations on the basis of their monetary costs. There is little doubt that what we love shapes our lives both individually and collectively, both who we are and what we do.

Again, ethical reflection will not provide absolute answers about what loyalties should dominate our lives. Such reflection and observation, however, can reveal to us the implications of living according to various loyalties. What would society be like if all members believed that their primary loyalty was self-interest? Here, as Hobbes rightly saw,[40] life becomes a war of each person against every other. Similarly, we can look at the lives of persons around us and in our history to see the shape of lives determined by various loyalties. We can also analyze various societies and communities to see the shape that various communal commitments give to particular communities.

Ethical reflection can also focus on the coherence between our professed worldview and our actual loyalties. To proclaim that our worldview demands that God be our primary loyalty, or our family be our primary loyalty, and then to discover that the bulk of our time and energy goes into accumulating wealth and power shows a profound discrepancy between what we claim to value and what we actually value. Ethics provides the tools for gaining a clearer insight into the motivations that determine both our personhood and the shape of our communities.

In conclusion, it is the job of ethical reflection to help us achieve some degree of independence from our loyalties, to "suspend" our lives temporarily, so that we might see more clearly who we are. As we decide how to act, ethical reflection helps with a similar suspension of our loyalties so that we might more objectively understand the empirical situation to which we are responding. Blinded by absolute loyalty to our nation, our nation's leaders and most American citizens were unable to see both the brutality of the use of atomic weapons on Hiroshima and Nagasaki, and the fact that such use was unnecessary for ending the war.[41] Likewise, loving our privileges and comforts, it is hard for many of us men to grant women equal social status, to surrender our domestic slaves. Because responsible moral action depends upon having as accurate an assessment of the empirical situation as time and resources permit, this ethical suspension of our loyalties is essential in order to avoid, as much as possible, a highly biased interpretation of the situation to which we are responding.

Norms and Values

As we move to the third component of the moralscape, I still want to retain a general conception of the terms "norms" and "values." In actual practice both norms and values are used more vaguely and generally than most philosophical definitions would permit. It is also the case that the full meaning of both our norms and values is enhanced by stories and narratives, and are not limited by their rational definitions. So, our working images of justice are informed by stories and images of just persons and just societies.

The concreteness of action demonstrated in these stories gives a fullness and richness to the concept of justice that the philosophical definition of justice—"giving to each their due"[42]—does not have. In addition, norms and values are given their full meaning by reference to the worldview within which they operate and by reference to the loyalties to which they are attached. The Soviet Union invades Afghanistan and it is an act of savagery, an attempt to deprive a people of its sovereign right of self-determination. We help to overthrow the democratically elected government of Salvador Allende in Chile, invade Vietnam, and pay for a mercenary destabilization of the popular Sandinista government of Nicaragua, and all are labeled acts of "liberation," attempts to keep the world safe for democracy, even though we replace popular regimes with brutal, unpopular, terrorist governments.[43]

Having made these stipulations, let me return to the definitions of the terms "norms" and "values" that I have already proposed. Values refer to things we desire. They may be goods or states of being. So we may value health, well-being, self-determination, or wealth. Norms, on the other hand, are rules and guidelines used to inform our behavior. Some concepts may function as both values and norms. We may value justice and also have rules that ensure just behavior. Norms and values are thus a kind of shorthand for guiding the moral life. They provide statements of what we should value and what rules we should follow if we are to live out the implications of our worldviews and loyalties. Norms and values also arise as we attempt to regulate our life together and give collective expression to our shared worldviews and loyalties.[44] Ethics has traditionally focused much of its attention on norms and values, but it seems evident that in terms of actually determining our moral lives, they are less important than our worldview and loyalties.

None of the above, though, should leave the impression that norms and values are not important. On a day-to-day basis, such norms and values have more impact on our moral existence than does any other element. It is a long and difficult process to sort out the implications of our worldview for all the situations that confront us each day. Society and tradition have done much of this sifting for us and have provided us with guidelines that we may use in governing our behavior. Should we steal something we would like to have or should we pay for it? In responding to such a situation we do not usually begin by referring to our notions about the human condition, the existence or nonexistence of God, or the nature of society. Rather, we make quick reference to a set of socially established norms against stealing and so pay for the item in question. Only on occasions when the norms do not seem to quite fit do we begin our reflection at a more basic level. Our family is starving and we have no money to buy groceries. If our only option for feeding them is to steal some money or food, is that morally acceptable? Here we are pushed back to a more fundamental level. Such situations remind us of the need to reflect critically upon our accepted norms and values. Here, too, ethical reflection is absolutely crucial to responsible action.

In the realm of norms and values, then, self-conscious reflection requires us to raise a number of important questions. Are our norms and values consistent with our worldview? Are our norms and values consistent with one another? Is placing a high value on material wealth consistent with a worldview that demands that we be concerned about others, especially if we live in a world of limited resources? Does a rule of justice that demands fair and equal treatment of all persons square with the high value we place on national strength and superiority? Can rules of justice be honored in the realm of international trade and international relationships if we value economic and military superiority? Ethical reflection, then, attempts to order our norms and values, and see that they are consistent with our worldview and loyalties.

Experiential and Empirical Elements

This category focuses more directly upon the external world, relationships, and circumstances that provide the context within which we build our personhood and the society in which we act. The external world imposes itself in two very distinct ways as it influences the shape of the moralscape and our decision-making process. First, it provides the experiences that develop, test, and challenge our worldview, loyalties, norms, and values. If we are born into a Christian community, we will be affected by the Christian worldview. On the other hand, the death of someone we love may call into question the very idea of a loving God.

Our experiences also shape our moral feelings and intuitions.

Growing up in a white, middle-class neighborhood may make it very difficult for us to empathize with the pain, desolation, and difficulties of minorities or the poor in our culture. Why do they not act as we do? If they are poor, why do they not get a job? Being immersed in a minority culture, becoming a minority in another culture, may help us to better understand and empathize with the situation of persons whom our society regularly degrades and dehumanizes. Such experiences may awaken new moral feelings in us and so offer us new moral possibilities.

Secondly, the empirical world presents us with moral situations to which we must respond and with moral problems we must solve. In the wake of a history of discrimination, should we now adopt affirmative action programs in order to create a more racially and sexually just and balanced society? Similarly, how do we respond to the poor of our society, what programs should we enact? Should we abort the child we had hoped to have when we discover that there is a high probability that it is afflicted with a defect that will cause it immense suffering? It is these specific dilemmas that we usually think of when we hear the word "ethics," and it is certainly the job of ethical reflection to help sort out the dilemmas that such problems pose. Having said this, let us look at the ways in which ethical reflection is helpful in clarifying the experiential and empirical components of the moralscape.

First, it is the role of ethical reflection to make us aware of the limits of our moral insights and feelings, which are a function of our limited experiential framework. We must realize that we comprehend only a small portion of human experience and are sensitive to only a small range of moral feelings because of our limited experiences. Ethical reflection reminds us that we cannot universalize our experiences. It also alerts us to the need to listen carefully and honestly to others whose experiences are different from our own, to search honestly to see if our worldview can incorporate the experiences of others. Christianity has often relegated non-Christian peoples, especially persons of color, to the status of nonpersons. As such we could treat Amerindian peoples and black peoples in the most vicious manner, or torture North Vietnamese, knowing that they were not really human. Listening to blacks, Amerindians, and Vietnamese presents us with experiences both similar to our own and quite different from our own. Hearing stories about their pain, their suffering, as well as their joys, shows us that their experiences cannot be incorporated in a worldview that views them as nonpersons. Our encounter with them forces us to reform and expand our own worldview.

Lastly, ethical reflection exposes to us our need to immerse ourselves in other cultures, classes, and racial groupings. It challenges us to roam about in the world's varying natural and social environments as we seek to enlarge our understandings of ourselves, our societies, and our world, and as we seek to develop the moral understandings, sentiments, and feelings that will allow us to live responsibly in these environments.

As we encounter particular moral problems, ethical reflection operates in a similar fashion. As noted earlier, it should serve as a check on our distorted perceptions and evaluations of particular situations. It provides a degree of objectivity that is missing when we simply approach such problems reflexively. Likewise, the search for a more objective understanding requires that we gather as much information about the situation as we possibly can. Here ethics is inescapably dependent upon history and the natural and social sciences to provide needed data and perspectives on the issue at hand. In order to decide the desirability of affirmative action, we need to know something about the numbers of women and minorities in various occupations, something about the barriers that exist for them in certain occupations, and some of the likely results of adopting affirmative-action guidelines. In order to decide whether to abort a defective fetus, we need to know something about the degree of probability that the fetus is defective, the actual effects of the defect, and the long-term prognosis. We cannot proceed responsibly in these areas until we have accurate answers to all the above questions. Ethical responsibility requires that we have access to, and make use of, the most extensive data that time and the situation permit. We will return to this issue in greater detail in chapter 6.

Mode of Decision-Making

This is another area to which philosophical, and more recently theological, ethics has devoted a great deal of attention. Standard introductions to ethics, like that of Frankena,[45] give the impression that the method of decision-making is the determining characteristic of an ethical system. Likewise, the situation ethics debate in theological ethics is largely a debate about methods of decision-making.[46] In general, a rough distinction is usually made between deontological approaches and teleological approaches. Deontologists are understood to put primary emphasis on adherence to rules and laws, and to believe that once the proper rules and laws have been discovered, then we decide what to do by simply obeying them. The morality of an action lies in its conformance to rules, and less attention is paid to its consequences. So, a strict deontologist who believes that we have an obligation to tell the truth would require that we tell dying persons that they are dying, even if the truth has a devastating impact upon them.[47] Teleologists, to the contrary, are supposed to be concerned about realizing some end or goal (embodying some value). As such, they are deeply concerned about consequences and they measure morality by the ability of an action to accomplish a desired end. Here adherence to rules and laws is important only if it helps achieve the desired end. For a strict teleologist who saw the goal as one of winning a particular war, the means used, even the killing or torturing of civilians, would be acceptable if it was the only way of achieving the goal.

From my perspective, the method of decision-making has an effect, but it is not nearly as important as the other factors in the moralscape. We discover that we can predict almost nothing about the behavior of persons or societies on the basis of their predominant mode of decision-making. What is decisive is what rules or laws the deontologist considers to be determinative, or what ends or goals a teleologist considers primary. These rules and values are not determined by the mode of decision-making, but rather by the worldview and loyalties of the persons and societies involved. The method of decision-making may certainly reflect something of the character of the person or society and reveal something of their fundamental commitments, but on the whole it provides us with very little information about the person or community.

Finally, this generally accepted distinction is not very useful, for in looking at the examples given—and granting that they are simplistic examples—most of us would conclude that there is something profoundly wrong with either a strict deontological approach to issues or a strict teleological approach. We are concerned about both the morality of particular acts and about the consequences of our actions. We appreciate the continuity and dependability that established rules give to our actions, yet we recognize with Joseph Fletcher: "If the end does not justify the means, what does?"[48] Simultaneously, with Gandhi, we recognize that means and ends are not really separable. The means we use partially determine the ends we are able to achieve.[49] This is especially the case when we recognize that all moral action occurs in the context of shaping both ourselves and our communities.

In conclusion, our method of decision-making certainly affects our decisions on particular issues and affects the shape and nature of our character and that of our communities. Nevertheless, it is not as crucial an aspect of the moralscape or of ethical reflection as some would argue. We will return to this issue in chapters 3 and 6.

CONFUSION IN THE MORALSCAPE

Before beginning a constructive attempt at presenting Christian ethics, I want to make a few comments about the society and age in which we live. Our context is marked by both moral confusion and intense moral concern. In some respects our age seems adrift, uncertain about the shape of the moral life and about what rules to honor and what to value. In other respects, churches, businesses, professions, and community groups are engaged in significant ethical discourse and reflection. I do not want to overstress the uniqueness of our age, or suggest that other periods of time were not marked by both moral confusion and moral earnestness. Still, our age and society, like all ages and societies, is unique in some important respects. I want to focus for a few moments on some of those elements that have altered our consciousness of the moral dimensions of our lives.

As we already saw, the emergence of pluralism has had a liberating effect on our relationship to our moral existence. In traditional societies persons are usually unaware that other moral alternatives exist. Rules and values seem to be dictated by the gods, or the fathers, and are not subject to critical examination. Everyone in the culture seems to abide by the same rules and accept the same values. In traditional societies there is a certainty about the moral life that obscures its contingent, social nature. We are now blessed and cursed with the knowledge of the varieties of moral life. Such knowledge frees us, but it also leaves us feeling adrift. Is all morality relative? Are all our norms and values just products of social conditioning? Is it possible that there is no right or wrong, that the moral life, like the esthetic life, is simply a product of personal and social preferences? We feel as if our moral lives have no grounding.

Similarly, the last century has been one in which change is so rapid that change itself has become one of life's few stable components.[50] This means that moral situations have arisen in droves for which there is no moral wisdom from the past on which we can draw. We are aware, as never before, that we must make choices that will affect our humanity, our society, and the very possibility of whether there will be a human future. Yet we feel alone and uncertain as we approach these decisions. Should we support or reject recombinant DNA research? Are there some types of new life forms that should not be created? Are in vitro fertilization and artificial insemination acceptable remedies to infertility?[51] Should we attempt to create an artificial womb? Do the benefits of nuclear power outweigh its risks? Is warfare acceptable in a world of nuclear weapons? We feel overwhelmed by the society we have created and the choices it requires of us. Lacking guidelines from the past, looking at our own record of disastrous choices, we doubt our wisdom and stand paralyzed in the face of the world we have created.

In a more positive light, we are more aware of our freedom to determine our lives, and, where such freedom is lacking, we are demanding greater control over our lives. The Enlightenment in the West marks the beginning of a period of history that has now swept the globe, a period in which persons have overthrown, or are attempting to overthrow, all arbitrary authorities. We began by overthrowing the arbitrary rule of gods and kings, and used our developing scientific knowledge to liberate us from many of the arbitrary constraints of nature. The second half of the twentieth century has been marked by worldwide revolutions aimed at overthrowing the arbitrary rule of totalitarian governments and oppressive economic systems. We are aware of our capacity for freedom and want the rights[52] and conditions that will allow us to have a significant voice in the decisions that will shape our personhood and societies.[53]

Finally, it is clear that we are profoundly confused about the answers to the fundamental moral questions: "What should we be?" and "What kinds of communities should we build?" In past ages persons have had at least tentative answers to these questions: we should seek to become fully rational beings; we should seek to control the natural world; we should build democratic societies; we should build capitalist economies. But today we are fundamentally uncertain about how to respond. We have become puzzles to ourselves.

We sense our incompleteness, that we are somehow unfinished, but we are uncertain about how to proceed in order to complete ourselves. Likewise, our historical communities seem to be in shambles. We live in an age marked by social revolution and marked by the debris of the failure of our social systems to provide humane, fulfilling conditions for their inhabitants. The world is marred by poverty in the midst of affluence, by terrorism, and by unprecedented rates of crime and mental illness. We no longer know what kinds of communities we should build. Rather we struggle both individually and collectively to hang on to what we have and prevent life from sliding into complete chaos.

Uncertain about how to answer the fundamental moral questions, deciding what to do on a day-by-day basis, becomes even more difficult, more arbitrary. Our decisions fit no coherent plan or pattern; they lack both internal and external consistency. And so, the specific moral decisions we do make seem only to contribute to our sense of moral confusion and uncertainty. Many of the "pro-life" opponents of abortion favor the expansion of our nuclear arsenal and support anticommunist, totalitarian governments that torture and murder their own citizens. Many of the opponents of the Tellico Dam project, who feared the extinction of the snail darter,[54] had no qualms about the free, open, and massive practice of abortion in our society. As a nation we give food to peasants who have been driven off their lands by the weapons we have provided for the military of their country. In a sense we have lost our moral bearings and it seems quite likely that we shall perish in our confusion.[55] Perhaps a new vision will emerge,[56] a "kairos,"[57] and we will be able, once again, to begin making our way, albeit tentatively, uncertainly, across the moralscape.

2

THE SOURCES OF
CHRISTIAN ETHICS

In this chapter I want to begin the constructive task of ethics—
that is, elaborating a framework, a vision, for Christian ethical
reflection and action. This framework is the base from which
answers to fundamental ethical questions will come. In fact, the
framework determines both the shape and types of ethical questions that are raised. Because this is an introduction, the framework will be abbreviated; nevertheless, I hope that its scope will be
sufficient to provide a starting point for Christian ethical responsibility. Likewise, because this is not a history of Christian ethics, the
framework I develop will select from among the various forms that
the history of Christianity has provided. As Beach and Niebuhr
indicate, however, in spite of the pluralism of forms, "there is a
certain unity in Christian writings, an inner resemblance shared
even by the most apparently diverse thinkers."[1] I feel that the
framework I am presenting reflects this unity of the Christian
tradition and also proposes some changes in the tradition, which
are necessary if persons who call themselves Christian are to be
ethically responsible in today's world.

Before developing this framework more fully, there are several
introductory matters that need to be considered. First, I want to
relate Christian ethics to the broader discipline (discipline understood as a human phenomenon and not exclusively as an academic
pursuit) of ethics in order to show both its uniqueness among and
its relatedness to other forms of ethical systems. Secondly, I want to
discuss the difficulty of doing "Christian" ethics in our age and

society. Thirdly, I want to discuss the two sources that are unique to the Christian ethical traditions: the Bible, and the person and teachings of Jesus. Following those discussions, I will return in the next two chapters to a more systematic development of the Christian moralscape.

THE SPECTRUM OF ETHICAL SYSTEMS

The various moralscapes from which persons try to answer the questions of what we should be as individuals and communities, and, on the basis of their answers, decide how to respond to particular situations, can be labeled "systems of ethics." There are numerous systems and variations on systems. Many Christians have claimed, and still do claim, that Christianity provides the only true, dependable ethical system. Therefore all other ethical approaches are viewed as either fundamentally flawed or, at best, incomplete.[2] In his classic work on Christian ethics, *The Divine Imperative*, Emil Brunner deals with the relationship of Christian ethics to other forms of ethics (primarily philosophical) and concludes: "Thus the survey of philosophical ethics brings us to the unsatisfactory conclusion that none of these systems achieves a real synthesis; . . . thus—in varying degrees—each has its own particular value, and each has its special weakness; thus the unsatisfactory situation cannot be overcome by any kind of 'synthetic ethics.' "[3] Brunner then goes on to ask, "Does the Christian faith give 'the' answer, the 'only' answer, and the 'whole' answer to the ethical problem?"[4] Brunner answers in the affirmative.

My approach is considerably different from Brunner's. Descriptively, as Brunner himself recognizes, there are many different ethical systems that persons and societies hold. I believe that ultimately none of them can be proven to be true in any final or objective sense, and that it is dangerous to hold them absolutely true in a subjective sense. Rather, many frameworks, including the Christian framework, give compelling descriptions of the situation in which we find ourselves as moral beings, and so offer morally defensible options for our responses. Likewise, all these frameworks, including the Christian, are unconvincing in some important respects, and so in some cases the alternatives they propose for action are suspect.

We are caught in a dilemma of needing to adopt some framework in order to merely live and breathe (even committing suicide requires a framework by which to determine that death is preferable to life); yet no framework, when carefully scrutinized, is fully consistent or convincing. We must, then, adopt our frameworks tentatively, openly, being able to hear and consider objections to the system we hold. Simultaneously, our adoption of a particular system means that we have found it to be generally more convincing than its alternatives, and so we must be willing to hold it with conviction and defend its strengths and insights. In this respect, H. Richard Niebuhr provides something of a model for the tension between tentativeness and conviction that should characterize our relationship to our moral framework. In discussing his own Christian beliefs, he offers the following insights:

> In one sense I must call myself a Christian in the same way that I call myself a twentieth-century man. To be a Christian is simply part of my fate, as it is the fate of another to be a Muslim or a Jew. In this sense a very large part of mankind is today Christian; it has come under the influence of Jesus Christ so that even its Judaism and Mohammedanism bears witness to the fact that Jesus Christ has been among us. But I call myself a Christian more because I have both accepted this fateful fact and because I identify myself with what I understand to be the cause of Jesus Christ.[5]

If a Christian ethical system is, then, only one of many possible systems, where does it fit in the spectrum of possible systems? Again, I will not provide a detailed typology of ethical systems; that has already been done.[6] What I want to do is simply make some general distinctions between types of ethical systems in order to put the Christian system into an overall perspective. First, a distinction can be made between religious and nonreligious—or positively stated, between religious and humanist or naturalist ethics. Religious ethical systems believe that some transcendental power reveals the good and empowers persons to do the good. Humanist or naturalist systems believe that either the good is contained in the laws of reason or being, or else they believe there is no good, no morality, only that which persons create and impose on existence.

Kant believed that moral codes are universal aspects of human reason and can be discovered and articulated.[7] Sociobiologists believe that moral codes are derived from our genetic impulse toward species survival.[8] Erich Fromm claims to have discovered in the human psyche a natural need and capacity to be loved and to love the other.[9] On the other hand, Nietzsche felt that there was no inherent moral structure and that it was up to the powerful to impose their superior standards upon the rest of culture.[10] Camus agreed that there is no objective morality, no meaning to existence, but concluded that we should respond to our situation by loving one another.[11] In all these systems, the good, the moral, is entirely independent of any concept of God or a power that transcends the human world. Persons are conceived of as capable of both knowing and creating the good, and of doing it if they but make use of the powers and capacities they already have.

In religious systems, persons are presented as being unable to fully know the good and incapable of doing it without outside assistance. The good must be revealed to persons by a power that transcends them in both wisdom and goodness. This power also empowers persons to do the good. The source of revelation can, of course, be understood and experienced in diverse ways. Consequently religious ethics take many forms: Hindu, Buddhist, Islamic, Jewish, Confucian, to name just a few. Christian ethics is thus a subset of religious ethics. Although traditionally most ethical systems have been religious systems, the Enlightenment in the West marks the beginning of a worldwide process labeled "secularization,"[12] in which religious explanations of the world, persons, and morality have been replaced in many spheres by humanistic or naturalistic explanations. The dominance of these newer explanatory categories has made it increasingly difficult to maintain religious systems in many parts of the world. I now want to look at the significance of this change for Christian ethics.

THE POSTRELIGIOUS AGE

There are a number of reasons why religious explanations of the world and human experience have become increasingly less convincing.[13] Most obvious is the rapid growth of scientific knowledge and its success in explaining phenomena in both the natural and psychic worlds. Such knowledge often directly contradicts the traditional explanations offered by religion. Creation did not take place in six 24-hour segments, nor did it take place six thousand years ago. Storms are caused by certain atmospheric conditions and disease by virus or bacteria. Neither is caused by angry gods or demons. In addition, we have flown into space and not found God, and burrowed into the bowels of the earth and not discovered hell.

Perhaps more important, science and the technology it has generated have proved much more effective in combating disease and hunger, and improving the human condition, than have prayer and sacrifice to gods. We are so convinced of the truth and power of our scientific knowledge and technology that stories about a "superhuman" being who sometimes sets aside the laws of nature to work miracles seem more and more like stories left over from some mythological past than accurate descriptions of the human situation. In fact, much of Christian theology since the eighteenth century to the present has dealt with finding ways of making the claims of the Christian tradition consistent with the findings of modern science.[14]

A related development has been a growing awareness of human freedom and power, coupled with the insight that both personal and social human histories are largely the product of human choices and actions, and not merely a series of fated events. This awareness poses many challenges to a traditional religious understanding of existence. Simply the assertion of human freedom, the elevation of the sense of human dignity, places humankind in rebellion against any concept of God to which persons must ultimately be subservient. Likewise, the sense of progress that has characterized human consciousness from the Enlightenment to the contemporary era has made God seem unnecessary. For a while, at least, we seemed quite capable of creating our own heaven on earth. In fact, religion was viewed by many as a prime impediment to human progress.[15]

In the West, the validity of a religious framework has also been eroded by the very history of its religious institutions and religious persons. Historically, the church has sponsored the Crusades, murdered millions of women during its witchhunts, and supported both the Holocaust and slavery. It has baptized wars of oppression and cruelty, and given its symbols for naming weapons of mass destruction.[16] Christianity was, and continues to be, a tool used for the cultural oppression of Third World peoples, and continues to be aligned with the rich and powerful[17] of the world and is regularly used as a defense of their wealth and power against the demands for justice raised by the world's poor and powerless.[18] Recent sociological studies also show that a close correlation continues between strong, orthodox Christian belief and various forms of racial, ethnic, and sexual prejudice.[19]

Perhaps the most telling indictment against a Christian framework of interpretation, however, has been the continued existence and intensification of human cruelty, evil, and destructiveness in this century. We have witnessed two world wars and numerous more localized conflicts whose destructiveness and brutality are unprecedented in human history. The occurrences of events like the Armenian and the Jewish holocausts make the claim that there is a loving God in control of human and natural history seem almost obscene. There seems to be no satisfactory way of explaining the persistence of such viciousness if God is a God of love. If we are honest, we are likely to agree with Michael Harrington who declares upon seeing the suffering masses in Calcutta:

> In Calcutta, I think, people are crucified by the thousands every day, and then those who have not died are crucified again and again. If he were half the God he claims to be, he would leave his heaven and come here to do penance in the presence of a suffering so much greater than his own, a suffering that he, as God, obscenely permits. But he does not exist.[20]

Of course, many persons still live with a religious interpretive framework. Unfortunately, many of those do so reflexively because they have been socialized to accept such a framework. Strangely, such reflexively adopted forms of religion have little to do with the traditional insights of the religion on which they are based, but are rather blends of personal needs for comfort and assurance, and social and cultural needs for control and legitimation. In the name of religion, popular religions often betray the best of the religious traditions themselves.

I want to proceed, then, in developing a framework for Christian ethics, recognizing that it will conflict with and challenge much that now goes by the name of "Christian." I also recognize that there are good reasons why any religious framework will remain unconvincing to many good, morally sensitive persons. I make no claims about the final truthfulness of the framework I propose. Nor do I claim that adherence to this framework will necessarily make persons "better" and more responsible. Other persons, using other frameworks, will often arrive at similar conclusions, and sometimes have more compelling insights than those offered by the framework I propose. I propose it merely as an understanding of human existence and the human situation which I believe—and the Christian tradition shows others have believed—makes sense of our experience as moral beings and offers us insights into how we might live together responsibly on this planet. As a prelude to developing this framework, I want to now look at two sources of ethical insight central to Christian ethics.

THE ROLE OF THE BIBLE IN CHRISTIAN ETHICS

In some important respects, all Christian ethics are rooted in the Bible. Christianity is a historical religion whose beginnings are related to specific historical occurrences. The Christian moralscape is a response to these particular sets of historical happenings. As Beach and Niebuhr observe, "From this point of view all later Christian life is but a continuation of that dialogue in which reference must always be made to what has gone before in the conversation and in which every generation needs to begin not where its predecessors left off but where the Bible ends."[21]

Certainly one can repudiate the Bible as a source of moral insight and wisdom, but then one is no longer doing "Christian" ethics, no longer employing a Christian framework. For those who want to retain a Christian framework, the question is not whether, but how the Bible should inform the shape of a Christian system of ethics. Certainly various traditions have given varying answers to the role of the Bible in Christian ethics. The discussion is still continuing as to the Bible's proper use.[22] Again, I will not provide a listing of the various alternatives for using the Bible in Christian ethics. Rather, I will attempt to sketch the role that the Bible plays in the system I am using, sometimes by making reference to other approaches.

Many persons have seen, and do see, the Bible as a source of specific guidelines and regulations that should be used to direct the moral life. When in doubt, this position contends, consult scripture for specific guidelines for action. Such an approach is usually based on the assumption that the Bible is the "literal" word of God. As such, it offers unerring guidance for the moral life. This approach is certainly appealing. It removes the need for careful, oftentimes consuming, sometimes painful reflection on complex moral issues. We can condemn all premarital intercourse or homosexual activity because Paul does not seem to approve of either (1 Cor. 7:1-8; Rom. 1:26-28). We are also relieved of personal responsibility for the consequences of our action, for we are obeying God's command, and only such obedience, not consequences, is important. Like the Nazi executioners of the Jews, or Nixon's presidential advisers, we can hide behind the claim that we are merely following orders. And such a moral position is attractive, for who wants to be held accountable for their actions?

There are, however, a number of obvious difficulties with such a use of the Bible. First, the biblical laws are not always clear; indeed they are sometimes contradictory. Certain Old Testament passages support capital punishment (Exod. 21:22-24; Deut. 22:23-25), whereas certain New Testament passages condemn such forms of retribution and even command that we love our enemy (Matt. 5:38-48). When laws of the Bible contradict one another, which ones do we obey? Certain other laws seem no longer applicable, such as laws dealing with dietary restrictions and cultic practices. Other laws violate our sense of what is morally appropriate. As Charles Curran notes, "There has been in theology an embarrassment about the attitude towards slavery and women in certain parts of the Scriptures, especially in Paul."[23] In addition, there are numerous moral problems for which the Bible offers no guidelines at all. There is no discussion of the morality of abortion, genetic experimentation, the use of nuclear power or nuclear weapons, or having children in an overpopulated world. Finally, the notion that the Bible is the "literal" word of God is a very recent notion, clearly a reaction to the challenges posed by scientific and rationalistic understandings of life. Even Luther, despite his claim that the forms of the Christian faith should rest entirely upon scripture, did not hold to the "literal" interpretation or inspiration of the Bible.

For Luther, rather, scripture was merely the medium through which the word of God sometimes revealed itself.[24]

The Bible, then, must be understood and used in a much more open and fluid sense.[25] Certainly it remains one of the starting points for Christian ethics and offers critical insights when answering the questions of "what we should be as individuals and communities." Nevertheless, as biblical study has shown, the Bible, like all literary works, is historically conditioned, the product of particular peoples responding to their understanding of God's activity in particular times and places. Calling the Bible a "revealed book" does not resolve the problem, for as Paul Tillich observes, speaking of those who understand revelation as a timeless event:

> They forget that revelation must be received and that the name for the reception of revelation is "religion." They forget that revelation becomes more revealing the more it speaks to man in his concrete situation, to the special receptivity of his mind, to the special conditions of his society, and to the special historical period. Revelation is never revelation in general, however universal its claim may be. It is always revelation for someone and for a group in a definite environment, under unique circumstances.[26]

In using the Bible, then, we must understand the historical conditions under which its particular writings developed, and try to understand the meaning they had for that cultural setting. We must also recognize that the Bible is not a single book, but many; that there is great diversity in the types of materials and in the responses to God's perceived activity. What holds the Bible together is the fumbling attempt of finite beings to be responsive and responsible to a God who is first acknowledged in the event of the exodus and who is perceived to be acting in subsequent historical events. What is important, if we are to stand in the biblical tradition, is not a slavish adherence to the literal meanings of the Bible, but our own attempt to be faithful to the God of the Bible, to the God who has acted and who continues to act in our history. The Bible thus serves as a source to tell us something of the nature of that God who is acting, of the nature of that God's activities, and of the ways that others have responded to that action. We can hope such knowledge makes us more sensitive to God's present action and helps us to respond more faithfully.

This means that our relationship to the Bible will be dialectical. We question the Bible and we must allow it to question us.[27] We must probe it for insights into the nature of the biblical God and that God's activities to determine what is required of us. This demands that we also allow the Bible to question us, to probe our self-understandings and the structure of our communities. The Bible provides an alternative framework by which we are able to see more clearly the conditioned, fallible nature of our own frameworks. It liberates us from the views and values that we hold unreflectively simply because they are part of our culture and social upbringing. Beyond this, the Bible plays a constructive function in forming our worldview, our character, and our basic norms and values. Nevertheless, even at this more general level the Bible is not always consistent in its presentation of God or its evaluation of what constitutes a faithful response: the God of the Old Testament is portrayed as commanding "holy wars" in which even women and children are to be slaughtered (Deut. 13:12–15; Josh. 6:21), whereas the God of the New Testament condemns such use of violence and even forbids insulting another person (Matt. 5:21–22). Hence a few more general guidelines are necessary for the use of the Bible in Christian ethics.

First, Christians make the claim that Jesus is the most complete revelation of God's intention for creation. Because of this, Jesus becomes the norm (the hermeneutic) by which other biblical claims are measured. Jesus' life, death, and teachings measure the biblical corpus just as they measure our lives and our societies. As Christians we are thus compelled to repudiate notions of a God who would command the slaughter of women and children, and we can set aside cultic laws and emphasize the primary importance of neighborly love in defining Christian responsibility. On the other hand, Jesus is a Jew and his life and teachings can be correctly understood only through the perspective of the Old Testament.

The spiritualization of Jesus' teachings is impossible when we understand him as a Jew. The kingdom of God is not a spiritual escape hatch, but the irruption of God's activity into history and the consequent transformation of personal, social, and political relationships. Love of neighbor is not a warm, fuzzy feeling, but a set of concrete acts to aid the real, embodied neighbor, after the example of the good Samaritan.

Secondly, because the Bible reveals a God who acts and a people that never fully understands the implications of that action, our increase in human knowledge, of both the natural and moral realms, needs to be used to supplement and sometimes correct biblical understandings. If we have new knowledge indicating that homosexuality has genetic or deep psychological roots, how can it be morally condemned? On the basis of our fuller understanding of the equality of all persons, how can we refuse ordination, or equal political and economic status, to women? Similarly, changed social and cultural contexts make certain biblical rules inappropriate. In an overpopulated world, obeying the command to "be fruitful and multiply" (Gen. 9:16) may be an irresponsible demand. As James Gustafson indicates:

> Scripture "alone" is never the final court of appeal for Christian ethics. Its understanding of God and his purposes, of man's condition and needs, of precepts, events, human relationships, however, do provide the basic "orientation" toward particular judgments. Within that orientation many complex procedures and appeals are exercised, and there is room for a great deal of argumentation.[28]

Finally, however, despite the great variety of material in the Bible (laws, histories, stories, wisdom sayings, poetry), and despite the long historical tradition it represents, Christian ethics is informed by the sense of unity that holds the materials together, the core understandings that unite the material. These core understandings have been articulated in different forms at different times, but nevertheless represent a common response to a God who is gracious, loving, creative, just, and who acts to save humankind and the whole of creation, and liberate them from the powers that constrict and restrict human and natural development (Isa. 66:22; Rom. 8:19–23).

The activity of God, as the Bible shows, is not always properly understood or embodied in the lives of God's people. But the Bible consistently portrays a God whose acts and demands attempt to soften the hardness of human institutions and coax persons into an awareness of the full implications of the liberation God is trying to enact. Israelite society, like surrounding societies, permits slavery and is very patriarchal in its family, social, economic, and political structures. Nevertheless, the Bible is marked by a continual pressure to modify these institutions and is informed by an understanding of the human that makes such structures incompatible with God's intentions. So, slavery is softened by laws that assert the rights of slaves, including prohibitions of the abuse of slaves and of lifelong slavery (Lev. 25:39–46). Similarly, in important respects, Israelite society is uniquely equalitarian in class structure[29] and women have higher status than in surrounding societies.[30] Likewise, the Bible is filled with sudden flashes of insight when the implications of God's intended liberation allow a particular biblical writer to suddenly transcend the practices and biases of a particular cultural setting. Isaiah (e.g., chap. 34–35) and Jonah have insights into God's universal rule and God's intention of uniting all humankind into one kingdom. Paul can utter, "There is neither Jew nor Greek, there is neither slave nor free, there is neither male nor female, for you are all one in Christ Jesus" (Gal. 3:28)—and at the same time he sends a runaway slave back to his master (Philemon), and teaches that women should not speak in public gatherings and should be submissive to their husbands (1 Cor. 11:3; Col. 3:18).

The Bible, then, portrays a God who coaxes us into freedom and responsibility, into community and life together. God softens the hardness of our heart, expands the limitedness of our vision, challenges our social structures, and demands a transformation of persons and societies. The Bible thus provides the backdrop for our ethical reflection and action by portraying a God of liberation[31] who, in the words of Paul Lehmann, is doing "what it takes to make and keep human life 'human' in the world."[32] As our new environmental awareness has allowed us to see, however, and as the biblical writers already understood, keeping human life human requires the liberation of the whole of creation.[33]

In conclusion, the Bible will shape the formation of Christian ethics in many ways, as will be seen in the rest of this work. The Bible will inform every aspect of the Christian moralscape. It will inform our understanding of the nature of persons and communities, and provide guidelines that can be used to make very specific moral decisions. The role of the Bible in Christian ethics is very complex, as is the nature of the ethical task itself. Nevertheless, the Bible is not the only influence on Christian ethics, nor is it the only source of wisdom and guidance. The Bible presents a God who acts in history, and who continues to act in the accumulation of knowledge about ourselves and our world, and in all that occurs in our lives and in the world. To be responsible to such a God means that sometimes Christian ethical reflection will lead us to repudiate some biblical insights or injunctions—in the name of the God of the Bible who continues to act. Finally, the Bible portrays a God who does not forsake us, and allows us to act uncertainly, yet courageously, in the face of the new and the perplexing, knowing that God will not desert us and will continue, through events and persons, to provide us with new insights and wisdom if we can just remain open to the voice and concerns of others.

Several times in this section I have made reference to the figure of Jesus and Jesus' central position for interpreting the biblical corpus. For Christians, of course, Jesus stands at the center of their understanding of existence and is definitive in some respects for their understanding of what it means to be human and how persons should organize their life in common. Before developing more fully the framework for Christian ethics, it is necessary to be more explicit about the role of Jesus in Christian ethics.

JESUS AND CHRISTIAN ETHICS

Christian ethics are, of course, defined by their understanding of Jesus, the Christ, for it is the Christian claim that in the person of Jesus we have the clearest expression of who God is and what God is doing.[34] In addition, the claim is made that in Jesus we have the clearest expression of what it means to be human. Finally, Christianity claims that the encounter with Jesus empowers us to do good, to become a "new being."[35] Thus, in the tradition, Jesus is portrayed as "fully God and fully human."

As the long history of christological debate shows, however, understanding who Jesus is, is not a simple task, nor is there any one answer that is universally accepted by all Christians.[36] Disagreement over Jesus extends all the way back to the competing views of Jesus that appear in the Gospels. In the synoptic Gospels (Mark,

Luke, Matthew), Jesus is a man whom God "adopts"[37] to be a special source of revelation to the people of Israel. Mark finds the life of Jesus prior to his adoption by God at the time of Jesus' baptism so unremarkable that his Gospel begins with the account of the baptism. In Luke, Jesus fulfills the role of a great prophet, the final prophet, who announces the imminent arrival of the kingdom of God. In Matthew, Jesus becomes a new Moses, a new lawgiver, who is ushering in a new age in the relationship between God and the people. Only the Gospel of John knows of Jesus as a preexistent being who enters human history, plays out a cosmic drama, and departs once again to the right hand of God.[38] Behind these various images is the problem of how Jesus understood himself and his role in God's activity. The quest for the "historical Jesus" has been fraught with problems.[39] There is still no absolute agreement about what can actually be known about the historical Jesus. Nevertheless, there are some general agreements about the person, Jesus, and his message.

The weight of biblical investigation shows that Jesus certainly understood himself as a key figure in announcing the coming kingdom of God, but suggests that he did not understand himself as the Messiah, a preexistent being, or one who would return to judge the peoples of the world. All these titles and concepts reflect, rather, the church's later attempt to explain its understanding of the significance of the person Jesus for human history. The question for us becomes, "How should we decide who Jesus is, and what are the implications of that understanding for Christian ethics?" Again, I will not provide a typology of all the responses that might be made to this question, but merely indicate my understanding of the person Jesus and the implications of that understanding for my construction of Christian ethics.

We must begin with what seems to be universally claimed about Jesus in tradition and what seems to be historically certain. Jesus is a Jew and his self-understanding and use of concepts can be understood only from the perspective of the Old Testament and the Jewish community. He comes demanding that sinners repent and prepare themselves for God's kingdom, which he believes is shortly to embody itself in human history. The coming of the kingdom will fundamentally alter human affairs and relationships. The kingdom will be a reign of justice and love, and so, to prepare for the inbreaking kingdom, persons should begin to live lives of justice and radical love, love even for the enemy. This love must be more than a feeling; it must display itself in acts that improve the situation of the neighbor, even the neighbor who is the enemy. Human love, like God's love, must show a special preference for the poor and outcast, the vulnerable of society.[40] Jesus further declares that those who fail to use their resources to aid society's powerless will be punished when the kingdom arrives (Luke 6:24–25).

We know that Jesus attracted many followers, most from the lower classes, and that he was perceived as being a great teacher and miracle worker. He came to be disliked by the religious and political leaders of the time, who saw him as a threat to social stability. Finally, he was executed as a political criminal and at the time of his execution all his followers deserted him. Beyond that, we know that at a later date some of his followers reconvened, claiming that the real significance of Jesus' life and teaching had been revealed to them in Jesus' resurrection from the dead.

Next, we have to say something about the significance and status of the person Jesus. With other Christians, I want to acknowledge that the person Jesus startles me into a new awareness of who I am and what it means to be human. The character, life, and teachings of Jesus call into question many of my assumptions and offer me new and fuller possibilities for human existence. In this sense, Jesus is "fully human," a symbol of human possibility that transcends my own understandings of what it means to be human and my own capacities for living out my humanness. In addition, I find convincing certain aspects of Jesus' understanding of the human situation (this will be developed more fully in the next chapter). Likewise, the life, teaching, and death of Jesus, like the exodus, convey a convincing notion of who God is and what God is about, and so in this limited sense Jesus can be understood as "fully God."

In developing an understanding of Jesus, however, it seems necessary to avoid developing notions that contradict the very insights into the nature of our situation and our responsibility to one another and the world that Jesus conveys. In this sense the liberation theologians are correct in maintaining that our theology must be a product of "orthopraxis"[41] rather than "orthodoxy." Both Christianity and Judaism are "moral" religions—that is, they define the God-human relationship in moral terms rather than cultic (worship) or gnostic (knowledge) terms. It is what we do, how we live, that is important, not the form of our worship or our doctrinal assertions about the nature of God. Our worship and theology are important only as aids to our moral life. And Jesus' life, teachings, and death are all quite clear about the nature of the lives we are to live: lives of love, justice, mercy, humility, and forgiveness. Our love, justice, and forgiveness are to be extended universally to all persons, and in our humility we must be open to, and thankful for, the gifts others bring to us.

From this perspective, some claims about Jesus seem unacceptable. Talk of a preexistent being who enters history, fulfills a prearranged task, and exits in glory, calls into question the significance of human history and undercuts the motive for actual, concrete, historical action. In addition, the doctrine of a preexistent Christ is embedded in a body/spirit dualism that makes salvation an event of spiritual escape from the world rather than an event of world transformation. To love the neighbor becomes too easily the proclamation of a message of spiritual escape while leaving the concrete person trapped in dehumanizing political, economic, and social situations. In addition, this christology presents a Jesus who is not "fully human" in any real sense. Jesus is not a person who confronts the ambiguities of human existence with any real anguish, but remains assured throughout his earthly ordeal, like a character in a "Star Wars" movie, that the "force" is with him and he will prevail. Such a Jesus knows nothing of the anguish we feel knowing that ultimately we may be mistaken and that all our struggle may have been for nothing. Finally, this christology makes history a product solely of God's planning and activity. We are fated beings. The acknowledgment of this fact by Judas in the musical *Jesus Christ Superstar* leads Judas to scream out in anguish, quite correctly, "I've been used."[42] We cease to be actors in the historical drama and become merely onlookers.

Similarly, understanding Jesus in a too literal sense as "fully God" has had profound effects upon women in Christian nations. God's maleness is confirmed and religious sanction is given to both benign and malignant forms of patriarchy.[43] Men become God's representatives on earth and it becomes their duty to rule over women and children both in the home and in society at large.

Women and children may be punished and used against their will for "their own good": "father knows best." The continued refusal of the Catholic Church, and some Protestant churches, to ordain women to the ministry shows the continued persuasiveness of the literal understanding of Jesus as "fully God." Likewise, the image of a white Jesus has been used for purposes of domination of people of color and to support the right of whites to rule over others.[44]

Perhaps, however, the most difficult claim to relinquish is the claim of Jesus' absolute uniqueness and the impossibility of attaining salvation, or becoming fully human, except through acknowledging his lordship. This claim has led to the persecution of Jews, Africans, Amerindians, and other non-Christian peoples. Because of this claim Christians have carried out, and continue to carry out, programs of brutal extermination of members of "pagan" faiths or adherents of "godless communism." The claim of the absolute lordship of Jesus has resulted in a cultural and personal arrogance and imperialism that has damaged both others and ourselves.[45] As Thomas Merton has written:

> This, of course, is the ultimate temptation of Christianity. To say that Christ has locked all the doors, has given one answer, settled everything and departed, leaving all life enclosed in the frightful consistency of a system outside of which there is the intolerable flippancy of the saved—while nowhere is there any place left for the mystery of the freedom of divine mercy which alone is truly serious, and worthy of being taken seriously.[46]

If we are to truly honor and respect the person of Jesus and live out the implications of his life, death, and teachings, we can no longer make claims about the absolute uniqueness of Jesus, or the necessity of the encounter with the person of Jesus for human liberation and salvation. To be true to the person of Jesus, his life of love and concern for all persons, his openness to persons of both sexes, all economic classes, all cultural backgrounds, we must repudiate a christology that measures the worth of persons on the basis of their relationship to Christ. All we can affirm in our encounters with others is that our encounter with the person Jesus has allowed us to discover what it means to be human in a new and fuller sense, and that we are willing to share our new understanding with others through the lives we live. At the same time, we remain open to the insights of others in order to yet more fully develop our personal and collective humanity.

What we are left with then is a very "low" christology. Jesus is more than just a teacher of moral wisdom. Jesus gives us new insights into our situation and challenges and empowers us to become more human. Jesus' teachings provide guidelines that help us arrive at decisions on particular moral issues. However, we must recognize that, like us, Jesus is a limited, historical being trying to respond to God's initiative in a particular historical setting. That is what it means to be human. If Jesus is not that, then Jesus is not human in any significant sense. It is the Christian claim, though, that Jesus has understood more fully and completely what God is about, and responds more consistently to God's will, than we have been able to do. We are provided with new insights and abilities in knowing and doing God's will. Nevertheless, Jesus' times are not our times; many of our problems were not Jesus' problems. Like Jesus, we must seek to be responsive and responsible to God's activity, and, like Jesus, we must take the risk of doing so in relation to our particular society and era. Jesus provides us clues, paradigms, and guidelines that help us to be more responsive, but he provides no detailed answers.

In conclusion, our relationship to Jesus, like our relationship to the Bible, is dialectical. We question Jesus and he questions us. By looking at this particular person we receive critical insights about what we have become and what we might be. We receive insight into what we should value and what guidelines are helpful as we set about developing our personal humanity and our communities. Finally, however, we are left to work out the implications of these insights and guidelines for our own lives and the life of our communities. All of this will receive further elaboration in the next two chapters as we develop a Christian moralscape that will be used in the remainder of the book to provide some tentative answers to our basic moral questions.

3

A FRAMEWORK
FOR CHRISTIAN ETHICS:
WORLDVIEW AND LOYALTIES

Chapters 3 and 4 will develop the Christian moralscape on which the remainder of this book will be based. I will use the five categories presented in chapter 1 to organize the pertinent materials and attitudes that provide the framework for my understanding of Christian ethics. Again, this framework will not be exhaustive of the elements and richness of Christian ethics. Such a task is impossible in a work of this length. It is also the case, as I have already mentioned, that some of the elements of the Christian moralscape are more emotive and intuitive, more dimly felt than clearly perceived and stated.

Finally, the effect of the Christian moralscape on our lives and society is determined by the way in which all the separate elements blend together and interact. This does not mean that the whole is harmonious, that all the parts relate smoothly to one another. It does mean that all the parts are related to one another and interact with one another. In using the above categories to describe the elements of the framework, it is easy to lose sight of the way in which the categories interact. Nevertheless, I feel that the method used in these chapters provides a general understanding of the Christian ethical framework I am using and a good insight into the prominent features that have given the Christian ethical tradition its distinctiveness and its power.

WORLDVIEW

The first category is that of worldview. As indicated in chapter 1, our worldview contains our general assumptions about the ultimate powers that determine existence, our fundamental understandings of the world in which we live, and our beliefs about human nature. Christian ethics is, as described in chapter 2, a form of religious ethics. As such it is grounded in the presumption of some transcendent power that constitutes "ultimate reality" and to which the whole of creation is related. In developing the Christian worldview that determines my ethical framework, I will look at five critical elements in that framework: (1) the nature of God, (2) the nature and role of evil, (3) human nature, (4) the natural world, and (5) the nature of society. Because God is the symbol used to describe ultimate reality, I will also discuss the way in which the four remaining subjects relate to God (ultimate reality).

God

To say that one believes in God[1] does not say much of anything, nor tell us much about the assumptions that control a person's selfhood and activity. What we need to know are what claims persons are making about ultimate reality when they talk about God. Only by knowing something about the nature of that God can we derive guidelines for developing our personhood and for our behavior. The Christian tradition has made a number of claims about God that inform the Christian understanding of ultimate reality. The first and most definitive claim is that God is good. This is an important claim because God may be defined primarily in terms of power or some other characteristic. Christians claim that ultimate reality is defined primarily in terms of goodness and so acknowledge an ontological priority of good over evil. There is a profound difference between acknowledging God because God is powerful and acknowledging God because God is good. If God is powerful, but not good, many of us might decide with Dostoevsky's Ivan Karamazov that even if we believe that such a God exists, nevertheless we would not worship such a God, or let such a

God shape our personhood.[2] Likewise Socrates in the *Euthyphro* raises the issue of the relationship of goodness to power by demanding to know from Euthyphro, "Do the gods love piety because it is pious, or is it pious because they love it?"[3] Christianity resolves this issue by declaring the priority of goodness over power. God's defining characteristic is goodness.

A second claim about God embodied in the Christian tradition is that of the relational nature of God. The distinctive doctrinal claim about God's trinitarian structure is the claim that, at the core, ultimate reality is relational. This means that reality finds its fulfillment in relationship. The whole of reality can be symbolically understood as a massive ecological system that works best when all the parts are properly related to one another. This contrasts dramatically with the Aristotelian God of the philosophers who is a radically independent, self-sufficient Being. It also stands in opposition to a particular scientific worldview that analyzes creation as a collection of distinct, mechanically related entities.[4] From such perspectives, God has no real need for creation and creation has no real need for God.[5]

The importance of the claims of God's goodness and God's relational nature becomes evident when we realize that persons try to emulate their gods. The Christian claim is that persons should seek goodness rather than power, relational fulfillment rather than self-sufficiency. It is quite clear that Christianity itself has all too often revered a God of power and self-sufficiency, the "omni" God (omniscient, omnipotent, etc.). As Beverly Harrison concludes, such an image of God is ultimately destructive:

> I submit that a theological tradition that envisaged deity as autonomous and unrelated was bound over time to produce a humanism of the sort we have generated, with its vision of "Promethean man," the individual who may, if he chooses, enter into relationship. Where our image of transcendence is represented to us as unrelatedness, as freedom from reciprocity and mutuality, the experience of God as a living presence grows cold and unreal. But even after such a God is long dead, the vision of the human historical agent as one who may, or may not, choose relationship lingers with us.[6]

But such a notion is a departure from the fundamental notions of God as found in the Bible and the best parts of the Christian tradition. From the claims about God's goodness and relational character flow other important claims about the nature and activity of God.

The God of the Christian tradition is described as the Creator. The claim is that all aspects of creation are grounded in and dependent upon a fundamentally good creative power. At the core, all that is, is good. Goodness has ontological priority over evil in the created world due to the nature of the Creator. The doctrine of creation further emphasizes both the goodness and the relational character of God. Creation is portrayed as an act of pure gratuity, a gift that is shared. It also represents God's desire to extend God's range and possibilities of relationship.[7] Finally, in the Christian tradition, creation is not simply a one-time event. Rather, it is a process, an ongoing, continuous event. God's grace continues in the constant creation of new possibilities and is portrayed as the ongoing attempt by God to develop a satisfying relationship with the whole of creation.[8]

The ongoingness of God's creative activity points to yet another important element in the Jewish and Christian understanding of ultimate reality. This is the belief that God acts not only in the natural realm but also in human history. God exercises an influence over the course of human events. Persons and natural laws are not the only forces that give shape to history. God exercises an additional influence. This claim about God's historical activity is so central to the tradition that Christianity and Judaism, along with Islam, are designated "historical" faiths. All three religions claim that God is most fully known through what God has done in history.[9] For Jews, of course, the central event is the exodus. For Christians it is the life, death, and teachings of the person Jesus. According to these traditions, these events provide us with insights into the nature of ultimate reality. Such an understanding of ultimate reality gives history itself a significance. It becomes an ongoing dialogue of words and activity.[10]

On the basis of the Jewish and Christian experiences of God's historical activity, further elements have been added to their understanding of the nature of God. Jews and Christians have concluded that God is just, loving, forgiving, and merciful, relating to us as an ideal parent, a father or mother.[11] God's love, however, extends to all human beings and the whole of creation. God is concerned about the fulfillment of all persons and all aspects of creation. This concern is expressed through God's justice: the demand that each person respect the rights and personhood of all others, and that each part of creation have at its disposal the resources necessary for its fulfillment. Additionally, God's love shows itself in forgiveness, in empowering us to escape the limitations and injustices of our past personal and collective behaviors, allowing us to live new, more constructive futures. Our errors do not condemn us to personal and corporate destruction. We are able to see new possibilities, to reach beyond the destructive patterns we have set in order to become something more.

One of the most unique aspects of this view of God is the belief that this God is merciful. Such mercy is shown to all persons and to all of creation, but is especially apparent in God's special love and concern for the poor, the oppressed, and the outcast. God is the God who frees a slave people and who empowers Jesus to heal the sick, feed the hungry, and proclaim a message of salvation to the outcasts of society. God is regularly portrayed as the one who cares for those whom others ignore.[12] God is the protector of the powerless, not because they have a special virtue and not because their poverty and simplicity free them to be more religious. God cares for them because they are the most needy and because their needs are so often overlooked by others.[13] This claim has profound implications for the way that Christians answer the fundamental moral questions: "What should we be?" and "What kinds of communities should we create?"

Finally, there is a disturbing acknowledgment in the Judeo-Christian faith of the limits of God's power. This limitation can be understood as God's conscious self-willing of those limitations, or as an awareness that once creation has been given a degree of autonomy, God has inescapably surrendered a portion of divine control. God is no longer the only actor and so no longer has complete control.[14] A useful analogy can be drawn with our relationships to other persons. We may have a degree of power over them, we may even be able to coerce them to do our bidding. Still, at their center, they remain independent from us, autonomous. True, through lobotomy or the use of drugs we may be able to destroy that autonomous center, but then we have also destroyed the person. God can be perceived as in the same quandary. Once there is an autonomous creation, God may retain the power to destroy it, but God does not have the ability to exercise absolute control over it. God retains some influence, remains one of the actors, but is no longer an all-powerful deity.[15]

Christianity, of course, has often failed to recognize God's limitations. It is frightening to think that we bear some ultimate responsibility for the course that history will take, that finally we have power to thwart God's intentions for creation. Nevertheless, any other conception of God portrays a God not worthy of our emulation. An all-powerful God is either the final cause of all the world's suffering and tragedy, or if not the cause, at least retains the power to end such suffering but chooses not to do so. In either case God becomes a monster, not something greater than humans but considerably less. Christianity in its symbolism has recognized this problem in the person and fate of Jesus. If Jesus reveals to us the nature of God and God's activity in the world, then we are forced to conclude with Dietrich Bonhoeffer:

> God allows himself to be edged out of the world and on to the cross. God is weak and powerless in the world, and that is exactly the way, the only way, in which he can be with us and help us. Matthew 8:17 makes it crystal clear that it is not by his omnipotence that Christ helps us, but by his weakness and suffering.[16]

But the understanding of the limits of God's control is no reason for absolute despair, for Christianity makes two additional claims about God. First, we do not suffer alone but rather our very suffering penetrates to the core of ultimate reality. God bears our suffering and suffers with us. As Hans Küng so eloquently recognizes, "Even Jesus did not explain suffering, but endured it as innocent in the sight of God, endured it however—unlike Job—to the bitter end. His story was different: real, not fictional."[17] This is a God who is saddened by the falling of a sparrow (Matt. 10:29). Additionally, this God is faithful and does not give up on us. God pursues us, chases us, hounds us with new possibilities.[18] God is constantly trying to lead us away from the edge of our self-created disasters. God is a God of life who goes ahead of us and calls us into a fuller future.[19]

In this respect even God's seeming absence can be viewed as a sign of God's faithfulness and encouragement of us.[20] For Christians, then, there is always a degree of hope even when all human possibilities seem to have been exhausted. The hope, of course, is not that of a sure and certain delivery, but rather the hope that rests on knowing that we have not been abandoned, that if we are simply wise enough, that if we have eyes to see, there are still possibilities that have not yet been attempted.

Evil

As we have already discussed, Christianity recognizes that God is not the only power at work in the world. Beyond that, it claims that powers are at work that are directly opposed to God's purposes for creation: powers that bring death, tragedy, and suffering into the world. The Christian tradition understands that such evil is radical in that it is embedded in the roots of all that is. There is no person, no aspect of creation, that does not deviate in some destructive way from God's intentions for it. Christianity has never given a clear, convincing account of the origins of evil or of the precise relationship of evil to God and the created world. It has, though, made a number of important claims that strongly influence the Christian response to moral questions.

Evil is understood as subordinate to good. Evil and good are not two equal powers locked in eternal combat. The good is ontologically prior; evil is the negation of good, the distortion of the true intentions for creation.[21] Creation, then, is not itself the source of evil. Matter, our embodiedness, is not the cause. Evil does not reside in our emotions, our feelings; it is not a product of our finitude. The created world is fundamentally good. Our embodiedness is to be celebrated.[22] Rather, evil is a force that misdirects creation and disturbs the intended harmony. We do not escape evil by escaping our embodiedness through some form of ascetic withdrawal or spiritual escape. Evil influences all aspects of creation and the self, the spirit as well as the body, the mind as well as the emotions.

If there is a cause of evil, that cause is closely linked to persons and their willful disobedience of God. The biblical writers understood that evil affects even the natural world, but viewed the disturbance of nature as closely connected to human disobedience

(Gen. 3:1-24). On the other hand, there is also the recognition that evil transcends, in some important respects, the human situation (Gen. 3:1-7).

Still, as more recent theologians have suggested, there is something about the nature of human existence that predisposes us to participation in evil, participation that is defined as "sin." Reinhold Niebuhr views sin as a product of the anxiety created by our dual nature: we are both angel and beast. We are finite, limited in all ways, yet we have the capacity to transcend our finitude, to see beyond our limits, to desire to be infinite, and so to become anxious about our finitude.[23] In our anxiety we desire to be God, to be the center of existence, to have the power to ensure the security of our lives. In order to guarantee such security, we dehumanize others in attempting to subject them to our control and we disrupt the ecological balance of nature in our quest for domination. As individuals and communities seek to be the center of existence, life becomes a war, a struggle in which persons and groups seek to gain power over each other and so the harmony of creation is destroyed. "Sin, all sin, is by nature a totalization. When we sin, we think we are all that there is and believe that our own totalized order is the kingdom of heaven."[24]

The recognition of the power and reality of evil is thus an important part of the Christian worldview. Evil does not so negate the goodness of the world or the goodness of persons that we should respond by world flight into a private religious world or a closed religious community. Likewise, the Christian doctrine of evil does not counsel flight into some otherworldly kingdom. Evil is also not understood to be so pervasive that it is impossible for persons or communities to do the good or reflect the goodness of their original nature. However, evil does distort all aspects of creation and of our lives. It means that all of us are capable of the most barbaric acts, and that none of our actions are free of the taint of sinful self-interest. The Christian understanding of evil knows it to be an inescapable part of all human action and structures, and sees evil as the perduring temptation to substitute our desires for existence and the shape of communities for those of God.

We will never become saints, never build utopias. Still, life can be improved, societies can be made better. In tentative ways we can experience the love of others and the justness of social structures.

But we are reminded that in all our attempts to do good, "to make and keep human life human," we must always plan our actions and social structures so as to control the inescapable effects of evil.

In conclusion, the effects and reality of evil cannot be allowed to blind us to the fundamental goodness of our lives and of creation, or to possibilities for improving the quality of existence of all beings on our planet. There is a strong temptation to despair in the face of evil, to lose hope. As Charles Curran notes, however, "For one who acknowledges the continuing reality of sin in our world, there is need to recognize that the existence of sin can never become an excuse for an easy acceptance of the situation as we know it."[25] The Judeo-Christian tradition claims that despite appearances, God continues to work to improve the human situation, to liberate creation. God cannot remove the suffering that evil imposes on the world, but God opts to bear the pain and continue the struggle. To be responsive and responsible to such a God means that we have no choice but to do likewise.

In a profound response to the problem of evil in our world and the overwhelming inclination to give up on the world, its human inhabitants, and God's goodness, Thomas Merton replies:

> It is only the infinite mercy and love of God that has pre-vented us from tearing ourselves to pieces and destroying His entire creation long ago. People seem to think that it is in some way a proof that no merciful God exists, if we have so many wars. On the contrary, consider how in spite of centuries of sin and greed and lust and cruelty and hatred and avarice and oppression and injustice, spawned and bred by the free wills of men, the human race can still recover, each time, and can still produce men and women who overcome evil with good, hatred with love, greed with charity, lust and cruelty with sanctity. How could all this be possible without the merciful love of God, pouring out His grace upon us?[26]

The Nature of Persons

I have already made some claims about the Christian assumptions regarding human nature, but will briefly restate them. Persons, like all parts of creation, have been created good and remain fundamentally good. They are given a unique role in creation, for the claim is made that they are created in "the image of God." When I discussed the role of Jesus in ethics, I showed the difficulty with understanding this "image" too literally. God cannot be correctly understood as a white male. If that were a correct understanding, all other persons would be, at best, inferior persons and, at worst, nonpersons. To say that persons are created in "God's image" does, however, make some significant claims about persons.

First, to say that we are made in God's image is to say that we are relational beings, that we find fulfillment in relationship. The creation story that touches on our creation as sexual beings (Gen. 1:27–28; 2:21–25)[27] and the biblical claim that our fundamental moral requirement is "to love our neighbor as ourselves" (Matt. 22:37–40) both emphasize this claim. We are created to live in right relationship with other persons, the rest of creation, and God. In addition, these three sets of relationships are understood to be inseparable. We cannot be in right relationship with God if we are not in right relationship with others or the rest of creation (1 John 4:7–12). To love God is to love God's creation and to be committed to doing God's work. And God's work is the work of reconciling all parts of creation, of liberating the oppressed, and of creating a just world order. Only participation in such tasks makes love of God both a possibility and a reality.

Secondly, to be created in God's image is to be created as an independent, autonomous being. We are gifted and cursed with self-transcendence; we are self-aware. We can contemplate ourselves and our behavior, we can imagine ourselves as different or altered beings. We can ask questions about what we should be, and take a role in shaping our personal and collective personhood. In sum, we can know the difference between right and wrong, we can choose to honor or ignore God's intentions for creation. In this respect, we become historical actors alongside God and help give shape to history, both social and natural.[28]

From the above flow several other claims about persons. We have a dominion over the rest of creation, a power over it. Our intelligence and freedom allow us to manipulate and use the rest of creation for our own ends. In this sense we become co-creators with

God, we have the power to transform creation.[29] The Judeo-Christian tradition talks about such power in terms of stewardship. We are to be stewards of creation, caretakers. We may use creation but we are also charged with preserving it, respecting its fragility, and recognizing its own integrity and fundamental goodness.[30] Nevertheless, we have the power to misuse creation, to subjugate it, even to destroy it if we so choose.

This brings us to the other side of the claims about human nature made by the Judeo-Christian tradition. Despite our being created in God's image, we are still creatures, attached to and supported by the natural order of creation. We are finite beings who cannot escape our dependence upon the rest of creation. Our finitude is not, in itself, evil. Acceptance of our creaturely status can bring peace and comfort to life.[31] Still our awareness of our finitude may create an anxiety that leads us to misuse our freedom. In our anxiety we attempt to dominate and control both nature and others, seek individually and collectively to overcome the limitations of our knowledge and wisdom. We try to use our freedom to become like gods ourselves (Gen. 3:5).[32] In the process the harmony of creation and the peace between persons is broken and destroyed.

Christianity claims that such anxiety is part of the life of all persons and all societies. To be human is to be anxious and our anxiety leads to sinfulness. We misuse our freedom because our knowledge and wisdom are limited, but more importantly and more unfortunately, we misuse it because we desire to transcend our finitude. This fundamental anxiety distorts our personal relationships and subverts our social institutions.[33] The Christian image of the human is thus one of a mixed, conflicted being, struggling to be more than human yet in the struggle becoming considerably less.

The Natural World

Much of what Christians believe about the natural world has already been stated. Still, I want to summarize a few of those important claims. First, the natural world is fundamentally good, a source of beauty and comfort intended for human enjoyment. Secondly, creation is a gift and it is a gift intended for all persons.

As such, all persons have a fundamental right to the productive and supportive aspects of creation that make human fulfillment possible. No one has the right to hoard the wealth of creation and so impoverish others. Creation is a gift that is meant to be shared. Thirdly, the above claims cannot be allowed to obscure the fact that creation itself has its own intrinsic goodness and value. In the Jewish creation stories, creation is pronounced good, full of value, before persons are created (Gen. 1:1-25). Our use of creation must include a stewardship that recognizes the intrinsic value of creation itself.[34] As we are now discovering, such respect may be necessary simply to assure our own survival. Our brutalization of the environment threatens us with ecological holocaust. In terms of the history of the Christian tradition, this concept of respect has not been as prominent an element in the moralscape as it needs to be. Christian thought has been strongly anthropocentric. A more recent theological trend has been attempting to correct this overemphasis.[35]

On the other side, the Christian tradition also recognizes the fallenness of nature. Nature itself is often a source of suffering and tragedy as well as delight. Diseases, birth defects, floods, droughts—all are the workings of a fallen nature. As beings created in the image of God we are charged with being co-creators, with working to remove and prevent the tragedies caused by the improper workings of the natural order. It is proper, in fact required, that we use our knowledge and skills to counteract and control the effects of disease or to minimize famine-caused hunger by working to eliminate the agricultural effects of erratic weather patterns. The challenge becomes that of controlling and containing the tragic effects of the natural world in a way that is respectful and supportive of the intrinsic value and fundamental goodness of the created world.[36]

The Nature of Society

Finally, I want to develop a Christian understanding of society. Here, again, some of the critical elements have already been discussed, but again I want to reemphasize some of the elements. First, humans are relational beings; we are meant to live in relationship. Communities are absolutely essential for meeting our basic needs, whether physical, psychological, rational, or spiritual. Economic communities produce the basic goods that support our lives and economic cooperation has allowed for a tremendous expansion of human economic well-being in some parts of the world. Additionally, stable political communities have facilitated the development of human communities that share common languages, cultures, and values—communities of persons who have created environments fostering a richer and fuller human existence. The accumulation and transmission of knowledge and of spiritual wisdom is also a corporate undertaking, and without basic familial communities, persons would not receive the love and care they need for authentic human development.

Our communities and societies are thus an intended, inescapable outgrowth of our nature and represent the relational drive toward community that characterizes ultimate reality itself. Our communities can be viewed as another of God's gifts to us. And, in fact, the exodus event is a declaration that the full development of persons depends upon their having free, responsive human communities. Only as persons are free to determine the shape of their families, the nature of their economy, and the form of their political order, will they be able to become fully human. Likewise, the concept of the kingdom of God is a declaration that human salvation (fulfillment, healing) can come only within the context of fully reformed, responsive communities. If human fulfillment is based upon our ability to live in right relationship with others, with the world, and with God, we can find fulfillment only if our communities support us in that endeavor and make such an existence possible. Salvation in the Judeo-Christian tradition is not salvation from our distorted, often tragic institutions and communities, but is salvation into a perfected community where true human life can be lived.[37]

A second claim, however, is that our communities, like all other aspects of existence, are corrupted, sinful, and misused. Human communities are intended to provide a context where all persons can develop fully and freely. The reality of our communities is that they are used by the few, the powerful, to control the lives of others and so make their own lives more comfortable and secure. Our communities thus become forces for dehumanization rather than human fulfillment. The family is used by males as a way of dominating women, of obtaining cheap housekeeping and needed emotional support.[38] The capitalist economic system is used to promote and protect the wealth and power of the few by allowing them to control the labor of the many. Our political systems are structured so that the powerful can use the laws, the police, and the military to protect their own power and interests. The gifts of our communities are turned into curses. Institutions formed to serve human needs end by victimizing persons for the glory of institutions. "Pro-family" groups advocate the removal of legal and social protections that prevent the abuse of women and children in order to strengthen the institution of the family.[39] Nations send thousands of young men off to kill and be killed in order to make the nation stronger. The poor have their scanty government benefits cut; the hungry have their food benefits withdrawn; the marginalized are made homeless in order to improve the economy.[40]

But the Judeo-Christian tradition does not conclude with a declaration about the sinfulness of our communities. It makes the claim that God is at work forming and reforming our communities. God is the power that assures that unjust institutions finally collapse or are toppled because of the instability that their injustice creates. In addition, God raises up prophets, persons who retain the understanding that our communities are meant to serve us, all of us; that we are created to serve one another, and not the many created to serve the few. God is identified with no final or fixed forms of human community but rather demands that in each situation we discover the types and forms of communities that create the greatest possibilities for the development of all persons. For, "The innate purpose and meaning of politics is the common good of all people and all groups. Good political activity is a way of helping people to live faithfully in the freedom and solidarity that befit human dignity and make possible the attainment of social justice and peace."[41] The difficult task we face is analyzing our particular situations to see what types and forms of institutions allow the greatest possibility for protecting and enhancing the humanity of all persons and the goodness of creation.[42]

Conclusions

The elements detailed above do not, of course, exhaust all the Christian worldview. They do represent its most prominent features and the prominent features of the worldview that informs my understanding of Christian ethics. Certainly others might emphasize different elements or a different mixture of elements. Still, the above elements are all central parts of the Christian tradition.

There is also the problem that the above description is an attempt at rational description of a particular worldview. As I have indicated, and will do so more fully in the section that follows and in chapter 5, we are motivated by more than the rational content of our worldview. Such a worldview must also be internalized in nonrational forms. It is not enough to describe ourselves as dependent beings; we must feel and respond to that dependency. The claim that creation has a fundamental goodness is meaningless unless we feel and resonate to that goodness. To state that creation is a gift to us is merely an empty phrase unless we are actually humbled and empowered by a sense of actual graciousness. The gap between the cognitive and affective aspects of our personhood is often great. The struggle for some consistency in these two aspects of our lives is difficult. I will deal with the important role of our affections in our moral lives in the next section.

LOYALTIES

I have already noted the strong emphasis that the Judeo-Christian tradition places on the role of love, emotions, and feelings in the moral life. This is a major distinction between the theological and philosophical traditions in the West. Christianity recognizes that we are divided beings, often failing to do that which we know to be good (Rom. 7:19–21), whereas much of the Western philosophical tradition accepts the Socratic principle that we cannot knowingly do evil.[43] For the rationalist tradition, a change of behavior, of personhood, requires a change in the rational construction of our interpretive framework. For Christianity, such a change might be required, but more fundamental is a change in what we love, what we desire, what we hope for. The primary driving force in our moral development is understood to be not the intellect but the will. We are governed by what we are more than by what we know. It is important, then, that we look at a Christian understanding of the role of loyalties in shaping our life and behavior.

The Christian tradition begins once again with the presumption of the goodness of creation, including the goodness of our feelings, desires, and capacity to love. In fact, inasmuch as we are understood to be fundamentally relational beings, the affective aspect of our being has primary importance for relationship and is grounded in our feelings, our emotions, and our capacity to love rather than in our intellect. In addition, Christianity affirms the goodness of our particular loves and loyalties. Unlike the Greek tradition, which celebrates the universal in persons and downplays the particular, the Judeo-Christian tradition celebrates our particularity. We are embodied, called to be particular persons in particular times and places. We are defined by our relationships to our communities, our societies, and to particular persons.[44] It is our embodiedness, our uniqueness, that gives life its richness and variety. In sharing with others what is unique about ourselves, all our lives are enriched. Variety of persons and communities is a fundamental gift to us, part of the beauty of the lives we have been given.

The implications of the above are obvious. We are to cultivate our loves and loyalties. We are to work to develop our relationships, to support our communities, to improve our societies. We have obligations to all the communities and relationships that have given us life and inform our particular lives. Again, however, the Christian tradition emphasizes the way in which sin and self-centeredness corrupt and misdirect our loyalties. At the personal level our desire for security, our intense self-love, means that we fail to accept the gifted nature of all our relationships and instead try to control them. We use various tricks of domination and submission to tie others to us and in the process corrupt the very relationships themselves.[45]

Similarly, our insecurity and egocentricity tempt us to make our relationships, our communities, our societies, the center of existence. Instead of seeing them as one among many, part of the richness of human social existence, we make our relationships, communities, and societies the center of value and the norm by which all other groups are measured. So a love relationship becomes a form of mutual egoism in which two lovers lose themselves in one another and withdraw from their responsibility to nourish other relationships and communities. Whiteness and its characteristics become normative for all other peoples, and racism is born.

Dark-skinned persons are viewed as culturally inferior, backward, and were constitutionally defined in the United States of America as three-fifths of a person.[46] Our immigration laws make it easy for white-skinned immigrants to enter our country, but throw up numerous barriers for persons of color, even for those fleeing war or political persecution.[47]

Similarly, our nation-state is portrayed as the center of virtue and value. What we do is good simply because we do it. If others disagree with our policies, they are by definition either mistaken, evil, or both. In this manner we morally justify economic, political, and military policies whose primary intentions are protecting and maintaining our national self-interest. Our selfish quest to be the strongest economic and military power on earth is cloaked in the rhetoric of morality. If the Arab nations decide to withhold their oil from our markets, we find no moral problem with using our military strength to forcefully ensure a continued supply of oil. Such a policy is right and just because we need their oil. On the other hand, the threat by another nation that it would use military force to ensure needed grain shipments from us should we impose a boycott against it, would be viewed by us as an act of international theft and military aggression. Our nationalistic loyalty blinds us to the broader perspectives of international justice and need.[48]

The Judeo-Christian tradition proclaims that all our loyalties must be ordered through reference to a primary loyalty to God. "Hear, O Israel: The Lord our God is one Lord; and you shall love the Lord your God with all your heart, and with all your soul, and with all your might" (Deut. 6:4–5). This does not mean that other loves and loyalties are excluded; it means that such love remains true love, true loyalty, only when subordinated to our love of God. But such love of God must be properly understood. God is the God of all humankind and of all creation. God is seeking to make and keep human life human, and to liberate the whole of creation.

Further, the claim is made that we are fulfilled, become more human, only as our capacity for relationship expands. We are, then, truly loyal to ourselves and to those we love only when we work with God in freeing ourselves and others, and liberating our capacities for love, care, and fulfilling relationships. Our concern for our communities and societies is authentic loyalty only when it empowers our communities to reach beyond their self-interest, beyond their racism and nationalism, to participate in and share the goodness and beauty of other communities. Only as we encourage the groups to which we belong to open themselves to the richness of plurality are we being truly loyal and loving to them.

What we know from history and our own experience is that the drive to make our relationships and communities secure ends up by destroying them. Locked into patterns of jealousy and possessiveness, our relationships collapse. When our communities are closed, rigid, self-protective, they finally collapse under the weight of hatred for, and fear of, other communities. Nations that seek only their own self-interest end up being destroyed by the forces of opposition that their global injustice creates. Unfortunately, such destruction usually brings intolerable floods of human suffering and social disruption. The injustice and viciousness of our ultranationalism now threaten with nuclear annihilation the earth and all humankind, guilty and innocent alike.

The Judeo-Christian tradition thus affirms both the goodness of our loves and loyalties, and the dangers of self-centered and nationalistic loves and loyalties. In the Bible such loyalties are called idolatry. Some particular finite relationship or community becomes the center of value for all our actions.[49] Our personhood and our communities are shaped and formed by a destructive, demoniacal commitment. The tradition claims that such narrow loyalties are not, in the final analysis, expressions of love for the persons or communities to which we are loyal. Such misplaced loyalty creates persons and communities that are narrow, anxious, cut off from the richness of other persons, communities, and creation. From this perspective, "Mortal sin is primarily, not an act against the law of God or going against the ultimate end, but rather the breaking of our relationship of love with God, neighbor, world, and self."[50] To properly love others, to be truly loyal to particular communities and societies is to do so within the context of God's love for and loyalty to the whole of creation. We must love others and our communities from the perspective of loving and caring for all persons and the whole of creation.

The Judeo-Christian tradition reminds us that none of our particular loves or loyalties must ever become our center of meaning and value. As H. Richard Niebuhr notes discussing his relational value theory:

With this beginning the value theory of monotheistic theology is enabled to proceed to the construction of many relative value systems, each of them tentative, experimental, and objective, as it considers the interaction of beings on beings, now from the point of view of man, now from the point of view of society, now from the point of view of life. But it is restrained from erecting any one of these into an absolute, or even from ordering it above the others, as when the human-centered value system is regarded as superior to a life-centered system.[51]

One task of Christian ethics, then, is that of developing character and institutional structures that allow us to love properly and to honor our loyalties in such a way that our particular loves and loyalties benefit the whole of creation. Such a task is carried out in the context of a contrary natural inclination to make our particular loves and loyalties the center of value, the norm by which all else is measured. The task is also approached in a fallen, sinful world where it is not always possible to honor some loves and commitments without disdaining others. It is in response to our need to act in such a world that the Judeo-Christian tradition has also affirmed certain values and norms, as well as some procedures to help us sort out our responsibilities. We will be looking at these remaining elements of the Christian moralscape in the next chapter.

4

THE CHRISTIAN MORALSCAPE: VALUES, EMPIRICAL FACTORS, AND MODES OF DECISION-MAKING

In the last chapter we looked at the two most influential aspects of the Christian moralscape—its worldview and its conception of our proper loyalties. In this chapter we will look at the remaining three categories of the typology I am using to describe the framework of Christian ethics: (1) values and norms; (2) the role of experiential and empirical factors; and (3) the method of decision-making. All the claims made in these areas have a direct relationship to the worldview and its concept of loyalties. Still, these additional categories flesh out and specify more fully the implications of these two broader, more general, categories. We will begin by considering the rules and values that the Judeo-Christian tradition has identified as being necessary guides for our personal and social development and our individual and corporate behavior.

NORMS AND VALUES

To begin, I return to the earlier distinction between norms and values. Values represent states or goods that we desire. They inform the affective motivations of our behavior and development, and define the goals and ends of our action. Values represent that which we love and that to which we aspire. Norms, on the other hand, are

72

rules and principles,[1] some formal and some informal, which provide guidelines for our behavior and which help us operate in a world of conflicting interests and confused loyalties. As we shall see, some moral terms refer to both values and norms. Justice is something we value; it may also be a label for a set of rules to regulate personal and social interactions. As in the previous sections, the treatment here will not be exhaustive of all possible Christian norms and values, but rather will attempt to articulate the more prominent ones that give the Christian ethic its distinct shape.

Values

I start with values because their influence on moral behavior is more pervasive and profound than that of norms even though, as a category, they appear more vague and their effects on our behavior less direct. Our values give a general directionality, a purpose, to our behavior. They define the goals of our activity. What is interesting about the values of the Judeo-Christian tradition is that they differ very little from the basic values of most persons whether they are part of this tradition or not. If there is a distinctiveness about Judeo-Christian values, it lies in the vision that orders these values, in the claims about how these values relate to each other and which should take precedence when values are in conflict with one another.

Like others, Christians value bodily and psychological well-being (health); access to basic resources of food and shelter; membership in caring communities and support groups that foster love, care, and a sense of self-worth. The tradition, however, expands this value to a vision of situations and conditions under which all persons have access to these basic goods and communities. Hence justice is a primary value in the Judeo-Christian tradition, and "giving to each their due" involves a right of each person to have these fundamental needs met. Here the value we place upon our personal well-being is expanded to a concern that all share a similar state of well-being.

Likewise, the Judeo-Christian tradition values political, economic, and religious freedom: the ability to have power over our lives and the life of our communities. There is a recognition that human well-being and development depend upon our being able to set the agenda for our lives and have the power to shape our personhood. When others can use political, economic, or religious power to control and shape our lives, we are dehumanized. The Bible thus begins with an act of political liberation (the exodus) and is the ongoing cry of a people seeking political, economic, and religious freedom (the Magnificat, Luke 1:46–56). Again, however, the concern for freedom expands to a concern for the freedom of all. Valuing freedom for others requires that we repudiate and surrender our power over others in order to assure that they have the same freedom we desire for ourselves.

In the Old Testament, all the above values are incorporated into the fundamental concept of shalom, a comprehensive vision of personal and societal well-being.[2] The concept of shalom is carried over into the New Testament in the vision of the kingdom of God, a state of total well-being for all characterized by a state of universal peace and reconciliation between all parts of creation. Both the Old and New Testament present this visionary longing for a world in which persons, and all aspects of creation, are open to the enrichment that the variety of creation and human interaction makes possible.

Embedded in the vision of shalom are two other important values already mentioned: peace and reconciliation. There is a tremendous biblical emphasis on peace; it is a fundamental value for what often appears to be a war-weary people.[3] Such peace, however, is not the mere absence of conflict, the peace that comes when one side intimidates the other into peaceful behavior; nor is it the cold war peace of mutual intimidation. This peace is a positive state of affairs based on a fundamental reconciliation of previously antagonistic groups.[4] Reconciliation is here understood as the mutual acceptance of the worth and value of the other; a recognition of the value and joy of differences; a willingness to allow others to develop their full humanity. This reconciliation, at its fullest, will include a reconciliation of persons with the natural world as well. It is this fundamental vision of shalom, of the kingdom of God, that gives meaning to, and orders, all human values.[5]

One could go on to list many other states of being and objects that persons might properly value, such as family, works of art, and peace of mind. The list would be almost endless, for it could include all those things and states of being that enrich and fulfill human existence. I will, however, focus directly on only one of these values because of its important implications for our current social situation.

This additional value is the value of expanding human knowledge about ourselves and the natural and social worlds. Our expanded knowledge offers unprecedented opportunities for human control and use of the environment in which we live, and even over our own biology. The Judeo-Christian tradition has always valued such knowledge. There is a fundamental understanding that we are to use our rationality to better understand ourselves and our world so that we can act more responsibly in all areas of our lives.[6] As cocreators, as persons living in a fallen world, such knowledge expands our capacity for responsible and loving action. Such pursuit of knowledge, however, is not pursuit of "knowledge for the sake of knowledge." Rather, this value, like all other values, finds its meaning and direction through reference to the kingdom of God. Our knowledge is to be used in the service of that kingdom. We are to work to build a just, peaceful, reconciled world.

This vision is balanced by the warning of our sinfulness that tempts us to use our knowledge to increase our power and security as we use our power to subvert others to our purposes.[7] Living as we do in a conflicted and fallen world, we need more specific guidelines to help us decide the appropriate use of our knowledge and to help us embody our values in our persons and communities. Norms and rules represent the wisdom of a tradition, and attempt to provide concrete guidelines to the living of one's faith.

Norms and Rules

Although our values and visions provide a general goal and direction for our moral activity, norms recognize that we live in an imperfect and conflicted world. Consequently, norms and rules provide guidelines that will guide us in conforming our personal and social development to our visions and values. These guidelines tend to be of two types. First are those that provide concrete guidelines to regulate our relationships to one another and our world. The second type are rules that regulate our deliberative processes in determining how to act in specific situations.

In looking at the first category of rules, we discover that the Judeo-Christian tradition provides a number of rules whose intent is to assure a minimum of respect between persons. The last seven of the Ten Commandments specify a number of rights that persons have in relation to their lives, property, and familial communities. These regulations are understood as protecting the necessary components of human fulfillment. These commandments also establish the basic conditions of truth-telling and respect for the personhood and property of others that make social life possible.[8] In addition, the tradition, as it develops, demands that we recognize the worth and value of all persons, not just that of members of our own community. All persons are presented as having equal worth in the eyes of God.[9] The equality and worth of persons is pushed to its most extreme possibility in the mandate to love even the enemy (Matt. 5:43–48). As Antoine Vergote notes, "This is undoubtedly the hardest of all the commandments. It is also the most specifically Christian among them."[10] According to this mandate, we are to give the enemy the same respect and recognize the same rights that we accord to friends and neighbors.

In addition, the biblical tradition draws a distinction between rights and wants. Rights are grounded in basic human need, whereas wants are a product of human desire. The rights (needs) of others always have a priority over our wants. So, as Beverly Harrison observes, "From a liberation ethics standpoint, no one has a right to luxury or even to less essential 'enhancement needs' if those needs are satisfied at the price of others' basic dignity or physical survival."[11]

At the level of specific action, the Christian tradition moves beyond the claim that we are to respect the rights and equality of others, to demand that we act affirmatively to enhance and improve the lives of others. We are required to work with God for the political, economic, psychological, and spiritual liberation of others, the world, and ourselves. Put more simply, "We are to love the neighbor as ourselves." We are to be actively engaged in the work of love. This is a critical distinction between Christian ethics and the philosophical traditions of the West. In these traditions, the claim is usually made that our primary moral responsibility is to avoid doing harm.[12] In the Christian tradition doing good is on an equal moral footing. We are held accountable not only for harming others, but also for failing to do the good that we could do (see the judgment story in Matthew 25).

In the complex world in which we live, deciding what is good for a neighbor is not always an easy task. We will return to this issue in the next section. Nevertheless, the Judeo-Christian tradition offers a general rule to guide us in determining our responsibilities to our neighbor. We are informed (the golden rule) that we are "to do unto others as we would have them do unto us." Clearly this guideline will not always provide accurate guidance; sometimes we may discover that neighbors are quite distinct from us in their values or wishes. Still it is a helpful general guideline for reminding us of our basic obligations to each other. If we are hungry, we want to be fed; if we are bereaved, we want comfort; lonely, we would like to be befriended; imprisoned, we would like to be visited and assured that proper justice is being done.

The issue of neighborly love is further complicated, however, by the fact that we are told that all persons, even the enemy, are the neighbor. But we cannot help all persons who need aid at the same time; in fact, sometimes helping one neighbor requires harming another. We might prefer a world in which such conflicts do not occur; we might be working to create just such a world. In the interim we must act in the fallen, conflicted world in which we live. How, then, do we decide which neighbor to aid? The general biblical guideline is to help those in greatest need. In a conflict between the powerful and powerless, we are to aid the powerless. Where the rights of the oppressed collide with those of an oppressor, we are to side with the oppressed. This prescription in favor of the poor, the powerless, and the oppressed is so strong in the biblical tradition that the justice of any society, its conformance to the demands of God's kingdom, is measured by reference to the conditions of the least well-off. A society of shared poverty is more just, more kingdomlike, than a society where the majority is relatively affluent and a small minority is dehumanized by poverty and lack of power.

Finally, the New Testament institutes a rule that governs the means that can be used in transforming others, our societies, and ourselves. The claim is that we should attempt to bring about such change through peaceful means, using the power of love and, where necessary, nonviolent resistance to accomplish such restructuring. Such forms of loving nonviolence respect the personhood of all parties involved, leave open the possibility of true reconciliation and peace, and offer greater opportunity for fundamental personal and social reform.[13] The use of violence simply replaces one form of repression and intimidation with another, and in the process erodes, and possibly destroys, the capacity for love and authentic human relationship in the persons who are the perpetrators of violence. The way of personal and social reform is one of suffering love, in imitation of Jesus who, instead of calling down armies of angels to fight for him, dies on the cross.[14]

In conclusion, I want to note that in the Christian tradition norms and rules are not absolute guidelines, but presumptions for behavior. Norms and rules, like Christian values, are informed by the vision of the kingdom and our concern to love the neighbor, even the enemy. At times it may be necessary to violate some of the norms and rules in order to truly love the neighbor and be true to the vision of the kingdom. Such suspension of norms and rules should not be done lightly. These guidelines represent the wisdom of a tradition that is thousands of years old. They represent the accumulated insight of a body of persons who have discovered that these rules and norms are important aids in helping us love the neighbor and actualize the kingdom. They should be set aside only after careful deliberation and scrutiny;[15] and only when, after such deliberation, it seems obvious that obeying the rules will actually harm the neighbor or when it is clearly evident that the neighbor will be better served and the ends of the kingdom furthered by setting aside particular norms and rules. Even under such conditions we must continue to monitor the actual effects of our rule-violating behavior to assure that it is truly serving the needs of the neighbor and God's kingdom. Such careful calculation is a requirement of responsible behavior and depends upon our ability to carefully analyze the existing empirical situation. It is to that category that I now turn.

EXPERIENTIAL-EMPIRICAL COMPONENTS

As I have indicated, no one feature of the Christian moralscape is necessarily unique to Christianity, although certainly many of the symbols used to describe the moralscape are unique to it. Still, the overall shape of the moralscape, its particular mix of features, does distinguish Christian morality from other forms. Particularly in its recognition of the role of human experience and the importance of the empirical world, Christianity is distinguished in some important ways from many other traditional theories of ethics.

Many traditional theories of ethics (Platonic, Kantian, Rawlsian) seek and assume the possibility of some objective, universally valid moral standards, but Christianity begins with an affirmation of the importance of our embodiedness for our moral concerns.[16] We are particular persons in particular times and places. All we know, feel, and observe is filtered through the lens of our experiences. We have, at best, a limited and partial view of the good and the true. We may, in part, be able to rise above our experiences, the factors that have determined our personhood, but we can do so only partially. And, although most ethical traditions would view such a limitation as tragic, a reason for despair, Christianity affirms the goodness of our embodiedness and so the positive nature of our seeming moral limitation. Our limited vision, if recognized, serves a positive role in the development of our personhood and our societies, and in our specific moral actions.

First, if we can recognize the skewed nature of our moral vision, the limits of our wisdom and goodness, we can be open to the goodness, insights, and corrections of others. We need not impose our views indiscriminately upon others or force our cultural beliefs onto "inferior" peoples. We can put down the "white man's burden" and be open to the richness that others can bring to our lives. As Camus presents so persuasively in *The Rebel*, it is our desire to impose our goodness, our knowledge of absolute truth, upon others that has been a fundamental cause of human suffering and tragedy.[17] Christians should be willing to suspend such claims and recognize the limitedness of their vision.

Additionally, a recognition of the limited nature of our insights and goodness means that in acting, Christians assume that the good will be done only partially and that, at times, evil will be done instead of good despite our best intentions.[18] Christians have no stake in proclaiming the absolute goodness of all that they do. To the contrary, they are ready to acknowledge and respond to the limitations of their actions. They are ready to repent the shortcomings of their actions, to acknowledge those occasions when they have actually done harm, and to admit that often they have failed to do the good. Because they have no need to proclaim their own absolute goodness, they stand ready to assume responsibility for their actions and to correct, as much as possible, their mistakes. They likewise do not expect perfection of others, but remain open to the tentative attempts of others to do the good, accepting the limited vision, the embodiedness of others' actions. This recognition puts human relationships on a very different footing and so offers new possibilities for human interaction and reconciliation.

Next, the recognition of our embodiedness is a reminder that our moral responsibility is to be particular persons in a particular time and society, and having particular relationships. We are called to live a life of responsibility within the context of a unique web of relationships and influences, to embody, in our small segment of history and geography, God's intentions for creation. Our primary moral task is not to envision some universal good or theorize about the abstract nature of truth, but rather to do the good in a particular time and place.[19] The recognition of our embodiedness drives us back to an awareness of our particular responsibilities, and so forces us to live out our understanding of what God daily requires of us. "Moral consciousness," as Daniel Maguire knows, "takes shape in a specific field of action and reaction to unique and unrepeatable challenges and in a web of collective and interpersonal relationships never found before or afterwards."[20]

The Judeo-Christian tradition, however, as I have already noted, understands that our anxiety drives us to proclaim the universal validity of what we know and do. We seem inescapably driven to make our notions of the good the standard by which all other persons and views are to be measured. Recognizing this temptation, the tradition emphasizes ways of overcoming this natural inclination. One, of course, is to measure our goodness according to God's standards. Looking at the Ten Commandments, or especially the Sermon on the Mount, we are driven to a confession of our own limited goodness.[21]

In addition, we are asked to enter empathetically into the lives of others. We have seen this demand in one of the central rules of the Judeo-Christian faith: "Do unto others as you would have them do unto you." We are asked to view situations through the eyes of others as well as our own. God's special love for the poor and oppressed requires that we look at our own actions and those of our society through the eyes of the powerless. We must view ourselves and society from the bottom, looking up.[22]

Because of the need for empathy, the tradition supports and demands the expansion of our own experiences. We become morally more sensitive as we immerse ourselves in the lives of persons and cultures different from ourselves and our culture. At its worst, the missionary activity of the church has incorporated an arrogant imperialism that has helped spread a dehumanizing form of Western culture and capitalism. But, at its best, it has led to the expansion of vision and moral feeling through the empathetic participation in the lives of other, culturally distinct, peoples.[23]

Lastly, the emphasis on embodiedness becomes a primary motivation for the building of new communities and the reform of old ones. Because we are inescapably formed and shaped by our communities, we are driven to develop communities that will allow us and others to expand and develop our personhood. The Jews understood that they could not live out "God's image" in their lives unless they formed a community, became a people that would permit and encourage such personal development. The early Christians, despairing at becoming God's people within the confines of existing social structures, withdrew to form new communities, communities in which they could support and encourage each other in the task of becoming more Christlike. But ultimately the love of neighbor drives us beyond social withdrawal to the reform of all aspects of society that currently lead to the dehumanization of others and ourselves. We must seek to restructure patriarchal family arrangements, oppressive political systems, cultures of poverty, and class- and race-based social systems. Proclaiming that we are embodied, that we are shaped more by the communities of which we are part than by abstract notions of the good, the Christian tradition demands such social transformation, for it is an inescapable task of human liberation.

The Christian concern for the neighbor, for the real embodied neighbor, means that the empirical world is important to Christian ethics in yet one more way. Love of the neighbor, even the enemy, does not mean that we are to have a nice, warm feeling about them. It is impossible to love enemies if by that we mean that we like them, that they warm our hearts. To love the neighbor and the enemy is to act in such a way as to respect, protect, and enhance their humanity. It is to act in such a way that we help liberate their humanity from that which restricts and oppresses it. From this perspective, we are required to love even those we do not like. But, in order to act in a loving, liberating way, we must know about our neighbors and the specific conditions that oppress them. In addition, we must be able to predict what kinds of actions will actually be helpful, and finally be able to analyze the actual effects of our actions to see if they have, indeed, had the desired effects. Such informed love requires that we be deeply enmeshed in the particularities of the persons and situations to which we are responding and sensitive to the actual effects of our actions.[24] Loving, responsible action requires the most careful analysis of the situation that we can make, including an analysis of our own motives for action. Responsible action is always informed action. Love requires that we make extensive use of the best historical and scientific insights available to us in each situation.

Christianity is thus very far removed from deontological theories of the right that are primarily concerned with obeying rules and principles, and are only secondarily concerned about the actual consequences of our action. Christian morality begins with concrete commitment to the particular neighbor (even the enemy) and is primarily concerned with improving the life of that person. Rules are important only if they contribute to the actual enhancement of the lives of others. In this respect, Christianity is much more closely aligned with teleological approaches to ethics than to deontological ones. As we shall see in the next section, though, a Christian mode of moral decision-making departs in important ways from both teleological and deontological methods.

MODE OF DECISION-MAKING

We have now arrived at the component of ethics that is commonly understood as "the task of ethics." Ethics is often presented as dealing primarily with providing us a method for solving moral problems and analyzing the rightness or wrongness of particular moral actions. As I have attempted to show, the task of ethics is much broader than this. In fact, the more prominent features of the moralscape so determine our behavior that most of our moral decisions are made reflexively without requiring elaborate moral deliberations. We do not stop to reflect upon whether we should or should not murder each particular person we meet or whether we should or should not rob each store or bank that we enter. Intense moral deliberation occurs only on those rare occasions when the situation or our moralscape is morally unclear or conflicted. Even in such cases, however, the broader moralscape will define the parameters within which moral deliberation will occur. We are convinced that the world is overpopulated and that population pressures are causing international tensions and leading toward environmental destruction. Our beliefs about the value of life and the comparative worth of persons will determine whether we entertain some form of genocide as an acceptable response to the problem.[25]

There are times and occasions when careful moral deliberation is both helpful and necessary in deciding how we should act. The Christian tradition has utilized a variety of methods for moral decision-making.[26] I want to support a method that combines elements from a number of traditions and, in fact, seems an adequate reflection of the way many Christians make moral decisions today and in the past.

Earlier I referred to two traditional methods for making moral decisions, the deontological and the teleological. As stated, the deontological approach demands that we look to the rules and norms that apply to a particular situation and then conform our behavior to the governing rules. A teleological approach requires us to decide what values we want to embody (what ends we want to achieve) and then perform the action that most fully accomplishes those ends. As I have suggested, neither approach seems quite complete, for most of us look to both norms and values, to rules and consequences, when we deliberate our actions. In addition, both approaches are flawed in that they tend to view each act as an isolated, coherent event. But moral action, as H. Richard Niebuhr observes, is more like carrying on a dialogue. We step into an ongoing process of events and influences whose origin predates us and whose effects will transcend us.

A member of a corporation's board of directors votes to close an industrial plant that is only marginally profitable. By his action, he helps set in motion a chain of events that will lead to increased suicides, child and spouse abuse, alcohol and drug addiction, increased crime, and marital breakups. Thousands of persons who have come to depend on the plant will be affected by a decision based upon rational profit-seeking calculations.[27] For most of us, the morality of the corporate decision will be determined not by the single, distinct act of deciding to close the plant, but by the corporation's long-term response to the employees and community it is deserting.

The moral worth of any action must be understood in the total context of the situation to which we are responding and by reference to our ongoing response to the new situation that our actions create. This means that an evaluation of our moral actions cannot be made solely on the basis of their "rightness" (conformance to particular norms) or their "goodness" (ability to accomplish some desired end), for neither standard is a fully adequate standard of measurement. Our actions are so complex in their motivations and effects, the consequences so ongoing, that neither evaluation can be finally or fully made. The evaluation that we can make is whether the action is "fitting." Does it make moral sense in the context of the dialogue in which we are engaged? Such an approach to moral decision-making is described by H. Richard Niebuhr as an "ethic of responsibility."[28] The method of decision-making I am proposing fits in the category of an "ethic of responsibility" and draws heavily on a refinement of this method proposed by James B. Nelson.

An ethic of responsibility demands that we first determine the context within which we are acting. This determination requires relating the particular situation to the broader aspects of our worldview. For H. Richard Niebuhr this means that responsible moral action must relate itself to an all-embracing context. "It is action which is fitted into the context of universal, eternal, life-giving action by the One. It is infinitely responsible in an infinite universe to the hidden yet manifest principle of its being and its salvation."[29]

However, it is also necessary to understand the empirical context of the particular situation to which we are responding. Is abortion right or wrong? In response to such a question, Joseph Fletcher is right in noting, "Right and wrong 'depend upon the situation.' Apart from helping or hurting persons, judgments—i.e., evaluations—are meaningless."[30] Aborting the fetus of a woman who has been raped, of a young girl who is the victim of incest, seems to be a different matter from aborting the healthy fetus of a married career woman. I do not want to argue here the morality of either, but simply to point to the fact that they are very different acts because of the context in which they occur. "Is capitalism better than communism?" is another unanswerable question. We need to know better for whom, and under what conditions.

Our method of moral decision-making must begin with a careful description of the context to which we are responding. We need to know something about its history, the persons involved, and the social forces at work. Any attempt to respond to a situation without significant information about how our actions will affect persons and the situation is irresponsible. It is like breaking into a conversation with one's own views and comments without first determining what the conversation is about. Once in a while we may be lucky and accidentally contribute a pertinent or valuable comment; more often our comments will be irrelevant; sometimes they will actually be harmful. Response, then, to particular moral situations requires a careful accumulation of information that allows us to describe as fully as possible the context to which we are responding.

So far, of course, most teleologists and deontologists would agree. We must describe the situation so that we know which rules are applicable, or how best to accomplish the ends we have set for ourselves. The most radical departure from these two other methods comes at the next step. Instead of moving to the applicable rules or values that govern a situation, James B. Nelson suggests a complex second step in our method of decision-making, a step that includes reflection upon our motives, our intentions, the nature of the contemplated act, and the likely consequences.[31] This second step thus includes a consideration of the character of the actor, the values we hope to embody or ends we want to achieve, the relevant rules and guidelines that have developed historically to deal with situations of this type, and the consequences of the action. The claim here is that by paying attention to each of these factors, we will be able to act more responsibly than if we rely on only one or two of them.

In step two, then, we begin by looking at the character of the actor or actors. What motivates their behavior? Why are we planning to act in a particular way? There is an entire moral tradition that argues that the goodness of an act resides in the motives of the actor.[32] If the actor sincerely desires the good, is genuinely concerned to do the right thing, the act is good. Certainly there is some truth in such a position. Few of us would consider the giving of money to charity simply for the purpose of reducing our taxes to be a good act even though it might have good consequences. Perhaps a more extreme example shows better the truth of this position. A person who inadvertently helps another even though he or she actually intended harm, has certainly not committed a "good" act. The goodness or rightness of an act certainly includes the motive for the action and the character of the person acting. On the other hand, proper motivation is not sufficient to make an act right or good. The person who desires to help another but who, through ignorance of the situation or personal incompetence, harms that person, has not done something good. Other factors need to be considered. Reliance on motives as the determining factor in deciding about the moral quality of an action is further complicated by the hiddenness of our real motives. Both personally and corporately we are adept at convincing ourselves that our petty, selfish acts actually have very altruistic motives.[33]

The second set of factors—intentions—helps offset the narrow focus upon the role of character in decision-making by requiring us to reflect upon the values we want to embody and the ends we want to achieve. One way of unmasking our actual motivations is to look at the ends we are actually seeking. All societies and politicians claim to be motivated by a desire to meet the needs of the citizens of that society, especially the least well-off. But what ends are actually sought in their concrete policies? Do the policies reflect a goal of actually ending poverty in a particular society or are they ill-conceived, underfunded programs whose primary goal is to appease the poor and undermine their demands for a truly just social order? In the first case the goal is meeting human need; in the second, it is the preservation of the benefits and status of those who are benefiting from the existing social order. Which values should be embodied, which ends pursued? Here reference to other aspects of the Christian moralscape provide clear direction in this instance. We are called to meet the needs of the poor. Inasmuch as the ends we envision are always limited, always benefit some more than others, responsible action requires further reflection.

Here, a third set of considerations comes into play, "the nature of the act itself." We are now concerned with applying the wisdom and insights of our moral tradition to the situation that confronts us. What rules and norms have proved helpful in regulating conduct in situations like these? What basic rights need to be acknowledged and recognized to assure that, in our attempts to do the good for some person or group of persons, we do not seriously harm or violate the rights of others? Our basic rules also function in helping us decide whether those persons who will benefit by our action are the persons we should be most concerned about benefiting. Which rights should receive protection as we develop our medical care system if there is a conflict between the rights of various parties? If there is a conflict between the rights of physicians to treat whom they please, to practice where they wish, and to establish their own fees, and the right of the poor and sick to medical care, whose rights receive priority? The wisdom of the Judeo-Christian tradition provides rules that clearly support a preference for the latter's rights.

Finally, we act responsibly only when we consider the various possible actions we might take and their likely consequences. Because Christianity is concerned about the actual effects of actions on actual persons, it is necessary to consider all the possible options for action and their likely consequences. In calculating consequences it is important to look beyond the obvious, immediate consequences and try to speculate upon the long-range impact on one's neighbors, one's society, and one's own character. Obviously we cannot know for certain all the effects of all possible courses of action, or even all the effects of any single course of action.[34] Still, we are required to consider historical precedents, and social and scientific projections, before we act. We ultimately should choose the course of action that is most beneficial, or, if none seems really beneficial, the course of action that appears least harmful. Again, a strong element for choosing a particular course of action is our assessment that it will set in motion a process of events that will allow for an ongoing, positive moral dialogue. All responsible action necessarily involves the calculated choice between carefully scrutinized alternatives. Certainly, in retrospect, we will sometimes have chosen the wrong alternative, but we can be spared the tragedy of knowing, "had [we] but thought about it before [we] acted, [we] would have acted differently."[35]

After Nelson has indicated that responsible action requires paying attention to motives, intentions, rules, and consequences, he goes on to affirm that the responsible act is one in which all the above aspects of the action are informed by love. That is, in Christian reflection upon moral activity, all areas of consideration are to be shaped by a concern for the well-being of the other, the neighbor, the enemy. In an extension of this claim, I would contend that the motives, intentions, rules, and consequences must also be informed by a vision of God's kingdom of justice, peace, and mutuality. Subjecting our deliberative process to the scrutiny of love, placing it before the light of God's kingdom, helps us discover the misplaced loyalties and the narrow self-interest that inform so much of our behavior.

As we have seen, Christianity recognizes the fundamental egocentricity that informs our relationship to the world and to others, and motivates our behavior. We are primarily concerned about ourselves, those we love, and those communities and organizations that support us and are part of our system of meaning. Christian love expands this vision, puts a check on our selfish loyalties, and demands that we evaluate our decisions from the perspective of the good of all. Dropping atomic bombs on Hiroshima and Nagasaki to end the war and save American lives discounts the equal worth and value of the Japanese lives. Supporting economic policies that use high rates of unemployment to lower the rate of inflation places the needs of the middle and upper classes ahead of the needs of the poor and unemployed. Assuring that each step of the deliberative process is informed by Christian love reminds us that at each step of the process we must be sensitive to the selfish distortions of our moral calculations.[36] It also reminds us at each step of the process that in a choice among neighbors, the most needy have a prior claim on our resources, time, and loyalties. Christian love also reminds us at each stage that there are no persons, not even the enemy, whose needs can be ignored. Finally Christian love drives us to look beyond the immediate situation and reminds us that all we are doing is being done in the context of a world where God continues to act to liberate and redeem the whole of creation.

The final step in moral deliberation takes place after we have acted. Christians refuse to call any act "good" in an absolute sense; refuse to see any act as finally past or completed. Rather, Christians model their action after the covenantal faithfulness of God.[37] Each act is merely a word spoken in an ongoing dialogue. The goal is to participate in a creative, ongoing conversation. In other words, Christians act in the hope of contributing to God's full liberation of persons and creation in the coming kingdom of God. Each particular act falls short of bringing such complete fulfillment, and so every act becomes the basis for further activity.

What is required, then, is that we continue our moral reflection after the particular act. We study its consequences; we attempt to learn from its successes and failures so that we can become better partners in dialogue. Most important, we attempt to see what action is now required by the consequences of the action we have just completed. How might we act to offset the negative consequences of a prior action? How might we act to further enhance its benefits? In all this, we must focus on the consequences of our actions for the personhood of others, the quality of our communities, and our own character. Because the goal is the creation of a community of love and mutuality, we must act to promote social structures that enhance human relationships, to liberate the loving, caring potential of others, and to contribute to our self-development and liberation. It is not only the other who needs liberation, but I too. Christianity, of course, is centered on a concern for the neighbor and the neighbor's need. Personal development is never the primary concern. As we shall see in chapter 6, however, there is a form of indirect care for the self that is absolutely essential if we are to be partners in cooperation with others and God, and be useful actors in the mutual struggle to liberate ourselves and creation.

CONCLUSION

In chapters 3 and 4 I have attempted to sketch the prominent features of the Christian moralscape that inform my response to both fundamental and derivative moral questions. As I will attempt to show in the remaining chapters, all these features, as well as some that have not yet been fully articulated, come into play in our lives as moral beings. Some responses will draw more fully on some aspects of the moralscape than on others. Sometimes responses will seem quite rational and articulate, sometimes they will seem more intuitive, based on a vague notion of what is fitting. In all cases, however, an attempt needs to be made, not in order to prove to others the correctness of our response, for such proof can never be given, but to show that our response is informed and intelligible, and not an ignorant or selfish act. Ethical reflection helps ensure that our action comes from a sincere attempt to be a responsible participant in an ongoing moral process. Beyond that, there is little that we can, or need, do.

In the following chapters I want to respond to the two fundamental moral questions: "What should we be?" and "What kinds of communities shall we create?" Then I will move on to a discussion of several derivative moral questions in order to show how the moralscape I have sketched shapes our responses to particular moral problems and situations. In all these chapters I attempt to show the ways in which Christian reflection and response share an immense common ground with other moral approaches, especially various forms of humanism.[38] However, I also try to point out the distinctiveness of Christian moral reflection and response.[39] At its best, Christian ethics is a partner to all those who are seeking to make and keep human life human, and trying to liberate the whole of creation. Like any good conversational partner, Christianity is willing to share its rich insights while remaining open to both the criticism and insights of other participants in the conversation.

5

SHAPING OUR HUMANITY

In this chapter I focus on the first of the two fundamental moral questions: "What should I be; what should I become as a person?" Treating this question first should not give the impression that it is more important than its companion question, "What should we be as a people, a community, a society; what should we corporately become?" As my treatment of both questions will show, the two issues are inseparable. It is impossible to treat the one without treating the other. It is impossible to make decisions about the nature of persons without simultaneously making decisions about the nature of societies, and vice versa. The two questions are related in the same way as the two great commandments of the Christian tradition: "You shall love the Lord your God with all your heart . . . and . . . You shall love your neighbor as yourself." Jesus declares the inseparability of these concepts, saying that the second commandment is like the first (Matt. 22:37–40).

The two fundamental moral questions are inseparable, part of a seamless cloth. Nevertheless, it is useful to distinguish the two questions for the purpose of emphasizing different aspects of human development and for the sake of clarity. The choice of a starting point is thus somewhat arbitrary, although the nature of Western culture makes it easier and more natural to start with the issue of the person and our individual identity.

As I indicated in the first chapter, our sense of morality, of being moral beings, is a function of our freedom, our self-transcendence, which both allows us and condemns us to create our own humanity. Certainly we do not create ourselves in a vacuum. There are biological and sociological determinants and constraints on our development. Despite these influences, each decision we make, each action in which we engage, helps determine the nature and shape of our selfhood and so of our humanity.[1]

Most of the time we are unaware of both our freedom and our self-creation. But during periods of crisis and uncertainty we become aware of our responsibility for shaping and developing our selfhood. Such crises and uncertainties take many forms. At the most simple level it appears in indecision about how to dress or where to live—simple choices, yet choices that make statements about us and determine, in some small degree, the kinds of persons we are and will be. Our recognition of our freedom also surfaces in the vocational anxiety of choosing a career, a sphere of work to which we will commit a significant amount of our time and energy.

However, as I indicated in chapter 1, our sense of moral freedom, though related to all these limited experiences, is the profound experience of recognizing that "truly the individual human person has the opportunity and the destiny to create one's own moral self."[2] To be moral beings is to have the power to determine the quality of our lives in a way that affects and colors all other aspects of our existence. The quality of our humanity will influence the vocational choices we make and also the way we perform that vocation.

Every year in the United States 20 percent of all operations performed by surgeons are unnecessary. The cost runs into the billions of dollars and the unnecessary loss of life is over ten thousand.[3] Many of these operations are performed by surgeons whose primary concern is the enhancement of their own reputations as surgeons or their own financial gain. Our system of medical care encourages such abuse for, as George Bernard Shaw observed in *The Doctor's Dilemma*: "That any sane nation, having observed that you could provide for the supply of bread by giving bakers a pecuniary interest in baking for you, should go on to give a surgeon a pecuniary interest in cutting off your leg, is enough to make one despair of political humanity."[4] Most physicians, of course, avoid such financial temptation and provide humane medical care because of their commitment to the well-being of their patients.

In a similar way, our moral commitments may influence what we wear or refuse to wear (animal furs, expensive clothes) or where we live (an exclusive segregated suburban neighborhood, or a modest home in an integrated neighborhood).

The awareness of our moral freedom, our ability to shape our basic humanity, takes two forms, each of which has been reflected by a particular ethical tradition. One experience is that of having violated some fundamental aspect of our own or someone else's humanity. It is an expression of an awareness that our humanity depends upon the nurturing of certain fundamental conditions and aspects of personhood; an awareness that violation or destruction of these conditions makes us and others "less human." This is a recognition that we do not have complete freedom to shape ourselves; that to be human we need to abide by certain "laws of nature." Awareness of these basic human requirements is coupled with awareness that we have the freedom to ignore or contradict the fundamental requirements that do, in fact, make us human. Part of our moral experience, then, is that of a moral law that confronts us as a demand, as an "ought," reminding us of what we are intended to be. This understanding of moral experience is expressed in Paul's confession: "I do not understand my own actions. For I do not what I want, but I do the very thing I hate. Now if I do what I do not want, I agree that the law is good" (Rom. 7:15–16). It is also embedded in the whole tradition of natural law[5] and is acknowledged in the concept of synderesis (a fundamental desire to do good, which is the source of human conscience).[6] This recognition of moral requirements, of laws of being, also stands at the core of Kantian ethics. We are confronted with an "ought," a "categorical imperative" that demands that we live out the law of our being, that we become what we are supposed to be.[7]

The whole deontological tradition thus represents a response to one aspect of our experience as moral beings, of having moral freedom. We are aware that we stand under a given law that must be acknowledged and lived if we are to be fully human. It is the experience of living under law that gives rise to concepts of human rights, of certain fundamental givens that must be respected if our humanity and that of others is to flourish. It is this experience that Tillich refers to as the experience of heteronomy.[8] We know that we live under a law that is not of our own making. It is a law that stands over against us, that predates us, and places constraints on the use of our freedom. This awareness of our "moral being" I will refer to as the "experience of our fundamental humanity." It is an experience that has content and helps to define our humanness and, in the process, gives guidance for practical moral behavior.

The sense of moral freedom appears to us in yet another way. We also have the experience of being incomplete, unfinished, and having the ability and autonomy to fundamentally shape our very humanity. We can set goals for ourselves and seek to achieve them; attempt to perfect or actualize those parts of our humanity that are only imperfectly or potentially present. Here our humanity is experienced "not so much [as] a 'being' [but] as a 'becoming.' This self-renewing potentiality means that any goal reached becomes a new beginning or, better, is then seen as only one element in a wider perspective. Present reality is merely an anticipation of something else to come."[9] Our ability to reach beyond ourselves is expressed in the Thomistic distinction between natural and supernatural virtues. All persons can, on the basis of their fundamental humanity, live a life of "natural virtue." It is possible to be just, prudent, temperate, and courageous. However, Christians can be empowered to transcend their natural humanity and live a life of an entirely different quality, a life of faith, hope, and love.[10] But we need not be familiar with Thomistic theology to understand the experience. All of us have the experience of wanting to become more than we are, of expanding our humanity, of reshaping the quality of our lives.

This experience of moral freedom is the basis for teleological forms of ethics. Here is an understanding that our moral life is characterized by a striving to become better, to expand our humanity. What is most distinctive about our humanity from this perspective is not the "laws of our being," but our incompleteness. We are human because we can set goals for our own development, because our lives are marked by intentionality.[11] We can, consequently, determine the shape and style of our personhood. We experience ourselves as still becoming, moving toward an indefinite future. As Paul acknowledges: "When I was a child I spoke like a child, I thought like a child, I reasoned like a child; when I became a man, I gave up childish ways. For now we see in a mirror dimly, but then face to face. Now I know in part; then I shall understand fully" (1 Cor. 13:11–12).

Paul Tillich is aware of this experience and refers to it as the experience of "autonomy."[12] It is based on a notion of having almost complete power in determining our selfhood. Like the experience of heteronomy, the experience of autonomy provides important insights into the nature of our humanity and also offers guidelines for practical moral decision-making. I label this experience of our moral being "the experience of our potential humanity."

Although both the experiences of heteronomy and autonomy provide information about what it means to be human, each, by itself, presents an incomplete understanding of the human situation. Deontological or heteronomous ethics presumes a set, static human nature. From this perspective, humans were created, or evolved, as beings with a particular identifiable structure. The human problem is our failure to recognize that structure and to live it out in our actual existence. Hence we are estranged, separated, from our real being. The function of ethics is to discover the essential laws of that structure and to develop guidelines that will allow us to embody it in our lives. Persons are viewed as inherently sinful beings who inevitably depart from their created nature unless restrained by law and some authority that enforces the law.[13] Dostoevsky experiments with the theme of the breakdown of such constraints on human behavior. He speculates, "Without God, there is nothing a man is bound to do."[14] Without God there is no absolute power to enforce the moral law.

Deontological ethics are correct in pointing to our distorted, estranged mode of existence. They are right in reminding us of our natural tendency to ignore the laws that govern and protect our humanity. This, however, is only a partial description of what it means to be human.

Teleological ethics, the experience of autonomy, rightly reminds us of our potential for doing good, for altruistic behavior and positive self-development. It properly points to our concern for moral improvement and perfection as a basic aspect of our humanity. We live in time, have the capacity for growth, and can live in futures very different from the pasts out of which we come. The ethics of autonomy also includes an understanding of the evil in the world but views it as residing primarily in structures, not in persons. The destructive behavior of persons is a product of socialization by defective social structures. Persons are not born greedy, selfish, racist, or sexist; they are shaped that way by their culture. Our radical freedom provides us with the possibility of reshaping our societies and recovering a basic goodness in ourselves.[15]

This account, too, is incomplete, for we are both constrained and free, good and evil, historical and ahistorical beings. The true description of our humanity is found in the relationship and tension between these two moral experiences: the experience of our fundamental humanity and the experience of our potential humanity. The interaction of these two experiences provides us guidance in our struggle to be the particular person we are called to become.

A number of contemporary Christian theologians have struggled to provide a model for the creative, historical interaction of our fundamental and potential humanity. Before discussing these broader interactive concepts, however, I want to first discuss the content of the deontological and teleological experiences separately to see what insights, guidelines, and directions they might provide for our moral reflection and action.

THE EXPERIENCE OF OUR FUNDAMENTAL HUMANITY

Simply to talk about our humanity implies that humanness, despite its open texture, has some fundamental givens, some structure. To be human means to be something different from an ape, a horse, or a dog. Clearly we share many characteristics with them and have many of the same needs, but there is also a difference or we could not differentiate between ourselves and these other beings. Again, the fundamental givens, the structure of our humanity, usually become apparent to us during those crisis periods when we violate the structure of our own being or when our fundamental human needs are not being met. We are unaware of our need for food except when we are hungry, unaware of our need for shelter and clothing unless it is cold or begins to rain, unaware of our need for love and support from others until that support is withdrawn or a loved one dies.

Although it is impossible to fully describe the structure of human nature, it is possible to isolate some fundamental human needs. In this section, then, I will be discussing our "fundamental humanity" by reference to basic needs that must be met if we are to maintain, in even a minimal sense, our humanity. To be sure, I will not attempt to identify all possible human needs, but only some that seem essential to our capacity to function as persons.

In developing a list of fundamental human needs, I use categories derived from the work of Abraham Maslow and William Temple.[16] The categories—physical, psychological, rational, and spiritual needs— are used for convenience, but clearly their relationship to one another is as important as the categories themselves. Both Maslow and Temple see the categories as being interdependent, with lower categories being most basic in the sense of being absolute preconditions for fulfillment of higher categories. If children are malnourished, there will be physical damage to the neurological system, which will affect the development of their intelligence. On the other hand, development of higher categories may expand our ability to meet more basic needs. The development of knowledge about agriculture and nutrition allows us to produce more and better food, and also meet the basic nutritional needs of more persons more efficiently.

The categories are a useful way for organizing discussion about our basic needs and so of drawing a sketch of our fundamental humanity. Each of these sets of needs provides insights into certain aspects of our fundamental humanity.

Physical Needs

We are physical beings, embodied. Like all other living creatures, our full development is dependent upon having our basic biological needs met. We need food, shelter, and appropriate clothing. Beyond that, we need a sanitary environment,[17] and, when injured or ill, we need appropriate care so that we can regain our health and return to normal functioning.

It is clear that the physical needs of persons are not identical. Persons have varying nutritional requirements, and persons in colder climates have needs for shelter and clothing different from those in tropical climates. The needs of a particular individual also vary throughout life. Infants do little except eat and sleep. As we age our needs get considerably more complex. Likewise, our need for medical care varies with age,[18] injury, or exposure to contagious illness. Nevertheless, our ability to develop as persons requires that these basic needs be met. It is also clear that the ease or difficulty in meeting these needs will affect our ability to develop in other ways. Persons who need to work twelve hours a day simply to meet basic needs have little time left for developing the more unique aspects of our humanity. This is the reason that the arts have flourished among the leisured, aristocratic classes, and why universities remain a center of intellectual life.

The upper classes have a parasitic relationship to the lower classes: the working classes sacrifice their own human development to produce the excesses of goods that allow artists and academics to live in leisure and develop the so-called higher aspects of culture. Theoretical Marxism gets its ideological power from its repudiation of this relationship between the classes, demanding that all persons share the productive work of society and that all have an equal chance for human development.

Psychologico-Emotional Needs

Persons are more than just physical beings. They are complex psychological, emotional beings. Full human development is dependent upon the development of these psychologico-emotional needs. Clearly these needs have a base in our physical being. All higher mammals seem to have a basic need for care and mothering during infancy. In humans, however, these needs become so significant, so extended, that they represent an existence of a different quality. Healthy human development seems to require significant amounts of parental affection and care. There are a number of instances where infants have had all their biological needs met, but were left uncared for, and who simply died, seemingly from lack of affection.[19] In humans, the need for stable patterns of care remains intense all the way through childhood and adolescence. No other being seems to require this extended period of nurture for its development and well-being.

In later life, this need for love, though in different forms, appears to be a human constant. Persons have a lifelong need for care from others and for human acceptance. We are easily socialized into the behavior patterns of our society because we need others' acceptance so badly. The most severe form of punishment we can imagine, and a technique used in brainwashing, is solitary confinement. The lack of human community and acceptance is felt as a deprivation more painful than the denial of certain physical needs. The entire hospice movement grows out of a recognition that even death is more easily faced if the dying are not isolated from the human community, but rather can face their own deaths in the context of continued human care and acceptance.

In addition, all persons have other psychological needs, which include the need for both stability and change in their environment; the need to feel that they have some power over their own destinies; and finally the need for productive work, which allows them to express their creativity and be reassured they are contributing to the human community.[20]

Rational Needs

The West has a long tradition that regards rationality as the distinctive mark of humanity. We are, after all, Homo sapiens (intelligent beings). As I will argue in the next section, it is not our rationality, per se, that constitutes our humanity. Still, our rationality is a distinctive feature of our humanity.

Our ability to reason is grounded in our physical being, the structure of our brain and nervous system. And it is evident that the proper functioning of this system depends upon having our basic physical and psychological needs met. To be physically starved leads to impairment of our rationality through physical brain damage. Psychological deprivation leads to a distorted, improperly functioning rationality, which evidences itself in neurotic and psychotic disorders.

Even animals perform feats of rationality. Dogs and horses are capable of learning tricks. Cats and monkeys can solve simple problems, and some apes even use simple tools. Porpoises have apparently developed a very sophisticated system of communication. Once again, however, there is a quantum leap between the ability of animals to solve problems, learn tricks, and communicate, and similar functions in persons. There is a difference between begging for a dog biscuit and playing basketball; a difference between using a stick to probe for grubs and insects, and planning, constructing, and using a tractor for farming. The gap is enormous; we are dealing with existence of a different type.[21]

As rational beings we have a fundamental curiosity about ourselves and the world in which we live. We have a need to understand the context in which we are operating and the forces at work. Our belief that human development is closely aligned with rational development is evident in the tremendous amount of time, energy, and money devoted to education. It is also evident in the reaction of the illiterate to suddenly being able to read. There is the explosive feeling of freedom, of shaking off chains, of becoming more human.

The power of education to free us and make us more human is also evident in the fear of oppressive governments to allow the education of oppressed groups. It was long illegal in the United States to teach black slaves how to read. Current educational policies and funding suggest that as a nation we still have an unacknowledged fear of educating blacks and other racial minorities. In Latin America, governments have regularly repressed literacy campaigns and programs. And it is interesting that one immediate effect of successful Marxist revolutions has been the establishment of large, successful literacy programs.[22]

To develop humanly we need education, rational development. We need to understand ourselves and our world, for such knowledge frees us from many natural and social constraints and gives us the power to more fully control our lives.

Spiritual Needs

Just as there is a tradition in the West that understands rationality to be the distinguishing mark of our humanity, so there is another tradition that sees our spiritual capacities as being our most important characteristic. It is our ability to be in relationship with God, our seeking after a religious answer to the question of existence, that makes us human. Again, our ability to develop, to actualize the spiritual dimension of our lives, depends upon the meeting of other needs. A severely malnourished person is likely to think of little else except food. And our ability to rationally understand the world and ourselves makes us religious beings in a very different sense.

The meeting of psychological needs also has a profound effect upon the nature and quality of our spiritual existence. The ability to have faith in the sense of accepting the trustworthiness of ultimate reality may be largely determined by the reliability of those charged with meeting our psychologico-emotional needs as children. If these persons were not trustworthy, if they provided erratic care, often responded with neglect or cruelty, it may never be possible for us to trust the fundamental goodness of existence.[23] Animals may have a fundamental spirituality, an unconscious, unarticulated relationship to the whole of the cosmos, but in persons the nature of spirituality is considerably expanded, and human existence is perceived to be existence of a different quality.

As humans, then, we have needs that reach beyond our rational needs; needs not only to understand ourselves and our world, but a need to understand both from a comprehensive framework of meaning. We want to know not only how the world came into existence and how human beings came to be, but *why*. As Tillich indicates, we are beings who ask the question of being itself, the question of what is "really real."[24] It is the question of the meaning or significance of being itself.

Our spirituality informs the psychologico-emotional dimension of our existence as well. It is not enough to be related to a few individuals, a small community, a particular place. We seek, at the psychologico-emotional level, to be related to all persons and the whole of the cosmos.[25] This striving for connectedness, for relatedness—in Christian terms, for reconciliation—is one of our most profound human needs.

OUR FUNDAMENTAL HUMANITY AND THE JUDEO-CHRISTIAN TRADITION

As we observe our fundamental humanity, our basic human needs, we observe nothing distinctively Christian. Although our basic human needs may express themselves differently in different cultures, they are still part of the structure of our humanity. Nevertheless, the Judeo-Christian tradition, especially in its biblical forms, recognizes these fundamental needs, and views their satisfaction as essential for human development. Both the Old and New Testaments are full of miracle stories that address the physical needs of persons. The people of Israel was fed in the wilderness (Exod. 16:9–36), and Jesus fed the multitudes (Matt. 15:32–38). The early church views the meeting of basic human needs as a primary moral requirement of the human community. The Bible is also full of miracles of healing. There is a recognition that human development depends upon physical health. And the Christian tradition has embodied itself in numerous hospitals and medical missions throughout the world.

In addition, the biblical tradition affirms the centrality of psychological needs. There is an obvious emphasis upon the need to provide care and support for one another, and a concern to maintain stable communities of care. Likewise, both Judaism and Christianity are religions that emphasize education. Part of parental responsibility in both communities is providing both religious and vocational education. And because both religions are religions "of the book," both give high priority to literacy. Both communities also have classes of professional educators, and Jesus affirms the need for the development of the rational capacities of women if they are to fully develop their humanity (Luke 10:38–42). There seems little need to indicate that both Judaism and Christianity see the need for spiritual development as well. What needs to be noted is that despite some distortions in the tradition, the tradition at its best always places spiritual development in the context of the development of all aspects of the human person.

Ethical Implications of Our Fundamental Humanity

Our humanity, then, has a basic structure. Our development as persons requires that our basic human needs be met. In this sense, there is a fundamental humanity, a fundamental structure, that cannot be ignored if we are to develop as human beings. This structure stands over against us as a set of demands, as a law of our being. Our failure to meet certain basic needs has profound consequences immediately apparent to ourselves and others. Our denial to others of the resources necessary for meeting these needs constitutes a dehumanization of them, a destruction of their personhood. As such, the Christian demand that we be concerned about others, that we wish to make and keep human life human, and its claim about the equality of all persons, have significant implications for us as we confront specific moral problems and seek to develop social policy.

We can view the Ten Commandments as a partial statement of fundamental human needs. The commandments bespeak a recognition of the need for physical security, respect for persons, stable communities of care. A more comprehensive set of guidelines appears in the United Nations Covenant on Human Rights. This covenant provides a list of basic human needs based on the fundamental structure of human nature. According to this document, persons have a right to food, shelter, clothing, education, medical care, and work. They also have a right to religious worship, freedom of expression, geographical mobility, and self-determination. Imprisonment without cause, torture, and suppression of dissent are seen as similarly illegitimate, dehumanizing acts.[26] The Covenant on Human Rights thus stands before us as a set of laws, as deontological commands that must be obeyed if we are to respect the fundamental humanity of ourselves and others.

Our Fundamental Humanity as a Set of Human Rights

As I will indicate in the next section, meeting these needs does not guarantee the full development of our humanity. We are more than just our needs; the fundamental structure of our humanity represents only the base from which we build and expand our humanity. Nevertheless, it is an essential base. This structure places limits on what is possible, but it is also the precondition for all human development. Our fundamental humanity can thus be largely described by reference to a set of human rights that may not be violated in the name of some higher cause or purpose for humanity.[27] We are bound by the law, the nature of our being, if we are to act in such a way as to preserve and protect our humanity and that of others.

THE EXPERIENCE OF OUR POTENTIAL HUMANITY

Although our Christian faith provides few unique insights about our fundamental humanity, this is not the case as regards our "potential humanity." Our *fundamental* humanity is a reflection of the structure of our common humanity and so serves as a basis for a shared, common ethic such as that described in the Universal Covenant on Human Rights. Our *potential* humanity, by contrast, presents itself as a question, an opening onto the future. What we can and should become is not self-evident.

Christianity claims to have access to a particular revelation that provides insight into the shape our potential humanity should take. The revelation, however, is not given apart from, and irrespective of, human experience. More importantly, the truth of the Christian revelation does not reside in the revelation itself, but in the ability of the revelation to provide a convincing interpretation of our experiences and to give us humanly satisfactory responses to the problems we face.

As I will go on to indicate, the Judeo-Christian tradition has identified the experience of our potential humanity with two elemental human quests: the search for personal integration, and the quest for relationship and social reconciliation. As we shall see, these are not separate goals, but are intrinsically related aspects of our humanity. Before studying this interrelationship, however, we will look at the two elements separately in order to better understand their implications for moral reflection and action.

Integrity

The Judeo-Christian tradition understands that we are more than just a collection of needs. In fact, as we are aware, especially those of us in affluent societies, even if all our fundamental human needs are met, we still may not feel fulfilled, may still experience ourselves as incomplete. Robert Heilbroner, discussing the discontent that plagues modern developed societies, writes: "The civilizational malaise, in a word, reflects the inability of civilization directed to material improvement—higher incomes, better diets, miracles of medicine, triumphs of applied physics or chemistry—to satisfy the human spirit."[28] Such discontent shows that meeting our fundamental human needs does not constitute the goal of our existence, but merely provides the base from which we construct our humanity. But what, then, is our task, what is the goal of human development?

Part of the goal of our human development presents itself to us once again through our experience of its absence. We discover that we are overwhelmed with the experience of personal "disintegration": the feeling that we are "falling apart." Or we have the experience of running in a "rat race"; we get nowhere because we are running in too many directions at the same time. In its absence we experience a need for wholeness, for integration; we sense the need for a personal center and for a purpose that can unify our work and striving. But such wholeness, such centeredness, is never fully and completely achieved. Hence it is always experienced as part of our potential humanity rather than part of our actual humanity. It always remains a vision toward which we are drawn. As Paul Tillich observes: "In man complete centeredness is essentially given, but it is not actually given until man actualizes it in freedom and through destiny."[29]

The experience of being a self seeking integration and identity is a universal experience and has resulted in various proposals for overcoming our sense of dividedness. Usually the proposed solutions include the suppression of some part of our personality by one dominant part, which is assigned the task of organizing and controlling the shape of our selfhood. The West, as noted above, has responded by proposing a personality type in which the body, the emotions, and even the spirit, are to be controlled and suppressed by our rationality. Any feelings or emotions that contradict or challenge our reason are to be ignored or resisted. This tradition has, from time to time, generated reactions in the form of romantic movements that attempt to resolve our dividedness by suppressing the rational on behalf of bodily feelings and the emotional. The East, by contrast, has attempted to transcend the experience of personal disintegration by suppressing all aspects of personal identity through spiritual discipline and mystical transcendence. And, modern forms of nationalism offer yet another alternative by requiring the surrender of personal identity to the goals and aims of the state.

The claim of the Judeo-Christian tradition is that any attempt to achieve wholeness through the suppression of parts of our selfhood is doomed to failure. In fact, the very attempt at such suppression exacts an immense personal and social cost. This insight has been confirmed and given elaborate expression in much contemporary psychological theory, but especially in the work of Freudians and Jungians.[30] The difficulties and costs of each of the above proposals could be analyzed here, but I will focus briefly on only one set of costs imposed by one of these alternatives: the traditional Western suppression of bodily feelings and emotions by rationality.

The West has been marked by a peculiar bifurcation of our humanity, which identifies the controlling principle—reason—with adult, white males, and the subordinate components—emotions and the body—with women, persons of color, and children. The West has assumed that white males are to govern all other persons in the same way that rationality is to control the body and the emotions. Women are to be subservient and live out their lives as emotional beings who nurture and care for the young and offer a haven, a home, for their husbands. Persons of color are suspect humans who threaten the social system with brute, animalistic rebellion, and must be kept under tight control and constant supervision.

The costs of such bifurcation have been immense. Women have been imprisoned in a small part of their own humanity, prohibited from developing the full spectrum of their capacities and abilities. Persons of color have been tortured, murdered, imprisoned, kept malnourished, and forced to live in carefully defined ghetto areas.[31] White males act like emotionally starved juveniles seeking mother's approval while playing at war and conquest. Society has been deprived of the gifts and contributions of countless millions. And, under the leadership of psychologically and emotionally retarded white males, we have developed a cold, calculating, bureaucratic society that daily threatens us with dehumanization and the possibility of ecological and nuclear extinction.[32]

The Judeo-Christian tradition, at its best, understands integration in a more "holistic" sense. True integration involves the harmonious functioning of all the parts of our selfhood, with each part contributing, in its particular way, to the richness of our personhood. This claim is so strong that the tradition has refused to identify our humanity with any of its specific qualities. Our humanity is not a function of our rationality or spirituality; our humanity is not restricted because of our emotions or embodiedness. Rather, our humanity is equated with the integrated functioning of all the aspects of our personhood. The self is actually the point at which these various components of our humanity intersect; it is the unique interrelationship of all these components, and defines our humanity and makes us a particular self.[33] Biblical tradition knows nothing of disembodied souls, or the dominance of human reason in creating integrated persons. When immortality is discussed, it is always done in the context of bodily resurrection, for it is presumed that we cannot be persons, cannot be human, without our bodies and all they contribute to our humanness. By the same token, biblical figures can use their reason, but their humanity is richer because of their ability to laugh, love, weep, and feel sorrow. True integration is not the product of a self-conscious act of organization, but rather involves allowing opportunity for all our human feelings and capacities to find room to express themselves and contribute to our selfhood.

Still, the Judeo-Christian tradition recognizes that the task of integrating our selfhood is never finally completed and that the shape of our integration varies with different individuals and with each particular individual over the course of time. The infant is clearly determined by physical and emotional needs, but there is also the need for rational stimulation and the beginnings of human spirituality. As the child develops, physiological and emotional factors become more predominant. The adolescent seems to be a bundle of raw emotions and new bodily experiences. Young adulthood becomes a time of increasing rational development, and old age seems to be a time of special spiritual sensitivities.[34]

Our personal health, our wholeness, is dependent upon our ability to integrate new feelings and capacities into a consistently functioning self. This task is difficult, for as Tillich notes, "Integrating and disintegrating forces are struggling in every situation, and every situation is a compromise between these forces."[35] And, as Tillich notes, disintegration can be caused both by our failure to recognize and respond to the need to incorporate new factors into our selfhood, and by the self's being overwhelmed by the number of new experiences that confront it. In Tillich's words:

> This failure [disintegration] can occur in one of two directions. Either it is the inability to overcome a limited, stabilized, and immovable centeredness, in which case there is a center, but a center which does not have a life process whose content is changed and increased; thus it approaches the death of mere self-identity. Or it is the inability to return because of the dispersing power of manifoldness, in which case there is life, but it is dispersed and weak in centeredness, and it faces the danger of losing its center altogether—the death of mere self-alteration.[36]

Nevertheless, the Judeo-Christian tradition affirms the inherent drive toward integrity and the possibility of its partial achievement even in the face of the forces of disintegration. In the words of Bernard Häring, "The deepest part of our being is keenly sensitive to what can promote and what can threaten our wholeness and integrity."[37]

In addition, the loss of integration or centeredness can also occur because of our lack of a coherent vision to shape and unite our various activities. So we have the sense of being divided, of working against ourselves. Persons spend a great deal of time and energy parenting, nurturing their children, giving them emotional support. However, their rational work life may be devoted to developing more sophisticated military weapons whose purpose is "peace through intimidation," but which have the potential for initiating a war that would destroy their children in the holocaust to follow. A sense of wholeness, of centeredness, thus also entails finding a purpose that integrates and makes sense of all the aspects and actions of our lives. As the next section will show, the Judeo-Christian tradition finds this purpose in relationship and reconciliation.

To summarize this section, the Judeo-Christian tradition affirms our potential humanity in its drive toward integration and centeredness. It repudiates any self-imposed form of self-identity that suppresses various elements of our humanity. Rather, it affirms a personal integration that is full and life-affirming, and includes a concern for the liberation and full development of others' humanity as well. In addition, it seeks centeredness in the vision of a reconciled world in which the fragmentation of personal and social life have been overcome. Personal integration is thus important, necessary for the development of our potential humanity, but such integration, such self-identity, is not itself the final goal of our human development; for our potential humanity exhibits itself as well in the need for others, and our need to be related positively to all that is.

Relational Existence—Interdependency

If the need for integrity is a demand that presents itself in experiences of personal disintegration, or fundamental conflictedness, the need for relationship presents itself as the drive toward reconciliation and reunification in a world of social and interpersonal alienation and division. Our earliest experiences of infancy are set in the context of the need for human relationship, and our vision of the most humane death includes death among our loved ones, holding their hands as we die.

The claim of the Judeo-Christian tradition, however, is more than the claim that we need relationships. Such need is part of our fundamental humanity. Rather, the experience of our potential humanity is the experience that the goal of our human development, its very fulfillment, comes in relationship. Human development is not essentially enhanced by the acquisition of goods, experiences, knowledge, or even a narrowly defined spiritual growth. Human development is marked by our ability to expand the range of our relationships. As Paul remarks (1 Cor. 13:2): "And if I have prophetic powers, and understand all mysteries and all knowledge, and if I have all faith, so as to remove mountains, but have not love, I am nothing."

The claim about relationship as being the sign of our full humanity stands at the center of the Judeo-Christian faith. As we have previously seen, this notion is fundamental to the biblical account of creation. God creates the world and is enhanced through relationship to it.[38] Persons are created male and female as a sign of the human need for relationship. And, as Augustine notes, even the story of a single, primal set of parents for the entire human race is intended to remind us of our inescapable relationship to one another: "God's intention was that in this way the unity of human society and the bonds of human sympathy be more emphatically brought home to man, if men were bound together not merely by likeness in nature but also by the feeling of kinship."[39] Likewise, as noted, the Christian doctrine of the Trinity is an affirmation that ultimate reality itself finds its fulfillment in relationship.

The doctrine of the Trinity, however, also makes some important claims about the nature of relationship. It is quite clear that our need for security distorts most of our relationships. Most of our relationships are relationships of unequals. In order to remain secure in their relationships, males often try to control and dominate relationships. They want to set the terms on which the relationship operates and place limits on the freedom of others to act as they wish. Much of the Old Testament sexual morality is based on a desire of males to control the sexual activity of females and to prevent any other male's offspring from being unknowingly raised as their own children. The power held by males in biblical society is evident in the sexual codes that prohibit extramarital sexual activity on the part of females, but allow it for males as long as their partners are unmarried females.[40] Then as now, male power was both psychological and economic. Even today, the price many women pay for asserting their own autonomy is that of impoverization of themselves and their children.[41]

The other side of such relationships, of course, is that of subservience. There is a temptation to surrender our power and self-development in order to be provided for and to gain a place in society. There is something appealing in losing ourselves in another, in allowing the other to take all the risks and to live vicariously under the protection of one's partner. Most of our relationships are informed by this inequality, resembling Buber's "I/It" relationships. Only one of the partners of the relationship is an autonomous, functioning being; the other is just an object who meets the partner's needs. The early Christian debate over the relationship of the persons of the Trinity to one another repudiated any notion of the inequality of the persons of the Trinity.[42]

It is at this point that the demand for personal integrity and the drive toward relationship, toward reconciliation, merge. For the true relationship of two or more persons requires that each be a functioning, autonomous center of being, each contributing their own wholeness to the relationship. Authentic relationship is possible only as each respects the integrity of the other, reaches out to the other not for purposes of domination, but for purposes of mutual enrichment; not as a flight from personhood and the subsequent loss of personhood in submission to another, but as a courageous affirmation of one's own personhood and worth. True relationship is, then, in the words of Buber, "I/You" relationship.[43] "The human being to whom I say You I do not experience. But I stand in relation to him, in the sacred basic word."[44] Our potential humanity is thus experienced in the complementary drives toward human equality and relationship. Reconciliation becomes a meeting of equals.

But the Judeo-Christian tradition pushes beyond the possibility of a few, fulfilling, I/You relationships. It witnesses to the claim that our human potential is experienced in our desire to live in right relationship with all other persons, the whole of creation, and ultimate reality itself. Our potential humanity exhibits itself in the capacity and desire to be in right relationship with all that is. Biblical visions of salvation present a cosmic drama of the reconciliation of all with all: of persons with persons, nations with nations, humanity with nature, and finally of God with all. So, "nation shall not lift up sword against nation, neither shall they learn war any more" (Isa. 2:4). "The wolf shall dwell with the lamb, and the leopard shall lie down with the kid" (Isa. 11:6). And, "Behold, the dwelling of God is with [the people]. [God] will dwell with them, and they shall be [God's] people" (Rev. 21:3).

In important respects this desire for reconciliation is evidenced in the human thirst for territorial conquest, for merging the whole of the world into a single empire that operates on uniform laws and principles. It is also displayed in the technologico-scientific imperative of our age, which seeks to submit the whole of the natural world to rational human control. But, as we have noted, the biblical vision is fundamental to such human enterprises. Here relationship is not based on domination, but on respect. The purpose is not the security that comes from controlling others or nature, but the enrichment that comes from sharing in their uniqueness and their beauty. This unity and equality is not the unity of sameness, but the unity that respects the integrity of others and glories in their particularity. As Holly Near sings of unity, "It doesn't always mean agreement, and it doesn't always mean the same."[45] True unity appreciates and respects difference.

From the Judeo-Christian perspective, then, human potential is as extensive as the whole of creation. We become more and more human as our capacity for love and relationship expands. We begin as infants able to love little but ourselves and our few caretakers, and grow by reaching out to others and to the world in which we live, being enriched and warmed by their love and presence and, through our love, affirming and enhancing their powers of life and creativity. As our humanity expands, we reach beyond our families, beyond our limited communities, beyond our nations, to embrace the whole of the world. We ultimately reach beyond our friends to embrace our enemies, for this becomes the real mark of our human development. For, "If you love those who love you, what credit is that to you? For even sinners do the same. . . . But love your enemies, and do good, and lend, expecting nothing in return" (Luke 6:32–35). Finally we reach beyond persons to the other beings of creation and to the whole of creation itself; to our animal friends, the snows of winter and showers of spring, to the wild flowers in the woods and to the air that sustains us.[46]

In reaching out to all persons and the whole of creation, we are put in relationship with ultimate reality itself, with the power that generates and sustains all that is. When I have become a fully responsive human being it happens that, according to H. Richard Niebuhr, "When I respond to the One creative power, I place my companions, human and subhuman and superhuman, in the one universal society which has its center neither in me nor in any finite cause but in the Transcendent One."[47]

However, just as we discover that it is difficult to retain a sense of wholeness, as we experience our integrity as limited and short-lived, so we find that it is difficult to maintain relationships of equality, and all but impossible to love anyone fully and consistently. Nevertheless, we do have fleeting experiences of reconciliation, moments when we can sense our interdependency with all that is; when we are able to love fully and properly "the enemy." "In struggle, we catch intimations of the face of God and a foretaste of a commonwealth where the genuine joy in life can be shared."[48] In these moments our potential humanity reveals itself to us and makes demands upon us. We understand its implications for developing ourselves and our societies, and its implications for specific moral problems and social policy. We will now look briefly at some of those implications.

ETHICAL IMPLICATIONS OF OUR POTENTIAL HUMANITY

The experience of our potential humanity, the awareness of our need for centeredness, integration, and of the desire for reconciliation, like our experiences of our fundamental humanity, provide a vision of what we should be. Our need for integration has both an inward and an outward focus. We look inward to discover psychic imbalances, obsessive drives and concerns, the disruptive tendencies of our personal life that destroy its wholeness. In their extreme manifestations, they lead us to seek counseling and help from those trained in probing the dynamics of internal life.[49] At the same time, the need for wholeness and integration draws us outward as we actively seek experiences that will develop and challenge the under-developed portions of our selfhood. The mother who has devoted her life to meeting the unceasing demands of her children returns to school. The business executive reduces his work load so that he can share in parenting and learn how to care for others and give of himself. Only the active development of our various personal attributes prevents our selfhood from becoming dangerously skewed and one-sided.

In addition, our striving for a centered existence requires that we find ways of integrating our personal and public selves and activities. This is especially difficult in the United States where the two spheres are so dramatically separated, and in the West in general where such a division is legitimated in much of the theological tradition. Luther's doctrine of the two kingdoms presumes that our private and public lives are of such distinctly different quality that different norms of conduct apply in the two realms. This distinction, in a modified form, reappears in Reinhold Niebuhr's *Moral Man and Immoral Society*, where love is understood as the norm of the private sphere and justice that of the public realm, for public life is not capable of attaining the same moral purity as private life.[50]

Such a distinction, of course, leaves us divided beings who live in two worlds, worlds symbolized by the suburbs where we live and city centers where we work. But our need for centeredness requires that we pull these parts of our lives together. This may mean changes in lifestyle so that the living of our private lives contributes to the building of a humane social order. So we may choose to live ecologically sound lives, conserving resources, eating and dressing simply, or not trashing recyclable materials. We may attempt to overcome our society's racial and social segregation by sending our children to public schools, and involve the entire family in projects for social reform.[51]

On the other hand, the integration of the public and the private may require us to refuse to engage in certain types of public work and activity, or to do public work in new and innovative ways. So, it may be impossible to continue to be a corporate lawyer who seeks to mitigate his company's responsibility for defective products or for the polluted environment. Or we may discover that we can practice corporate law, but can do so only as an internal advocate for greater corporate responsibility.[52]

The quest for personal integrity will also require us to value wholeness and to see it as more important than many of our traditional values. So, we must now measure success not by how much money we have made, or by what we have accomplished, or by the power we have acquired. Our success is now measured by the degree of our personal wholeness. Howard Hughes becomes a symbol of human failure rather than success, as does any great achiever whose capacities for love, care, and personal integration have been diminished by their quest for greatness. Placing such a value on wholeness is very difficult in a society that measures individual worth on the basis of money, power, and achievement. But the insignificance of such values is central to the biblical understanding of our potential humanity. "For what does it profit (persons) to gain the whole world and forfeit their life?" (Mark 8:36).

The Christian concern for the neighbor, for the other, also means that the experience of our need for wholeness demands that we help create conditions under which they, too, can achieve a degree of integrity. This requires that we develop an attitude of openness toward others, that we offer them our care and support as they attempt to achieve personal integration in a world dominated by disintegrative forces. It means that we offer our support in a context of freedom—that is, a context that allows them to achieve wholeness in terms consistent with their own potentialities, abilities, and values.

The concern for integrity forces us beyond the concern for changing our attitudes and values to attempted reform of the social system in which we live. I will treat this issue in more detail in chapter 7. We become aware of the need to transform education so that it educates the whole person and not just the intellect. Jobs need to be shaped so as to allow a better integration of home life and work life, and in such a way that they challenge the whole person and provide ongoing meaningful activity. Certainly we are required to reform the political system so that all persons feel a part of it, so that they know their views have an impact in the shaping of their communities and society.

In all areas—personal attitudes and social reforms—special attention needs to be given to minorities, women, and the economically disadvantaged. They have been given few opportunities to develop their own integrity, to achieve wholeness. It is important that they be provided the optimum conditions for exploring their own potential and finding unique forms of wholeness and integration. Women cannot be expected to become like men, blacks like whites, blue collar workers like the white collar elite. Nor can we expect all women, or all blacks, or all Hispanics, or all low-income persons to be the same. As particular groups, they share common histories and common problems, and can work together to overcome personal fragmentation and distortion. As individuals, each will find unique ways of expressing their potential wholeness. It is likely that those in power will be frightened by the new patterns they see emerging, to see in "black consciousness" a threat to white survival, or in feminism a challenge to the family and so to social stability.

Nevertheless, such fears must be overcome and all attempts made to create attitudes and conditions under which the oppressed can regain their sense of integrity and personal wholeness. As we will see in the next chapter, the liberation of the oppressed brings great benefits to oppressors. The humanity of both is enhanced. This overcoming of divisions brings us to the second aspect of the awareness of our potential humanity: the quest for reconciliation.

Just as our experience of the possibility of personal wholeness makes demands upon how we live our lives, so does the experience of the possibility of reconciliation with others, with our world, and finally with ultimate reality itself. Again, much of the change required is experienced as the need for new attitudes. We are required to acknowledge the fundamental goodness of all persons and of all that is, and to respect this basic goodness.

In addition, we need to become more sensitive to the networks of interdependency that hold everything together and account for the fact that actions have effects that extend far beyond what we initially imagine. Both the sins and the accomplishments of fathers and mothers are visited upon their daughters and sons. We know that abused children usually have parents who were themselves abused as children. Similarly, the prosperity that some of us enjoy in the United States is a product of the genocide of Amerindian peoples and the brutal enslavement of black peoples, as well as a product of the fundamental disregard of the natural environment. We also know that a small conflict in the Middle East or Central America may result in the nuclear annihilation of the world. Positively, we know that a new respect for the environment and for one another can help create a just, sustainable world society.[53]

Recognition of the worth of others, and of the interdependency of all that is, requires the displacement of our basic egocentricity. Affectively and rationally it requires viewing the world and our experiences from broader, more inclusive, perspectives. Again, this requires an active seeking of experiences that will increase our understanding of others and our empathetic relationship to them. It requires us to learn to listen to others openly, honestly, and nondefensively. In addition, it requires us to recognize our own neediness, our own finitude, and to view both as points of connection, as grounds for reconciliation, rather than as threats to our imagined self-security and independence. We need to also cultivate our sense of connectedness to the natural world and to the ongoingness of human and natural history, to see ourselves as part of a much broader, inclusive whole. From this perspective we can more easily see the sources of division and animosity in our world and of our complicity in them. When we understand the abject poverty of much of the world, we can better understand hostility toward us and toward our flagrant display of affluence. As a male I can then more readily see the reasons for women's anger at men. As a white person I can then better understand the resentment by persons of color.

We also need to work to enhance our capacity to forgive and accept both ourselves and others. Reconciliation means an ability to forgive, to forget. "This kind of forgetting is decisive for our personal relationships. None of them is possible without a silent act of forgiving, repeated again and again."[54] We must be willing to forget others' real and imagined offenses against us. We must also work on our ability to move beyond personal self-defensiveness, to admit our own sinfulness: our sexism, our racism, our cruelty to others and the environment, and to forgive ourselves and move on to more positive, life-affirming ways of relating to others and the world. Forgiveness always entails acceptance, acceptance of incompleteness as well as sinfulness. There is a slogan that readers may have seen or heard: "Don't be impatient; God is not finished with me yet." We must see reconciliation as a process, a journey of mutual support and tolerance, not a once and for all, completed event.

Finally, such changes require that all our relationships take on a new form. We must repudiate all forms of hierarchical relationship that divide persons and creation into categories of varying worth. We cannot relate to one another as if males were superior to females, whites superior to persons of color, human beings superior to the natural environment. This requires a suppression of our instinctive attempt to control relationships through domination or to escape the risk of selfhood through submission. Rather, we must take the risk of partnership,[55] of having both the courage to affirm our worth and selfhood, and the humility to allow others the freedom to affirm and develop their worth and selfhood. Our relationships must be relationships of respect and equality.

In this area, too, the implications of our desire for reconciliation move beyond the realm of personal restructuring to social change. We must create structures that affirm both the equality of persons and their interdependency. Such structures might include educational institutions that obscure the definitions of teacher and student so that all become students and all teachers. It might involve the expansion of worker-owned cooperatives giving workers greater control over their lives and a greater share of corporate profits. It certainly includes the development of forms of democracy in which all are, in reality, both rulers and ruled. And it certainly demands new forms of production and styles of living that respect the integrity of the natural world and our dependence on it. We will return to all of these themes in chapter 7.

In conclusion, social restructuring must pay careful attention to the needs of those who have traditionally been treated as persons of inferior status. Until they share equitably in our society's power, knowledge, and wealth, they will not be treated as equals in fact. Social restructuring informed by the desire for reconciliation will require a radical redistribution of wealth, knowledge, and power, and perhaps a different understanding of the nature and uses of all three.[56]

6

MORAL DEVELOPMENT
AND RESPONSIBLE EXISTENCE

In the last chapter we looked at the moral experiences that generate deontological and teleological approaches to ethics. As we saw, both are derived from valid, important, moral experiences. We are aware of a moral law that reminds us of, and seeks to protect, the needs of our fundamental humanity. On the other hand, we are aware of our incompleteness, of the possibilities for human growth and development, and of the desire for personal wholeness and social reconciliation.

Although both experiences are important and provide clues about what it means to be human and what is required of us if we are to live "humanly," the two ethical approaches described as deontology and teleology provide incomplete descriptions of what it means to be a moral being. This results from the failure of each approach to fully acknowledge the legitimacy of the moral experience on which the other approach is based. It is also the case that both overlook the radically historical nature of human existence. I want to discuss a bit more fully some of these inadequacies and then present an approach to ethics that draws more fully on our experience as moral beings.

INADEQUACIES OF DEONTOLOGICAL AND
TELEOLOGICAL APPROACHES

First, the problem with both the deontological and the teleological approach is that they fail to see the importance of the moral experience on which the alternative theory of ethics is based.

118

We are, in fact, grounded in a fundamental humanity that cannot be fully divorced from our biological, psychological, rational, and spiritual needs as an organism. To overlook or deny these needs is to dehumanize ourselves and others in the most fundamental way. To deprive persons of their nutritional needs, especially during infancy, irreparably damages their humanity. In our treatment of ourselves and others, and in the development of social policy, we always need to be aware of the fundamental requirement to meet basic human needs. Unless these needs are met, the possibility of achieving more complex forms of human development will be thwarted.

Students who shut themselves off from human contact in order to become "better" students and so get into medical school, repressing the need to care for others and to be cared for by them, become so fundamentally dehumanized that they will probably never become "good," caring physicians, no matter how technically astute they may be.[1] Similarly, to exact massive sacrifices from the general population—as has been done in Brazil, where millions are malnourished, homeless, living on garbage heaps—in order to extract funds for the development of a "democratic" capitalist society,[2] entails a blatantly immoral destruction of the humanity of the populace. We can never legitimately disregard the fundamental human needs of others, for it both violates our experience of the demands of our fundamental humanity and obstructs the possibility for the further development and expression of our potential humanity.

Just as the development of potential humanity depends upon fundamental humanity, so our potential humanity completes, extends, and gives a purpose to our fundamental humanity. Simply meeting fundamental human needs does not, finally, give us a sense of wholeness or completeness, nor does it satisfy our religious questioning about the "meaning" or "purpose" of our existence. Certainly we need to meet our fundamental human needs, and the advertising industry in the United States has worked hard to get us to believe that our basic needs are unlimited. Still, there are moments in the lives of affluent persons when they are suddenly struck with the emptiness of accumulating goods and experiences. Such accumulation is not a satisfying end in itself. We are beings who have a need to place all our actions in some broader, more comprehensive, framework of meaning.

Likewise, at the social level, an economic policy geared exclusively to an annual increase in the GNP hardly makes sense. There is nothing about a continually rising GNP that guarantees improvement in the life of a society. In Brazil a rising GNP has accompanied an increase in the number of poor and the severity of poverty.[3] In the United States a rising GNP has had little effect on reducing the numbers of poor and has been accompanied by significant increases in crime, mental illness, drug addiction, child abuse, divorce rates, a depletion of natural resources, and destruction of the environment. It is quite clear that both personally and socially our humanity is defined by its openness, its potential, its striving for a fuller, more developed future. To overlook this dimension of our humanity is thus to make us less than human.

A second problem with both the deontological and teleological approaches is that they make decision-making seem much too easy because of their failure to understand the radically historical nature of human existence. Although the deontological approach is correct in pointing to certain laws of our nature, the exact expression of these laws is not obvious and apparent. We have certain fundamental human needs, but there may be various ways of meeting them and, especially in cultures of scarcity, decisions need to be made as to which needs receive priority. Decision-making is not a matter of finding the appropriate law and applying it, but finding ways of meeting fundamental human needs under particular personal and social conditions. Thus, we need to provide both physical and emotional care for the elderly, but we also live in a highly mobile society. Should care be provided in the home of the extended family or in an institution? There are no easy answers. It depends on the home and the institution and the particular persons involved. The need for care remains; how we meet it depends upon the persons and the situation. In a developing country with limited resources, do we first develop a system of universal education or of universal medical care? Again, there is no set law that provides us with an easy answer.

Similarly, the teleological approach assumes that we can set goals for ourselves and then map out a strategy to achieve them. What is missing is a recognition that we are such historically contingent beings that new information or experience might radically alter our goals. There is also the problem that our finitude limits our perspective and often leads us to choose goals and strategies that are incomplete or misguided. Finally, as historical beings, our actions have ramifications that we do not anticipate, ramifications that may reveal the lack of wisdom in the goals we have chosen, or may open previously unanticipated possibilities for further development.

Both teleological and deontological approaches are ahistorical in yet another sense. Both approaches assume that our actions have a certain completeness to them. We find the proper law and apply it, and the act is completed. We set a particular goal, achieve it, and we have fulfilled our moral responsibility. But this does not fit our experience. We know that our decisions leave loose ends or create new problems and possibilities to which we have to respond. Meeting the fundamental human needs of ourselves and others is not a once and for all event, but an ongoing process under changing circumstances and conditions. Achieving integrity or social reconciliation is not a goal that we achieve and then move on to something else. Both are ongoing processes. Integration, wholeness, needs to be continually reestablished under changing conditions. Reconciliation is not an event, but the achievement of a relationship. Relationships require continual, ongoing commitment and attention. One does not "fall in love" and get married the same day, or become "friends" in one day. Both are ongoing events, changing relationships. Neither deontological nor teleological approaches take seriously the necessity of living out both our fundamental and potential humanity under changing historical conditions.

THEONOMOUS-RESPONSIBLE EXISTENCE

As a response to the inadequacies of the deontological and teleological approaches to the moral life, theologians as different as Paul Tillich, H. Richard Niebuhr, Bernard Häring, Charles Curran, Beverly Harrison, and Daniel Maguire have worked to develop new categories for studying our experience as moral beings. They are representative of an approach to ethics that recognizes that our humanity is characterized by both the givenness of our human nature, the constraints placed on our development by our fundamental human structure, and the openness of our humanity and its potential for further development. In addition, these approaches incorporate an understanding of the radically historical context of human existence, which sets the conditions under which we must affirm our fundamental humanity and develop our potential humanity. Theologians like Tillich or Häring place more emphasis on the experience of our fundamental humanity, and others, like Niebuhr or Harrison, on our potential humanity; but all of them recognize the dialectical relationship that exists between these two moral experiences.

Paul Tillich uses the term "theonomy" to discuss his view of human moral experience, and contrasts it with the experiences of "heteronomy" (standing under a law not of our own making), and "autonomy" (having complete freedom to determine and develop our humanity).[4] In discussing these three terms, Tillich writes:

> Autonomy asserts that man as the bearer of universal reason is the source and measure of culture and religion—that he is his own law. Heteronomy asserts that man, being unable to act according to universal reason, must be subjected to a law, strange and superior to him. Theonomy asserts that the superior law is, at the same time, the innermost law of man himself, rooted in the divine ground which is man's own ground: the law of life transcends man, although it is, at the same time, his own.[5]

Ultimately heteronomy is destructive of human development because it ignores the experience of human potential and undermines our attempt to perfect and extend our humanity. "It destroys the honesty of truth and the dignity of the moral personality. It undermines creative freedom and the humanity of man."[6] At the same time, autonomy loses sight of the fundamental structures in which our humanity is embedded. Because of its lack of rootedness in our fundamental humanity, "it becomes emptier, more formalistic, or more factual and is driven toward skepticism and cynicism, toward the loss of meaning and purpose."[7] According to Tillich, our age is dominated by heteronomous and autonomous understandings of the human, systems of thought drastically opposed to each other and destructive of the conditions under which human life can be made and kept human. He concludes that we must engage in a struggle to create conditions under which our humanity can fully develop. According to him: "'The double fight against an empty autonomy and a destructive heteronomy makes the quest for a new theonomy as urgent today as it was at the end of the ancient world."[8]

In addition to recognizing the importance of both moral experiences—those of our fundamental humanity and those of our potential humanity—and of the need to hold them together in a creative synthesis, Tillich also responds to the fundamentally historical nature of the lives we live. We do not reach a stage of personal integration that is final and complete, or finally create a utopian, static society. We live under conditions of constant flux. Changes in the social and cultural environment, even our own aging, present new problems and new conditions under which personal integration must be reasserted and cultural forms renewed. There is no end point to the task of our human development or to the job of structuring our communities and societies. Each moment offers both new possibilities and new challenges for our personhood and for our communities. Our self-creation as persons and communities is ongoing as we try to re-create in new forms the conditions necessary for human fulfillment, allowing the expansion and extension of our personal and corporate humanity. Even though moral experiences and visions may remain constant, still, Charles Curran notes, commenting on his own ethical methodology:

> A more historically conscious methodology does not pretend to have or even to aim at absolute certitude. Since time, history, and individual differences are important, they cannot be dismissed as mere accidents which do not affect essential truth. This approach does not emphasize abstract essences, but concrete phenomena. Conclusions are based on the observations and experience gleaned in a more inductive approach. Such an approach can never strive for absolute certitude.[9]

In a similar fashion, H. Richard Niebuhr recognizes the validity of the deontological and teleological moral experiences. In describing the teleological experience, he writes: "Two things in particular we say about ourselves: we act toward an end or are purposive; and, we act upon ourselves, we fashion ourselves, we give ourselves a form."[10] That is, we are aware of our ability to make and transform both ourselves and our communities. On the other hand, we are also aware that much of our personal and social behavior seems to be determined and sets limits on our development. There are needs that must be met regardless of the goals we set for ourselves. So, Niebuhr describes the deontological moral experience in the following terms:

> Our body, our sensations, our impulses—these have been given to us; whether to have them or not have them is not under our control. We are with respect to these things not as the artist is to his material but as the rules of a city are to its citizens. He must take them for better or for worse.[11]

Niebuhr recognizes the legitimacy of both experiences, and the weakness of moral approaches that recognize the validity of only one of these experiences. His primary criticism of both is their failure to understand the radically conditioned historical context in which we live out and develop our personal and collective humanity. We must develop our humanity, not in a vacuum or in an internal sphere of personal privacy, but in the context of thousands of interacting, changing, relationships.

This context of relationships is so critical to our moral experience that Charles Curran appropriately relabels Niebuhr's approach a "relationality-responsibility model." He goes on to observe, "The Christian is related to God, neighbor, the world, and self. The failure to give due weight to all these relationships will distort the meaning of the Christian life."[12] It is our ability to become human and to humanize others in our relationships that characterizes us most fully as moral beings. These relationships, however, dare not let us overlook the experience of our fundamental humanity, the reality of the "givens" of human nature. We must recognize them and draw upon our potential for human development and expansion.

In contrasting the ethics of responsibility with those of deontology and teleology, Niebuhr shows the way in which his understanding of moral experience both includes and transforms the other two approaches. This becomes clear in his discussion of the standards of judgment which emerge from each of these moral experiences:

> If we use value terms then the differences among the three approaches may be indicated by the terms, the "good," the "right," and the "fitting"; for teleology is concerned always with the highest good to which it subordinates the right; consistent deontology is concerned with the right, no matter what may happen to our goods; but for the ethics of responsibility the "fitting" action, the one that fits into a total interaction as response and as anticipation of further response, is alone conducive to the good and alone is right.[13]

The concepts of theonomy and responsibility thus provide a good summary response to the moral question: "What should we be, what should we become as persons?" The response to the question is informed by three experiences: the experience of our fundamental humanity, the experience of our potential humanity, and our experience of ourselves as historical, conditioned beings. The shape of our humanity will be determined by our ability to meet our basic human needs—to achieve a sense of personal wholeness and to discover a sense of relatedness to all that is—and our ability to assume the tasks of both our fundamental and potential humanity under constantly changing conditions and within regularly changing patterns of relationship. The task seems awesome, but it is inescapable. The issue is not whether we will actively take part in the shaping of our humanity, but the quality of the humanity that we will shape.

As I have mentioned earlier, the quality of our personhood is largely dependent, both positively and negatively, on the type of communities in which we live. In the next chapter I shall address the issue of what responses must be given to the basic moral question: "What should we become as a people; what kinds of communities should we create?" I shall respond to the question in terms of creating communities that will help us live out the vision of humanity, of personhood, we have explored in these chapters. Before proceeding, however, I want to look briefly at a claim made by the Christian tradition about the process of responsible, theonomous moral development.

PERSONAL DEVELOPMENT AND
THE CHRISTIAN TRADITION

There is currently a great deal of attention being focused on personal and moral development. Erik Erikson has devoted his life to defining stages of personal development and isolating the tasks that must be performed and the problems that must be solved if a person is to move successfully from one stage to another.[14] In a more popularized form, Gail Sheehy in her book, *Passages*, provides similar clues for personal development.[15] Various human potential movements and popular religious movements offer meditative techniques or religious formulas for personal development. In the area of moral development, Jean Piaget and Lawrence Kohlberg have spawned a whole discipline concerned with the study of moral development,[16] and other contributors, like Carol Gilligan, have begun to correct some of the biases of earlier research.[17] James Fowler has initiated a new field of study that is trying to analyze, in a systematic form, the process of religious development.[18]

Despite the new interest in human development, concern for understanding the dynamics of human development so that "proper" development can be encouraged is nothing new. Plato's *Republic* and later, *The Laws*, are attempts to understand human development and encourage it in positive directions. Likewise, Aristotle's notion of "virtues" and his program for cultivating them initiated a still ongoing tradition concerned with developing aristocratic virtues.[19]

The Christian tradition, too, has a long history of concern about human development. The entire monastic movement was organized around a detailed program for building proper Christian character and virtue.[20] Similarly, John Wesley's societies were communities whose primary concern was the moral development of their members.[21] Today this concern for moral development is evident in Christian programs for self-renewal and development.[22] Despite claims that moral renewal is solely a function of God's activity in us, the Christian tradition, in its many programs for moral reform and its use of preaching as a tool for encouraging moral reformation, has recognized the human role in moral development and has shown a concern for proper moral development.

A Theory of Personal Moral Development

In this section, I will not elaborate a complete theory of personal moral development. Some aspects of such a theory have already been discussed. Much of our development is a product of family experiences and socialization into cultural norms. Our development is strongly influenced by the groups and communities to which we belong. Moral development requires recognition of these social influences and a conscious decision to either affirm or reject them. Additionally, it seems likely that we go through various phases of development that are related to life stages, and that our ability to solve the problems presented by the various life stages has an effect on our development. Much of what I say, then, is not meant to contradict the work on personal and moral development being done by the human sciences. Such work provides important insights into our development and may offer helpful clues for personal development and social renewal. What I want to do is focus on some important claims about moral development that are central to the Christian tradition.

Paradoxically, the Christian understanding of character development begins with the claim that "love of the neighbor, of the enemy," is more important than our personal quest for moral perfection. Our primary concern should not be our own righteousness, but rather the needs of others.

The centering of concern on the other rather than on self-development seems to be informed by three insights concerning the nature of being human and the dynamics of human development. First, we are to conform ourselves as much as possible to the likeness of God. God, we are told, is concerned about all others, seeks their welfare regardless of their response to God. So we are told, "Love your enemies and pray for those who persecute you, so that you may be [children] of your Father who is in Heaven; for [God] makes [the] sun rise on the evil and the good, and sends rain on the just and on the unjust" (Matt. 5:44–45). In addition, Jesus, as a revelation of God's activity in history, portrays a God who becomes the servant of others, placing their needs ahead of his own, accepting suffering, making sacrifices, placing concern for others ahead of concern for personal fulfillment and development.[23] We find no indication in the New Testament that Jesus' major concern was to make himself a good person.[24] Rather the concern is always for doing God's will by meeting the needs of others.

Secondly, there is a recognition that the personal quest for goodness, for virtue, destroys the possibilities for human reconciliation by creating classes of persons who view themselves as bearers of a special righteousness and are intolerant of the weaknesses of others. As Leonardo Boff knows, "Those who regard themselves as righteous, with no sins and with no need for conversion, also see no real need for forgiveness."[25] The New Testament, as Boff goes on to show, is full of stories of Jesus' mixing with outcasts, persons of little virtue (e.g., Matt. 9:10–13), and of his repudiation of the self-proclaimed righteous and virtuous (e.g., Matt. 15:1–20). Their self-righteousness is only apparent, for goodness is ultimately measured by our concern for others and by our recognition of our interdependency with all other persons.

Christianity, of course, has often yielded to the temptation to become a society of the virtuous, which, from its elevated position, seeks to lift up the rest of a degenerate society,[26] but this runs counter to its own best insight. As Luther acknowledged, we are always both "saints and sinners." Any goodness we have is merely ascribed to us by God and is not real.[27] Luther's concern, in part, grew out of the awareness that the claim of having special virtue leads to the destruction of human relationships, for it creates new hierarchies in society, hierarchies based on the supposed virtue of those members who compose the various tiers of the hierarchy. His proclamation of the "priesthood of all believers" was an attempt to repudiate the claim that the training and subsequent ordination of the clergy created a class of persons who were of a different moral and spiritual quality, superior to the laity.[28] The emergence of "base communities" as a response to contemporary forms of the Christian church is a modern embodiment of the belief that, "the Church should exhibit a radical egalitarianism."[29]

The idea of a special virtuousness always precedes the claim by some that they have a right to rule over others: whites over blacks; men over women; Nazis over Jews; upper classes over lower classes.[30] But such a denial of the possibilities for open, creative relationships between persons destroys rather than enhances our real humanity, for human development is actually a function of our ability to relate to, and be reconciled with, others. The extension of our capacity for relationship marks the expansion of our humanity. The destruction of that capacity diminishes us.

The third insight about the priority of the needs of a neighbor over personal righteousness grows out of the claim that human development is a product of our ability to be in positive relationship with others and the world in which we live. If this is true, we are caught in a peculiar paradox. Directly focusing on our personal development makes us more self-centered, more egocentric, and so reduces the possibility of our relating positively to others. If our self-development becomes our primary concern, then we become the center of our world and all else is measured by its ability to contribute to our self-development. According to the Christian concept of moral development, such a focus destroys our ability to respond honestly to the needs of others. In addition, such self-focus destroys the possibility for personal integration. We may be able to impose a form of integration upon ourselves, but such self-conscious integration is not able to incorporate all the aspects of our unconscious and subconscious selves, nor all the nonrational components of our selfhood.[31] Rather, Christianity makes the startling claim that integration, wholeness, salvation, comes as a gift when we are concerned about meeting the needs of others.

Wholeness, then, comes not through focusing upon the self and its development, but is given to us at the moment we look away. In this sense, the long-standing claim of the Christian tradition that we cannot earn our salvation, cannot make ourselves righteous, is a claim about our human development. Wholeness, integration, is given to us, appears mysteriously when we are least expecting it. Intense focus upon, and concern for, our own salvation is a primary inhibitor to ever achieving such wholeness. Becoming whole is much like gaining happiness. We cannot really make ourselves happy. We have all had the experience of being depressed, of wishing to be happy, of focusing upon our depression and trying to snap ourselves out of it. As long as we focus on the depression, on our unhappiness, we are unable to escape it. Suddenly, however, we discover we are no longer depressed, we are actually happy, but it is not something we have done. We have changed because we have been distracted, looked away from ourselves and our unhappiness, and suddenly discovered that what we could not do for ourselves has been done for us. This is the paradox embedded in the New Testament claim, "the one who finds his life will lose it, and the one who loses his life for my sake will find it" (Matt. 10:39). We are given our lives, our selfhood, at the moment we offer it to another.

The destruction of our self-centeredness, however, is not an easy task. We are born as a totally self-centered infant and as a small child we learn only very gradually and imperfectly that others have feelings like our own and needs that often equal or exceed our own. Even in adulthood, our ability to break from a self-centered existence requires a profound self-scrutiny and repentance. Jesus comes proclaiming, "The time is fulfilled, and the kingdom of God is at hand; repent" (Mark 1:15).

We must learn to look at our life and see the full damage that our self-centered existence has had on ourselves and others. Such insight might force us to search for an alternative way of living our life, a way of living that seriously considers the needs of others. But such repentance, along with the humility it produces, is only a prelude to a more profound shift, a change in the "fundamental option" informing our life that must occur if we are actually to begin living a life of a different type.[32] This change is understood in the Christian tradition as the change from a life of unfaith to one of faith, or from idolatrous faith to living faith. This faith is much more than the rational assent to a new set of religious doctrines; it is a total transformation of the orientation of our being.

Faith and the Covenant Tradition

Escape from excessive self-concern, a totally one-sided search for personal security, requires a fundamental shift in our perception of the human situation and a shift in our basic attitudes and feelings toward ultimate reality. We must move from a situation of distrust to one of trust; from one in which we view the other not as an enemy, but as a friend. We must come to believe and feel that at the very center of existence is a power that is trustworthy;[33] that ultimately forces of love, care, life, and integration have primacy over their opposites. We must affirm finally that life not death, love not hate, has the final word. We must come to feel that, despite all appearances to the contrary, we and all that is are finally and fundamentally cared for.

It is this change in our perception of ultimate reality that constitutes faith. Referring to this change, Donald Evans writes, "The most crucial personal struggle in religion, morality and life is between trust and distrust." But this is trust of a particular type, it is "basic trust" and "it pervades the whole personality and it is brought to every individual whom one encounters."[34] It is this experience of "basic trust" that allows us to quit living a life of self-defense. As H. Richard Niebuhr writes, "With our ethics of self-defense or survival we come to each particular occasion with the understanding that the world is full of enemies though it contains some friends."[35] Knowing that we are cared for, that we need not trouble ourselves with our own security, we are freed to meet others as friends and freed to be concerned about their needs.[36]

To experience life as trustworthy, to see "the Other" and others as partners, friends, not enemies, opens up the possibility for human development and reconciliation in yet another way. Living a life of "concern" for the other can be a disguise for living a very self-centered existence. The needy neighbor can become a means for our own personal aggrandizement. Giving to the other may become a way of making ourselves feel good and righteous; it may be a way of demonstrating to others our self-sufficiency and superiority. It may also become a disguised form of the search for personal security, for in always giving, and never accepting, we prevent ourselves from becoming dependent on others, others who may prove untrustworthy and desert us.

The experience of faith includes our experience of needing care and of being cared for. It affirms the properness of our need for others and allows us to risk dependency on them. We still know that others will often disappoint us, harm us, desert us, but we now experience all of this as taking place in the context of a more fundamental care. We can begin to live together in gratitude, in partnership, caring and being cared for, empowering one another to expand our capacities for positive, life-affirming relationship with all that is.

Our ability, then, to leave the self behind, to gratefully accept the care that others offer and to make the needs of others a focal point for our own lives, depends upon our surrendering our personal quest to achieve security. "Therefore . . . do not be anxious about your life, what you shall eat or what you shall drink, nor about your body, what you shall put on. . . . Your heavenly Parent knows that you need them all. But seek first God's kingdom and God's righteousness, and all these things shall be yours as well" (Matt. 6:25–33). The acceptance of such a view of life is tremendously difficult; it runs counter to many of our natural instincts and seems inconsistent with much that we actually experience. In addition, like happiness and wholeness, we are told that the experience of faith, of a fundamental trust in all that is, is not something we can create in ourselves or force upon others. It happens to us, appears as a revelation, a gift. We are simply given a new way of being. Such a claim seems to offer little comfort or hope for our fulfillment or for social reconciliation, but this is only part of the message.

The Judeo-Christian tradition has always affirmed that, although we receive faith as a gift, the gift giver is not an arbitrary power. God is portrayed as seeking the good of all that is, of offering gifts freely. We are the problem. We fail to prepare ourselves for the gift; the reception of faith requires preparation. We begin by committing ourselves to a different way of living. Such change may be a response to the frustration that our current style of living brings, or a reaction to the destructive consequences our life is having on others. Nevertheless, we make an effort to begin to live a life of faith even if we have not yet experienced life as trustworthy.

We can train ourselves to attempt to live an "in spite of" existence. "In spite of" the fact that death seems in control of life; "in spite of" the fact that our social history is riddled with acts of unbelievable cruelty; "in spite of" the fact that our personal relationships are marked by experiences of desertion and betrayal; nevertheless, we shall live as if life were victorious over death, kindness over cruelty, love over hate. "In spite of" the fact that our actions seem absurd to others, that we appear foolish, as "suckers," "easy-marks"; nevertheless we will continue to live as if the other were trustworthy. Recognizing our profound neediness and the frequent failure of others to meet our needs, we will still live as if our needs will be met.

Such a life is not easy. It offers no guarantees of peace of mind, no assurances of success or acceptance by others. Jesus dies on a cross; Gandhi and Martin Luther King, Jr., are killed by assassins.

And, if we read carefully in the works of Christian tradition, we discover that even its more "faithful" adherents are troubled by periods of doubt, periods of uncertainty about whether, ultimately, life is to be trusted. Saint John of the Cross writes of the "dark night of the soul," a portrayal of faithful despair over the goodness of life and the trustworthiness of God.[37] The "death of God" movement may represent a general cultural situation in which life is generally viewed as precarious, marked by betrayal, and moving toward an inevitable doom.[38] But it is precisely in these periods that we must live "in spite of."

Jesus is dying on the cross, deserted by all his followers, aware that the kingdom he proclaimed as imminent is not about to break into human history. He hangs on the cross, feeling deserted, betrayed, a failure, declaring, "'My God, my God, why hast thou forsaken me?" (Mark 15:34). Jesus senses the absolute power of death, the untrustworthiness of all that is. But the words he recites are the opening lines of a Jewish psalm that goes on to reaffirm faith in God, trust in God's care, despite the experience of having been abandoned by God (Psalm 22). Jesus affirms in his suffering and death his continued commitment to the style of life he has lived and advocated "in spite of" being deserted, abandoned, left to die as a failure.

Faith, then, is a risk. But so is lack of faith. We know the consequences for ourselves and others of living a life of unfaith, of personal and social self-centeredness and distrust. We are challenged to live a life of faith, trust, concern for others, "in spite of" what we experience and know about ourselves, others, and the world in which we live. Such a life offers no guarantees, no assurances, no easy peace of mind. However, we are told by others, who have attempted to live the life of faith, that if we persevere, there will be rare moments when we shall experience the power of life over death, love over hate; when we will have insight into the trustworthiness of God, the dependability of ultimate reality. Because of their witness, we, like the children of Israel, can commit ourselves to lives of covenantal faithfulness.

Earlier I discussed the concept of the covenant from the perspective of God's faithfulness to us. But, given what we know of life, given what we have experienced, faith requires a covenantal loyalty on our part as well. God's love, care, trustworthiness, is not always evident in our experiences. We, too, must be willing to take a risk, just as the Bible claims God is taking a risk with us. We must act as if God really were trustworthy, loving, caring, and ultimately able to make some difference in the lives we live and the communities we create.

A CRITICAL RESPONSE

Having emphasized the paradoxical claim of the Christian tradition that true self-development occurs when we focus on the needs of the other and not on the needs of the self, I must now offer a critical rejoinder. For, though I still believe in the truth of this paradox, it is clear this claim has been used by dominant members of "Christian" societies to suppress and control subordinate members. Thus the claim that we should be concerned about others, not ourselves, has been used to discredit demands by women and persons of color for equal treatment. The practice is not new. On the grounds that self-concern is inconsistent with the Christian faith, Luther repudiates the demands of oppressed peasants for adequate food, shelter, and just treatment under the law.[39] Likewise, James Cone is right that the dominant classes have demanded that oppressed persons honor the command "love the enemy," and avoid the use of violence in attempts to achieve their liberation. But as he says, "It is interesting that so many advocates of nonviolence as the only Christian response of black persons to white domination are also the most ardent defenders of the right of the police to put down black rebellion through violence."[40]

In addition, the internalization of such self-denial by the oppressed may become a barrier to authentic human development. Women, believing that their place was in the home meeting the needs of their husbands and children, did not develop the whole range of their intellectual, social, and artistic abilities.

In a seemingly opposed way, emphasis on the virtue of giving can create a destructive paternalism in which one partner or class views itself as the all-wise, good giver, and the other party becomes the servile recipient of the other's generosity. In this way political, economic, social, and sexual oppression can be masked by charity. The Rockefellers, the Carnegies, can exploit their workers and defile the environment but use their wealth to build libraries, museums, and to create foundations as masks for the injustice of the financial empires they have created.[41] Physicians, who in our country collectively support a medical care system that denies medical care to millions of low-income persons, provide free treatment for a few patients and so convince themselves of their own kindness. In this and similar ways, "giving to others" can be used to support and maintain unjust personal relationships and oppressive social structures. For this reason, several critical responses need to be amended to the paradoxical notion of "finding one's life by giving it for others."

The first response to be made draws on the idea of reconciliation, which must inform the Christian concept of "love for the other." As already pointed out, reconciliation requires respect for the integrity of others and recognition of their value. It requires an affirmation of the equal value of all persons. Love, then, is never an act of pity, never a reaching down to another. Love is an act of justice, of giving to others "their due." It means extending to another what we wish another would offer to us were our places reversed.

Additionally, reconciliation requires that we listen to others to hear what they want from us. We cannot presume to know what others need without first hearing from them.

Finally, reconciliation is based on mutuality, a recognition that the other has something to offer us. It is based on a recognition of our neediness and a graciousness in accepting what is offered to us. There is no place for paternalism in love, for the goal of love is authentic reconciliation, the coming together as persons who know and respect each other's humanity.[42]

The second response is based on the criticism of Christian self-denial by the various liberation theologies. As these movements recognize, reconciliation requires the possibility of persons meeting as equals. An early statement (1966) by the National Committee of Negro Churchmen affirms, "We must rather rest our concern for reconciliation on the firm ground that we and all Americans are one."[43] True reconciliation cannot occur where one person or group of persons is kept subordinate to another, considered to be inherently inferior. Persons have a right, in fact a duty, to meet their fundamental human needs and develop their human potential if they are to be full partners in their relationships with others. The demand that some persons suppress their self-development in order to meet the needs of others, especially the needs of privileged persons, is an unjust, unloving demand. Women, persons of color, must work to recover their suppressed personhood, to reclaim the value of their own lives so that they might assume a position of equality in all social relationships.

As we look at the numerous liberation movements that have arisen in the country and globally in the last thirty years, it seems evident that movements to reclaim the identity of a group of oppressed persons are absolutely essential to the development of personal and collective selfhood. The "black power movement" is a necessary affirmation of the fundamental goodness of blackness and its cultural attributes in the face of a culture that has for generations made blackness a symbol of disgrace and so filled black persons with self-hatred.[44] As James Cone writes, "Black Power, in short, is an 'attitude,' an inward affirmation of the essential worth of blackness."[45] Likewise, the radical feminist movement includes a necessary affirmation and recovery of the goodness of the feminine in a culture where the greatest insult one man can give to another is to call him "a woman." It seems likely that every oppressed group and person will necessarily pass through a phase of what may seem to the outsider excessive self-preoccupation and self-affirmation. But such a process may be absolutely necessary for the recovery of a lost selfhood and as such is a prerequisite to full human liberation.

Despite these critical responses to the claim that the Christian's primary orientation must be toward meeting the needs of others, still I want to affirm what I believe is the essential correctness of this claim. Even as we look at the claims of liberation movements, we discover that these movements truly liberate their followers only when the movement is guided by a comprehensive vision incorporating the needs of others and the desire for reconciliation with others. At the personal level, concern for self-development ends in the betrayal of one's own people if the purpose of self-development is merely self-aggrandizement. Individuals who overcome racial, sexual, or economic prejudice and then conform to the norms and demands of the dominant group in order to assure their success, end up alienated from their own roots and their own people. Their personal achievement is paid for by the loss of part of their humanity.

On the other hand, concern for personal development is fulfilling when it includes a concern for all other members of one's group. One's personal development then becomes a means for the liberation of all one's people. In this context, love of one's neighbor, of one's sister and brother, requires concern for personal liberation and development.

The path to authentic self-development, then, is very different for the privileged and for the oppressed. For the privileged, loving the other requires the suppression of an overgrown sense of self-importance and an exaggerated egocentricity. For the oppressed, loving the other requires a long process of self-actualization and recovery of a lost personhood. Still, the dynamics of true human development remain the same. True human development is reflected in our ability to move out of the self to the other in genuine love and concern. The purpose of authentic black liberation is not, in the final analysis, that of liberating blacks to become as oppressive, hedonistic, and self-serving as the whites who now dominate our culture. As Dorothee Sölle tells us in "The Emancipation of Women":

> We don't want
> to be like the men
> in our society
> crippled beings
> under pressure to excel
> emotionally impoverished
> molded into bureaucrats
> functionalized into specialists
> condemned to make good.[46]

Self-centered forms of liberation condemn oppressed groups to repeat the mistakes of their oppressors. It condemns them to lives of empty pursuit, domination of others, and fear that those they now dominate will some day rise up in revolt. It condemns them to continue the work of today's privileged classes, to:

rule and command
conquer and be waited on
hunt capture subdue.[47]

At some point in the liberation process, then, all inward-looking liberation movements must again look outward and find their meaning in the pursuit of a fundamental reconciliation of all with all. According to Major Jones, "For the black awareness movement, rightly interpreted—the emergence of black selfhood—is not to be taken or conceived as a thing in itself; rather it is to be viewed against the background of an emergent community."[48] From this perspective concern for the self-development of oppressed persons and groups takes on a new meaning. If the good of all human development is marked by a drive toward reconciliation, the act of personal development by the oppressed becomes an act of love toward the oppressor, for it creates conditions under which the two can meet as equals, a prerequisite for reconciliation. Thus Martin Luther King, Jr., was concerned to humanize whites as well as blacks by allowing both to recognize their common humanity.[49] And the struggle for women's liberation is finally, as Letty Russell writes, a struggle for the liberation of all, for, "The struggle is basically for a 'new human being': one that is whole; that moves beyond social stereotypes of masculine and feminine, dominant and subordinate, to an understanding of human sexuality that recognizes that variety of sexual characteristics in each person."[50]

In important respects, then, the priority given to self-development by the oppressed does not contradict the Christian claim that concern for the needs of others has priority over one's concern for personal development. In the case of the oppressed, the only way they can love the neighbor, even the oppressor, is through the intentional development of their own personhood.

Concern for the other is thus not opposed to self-development. In fact, it is required. As Patricia Wilson-Kastner recognizes, the ability to love requires a self-conscious "I" that is able to recognize the value of others and offer them love. Only "persons" are capable of love in its fullest sense:

One who is fully a person is not obsessed with self to the point of excluding concern for others and using them to serve his or her own ends. At the same time, she or he is not so other-directed and attentive to give to others, serve them, and find satisfaction by filling their needs that she or he is void of self-centeredness, the consciousness of the "I" who is dedicated to others. These dimensions of the person are not opposed to each other, but are essential polarities which must be both active and interacting for a person to be truly human.[51]

That the various liberation movements have recognized the need to have a vision that extends beyond the limited aims of their personal and group development is evidenced in the exciting dialogue beginning to emerge among the various liberation movements. These movements have passed through a period of self-defensive development to a position that now allows one of the leaders of the black theology movement, James Cone, to admit: "There are various reasons for this silence on feminist issues among Black male theologians. Some Black male theologians are blatantly sexist and thus reflect the values of the dominant society regarding the place of women."[52]

Recognizing this sexism, Cone goes on to propose an expanded program for the black liberation movement: "But whatever the reason for our silence on the unique oppression of Black women, we now must realize that our continued silence can only serve to alienate us further from our sisters. We have no other choice but to take a public stance for or against their liberation."[53] And finally, the vision must extend beyond national boundaries and include an "independent dialogue among the poor," whose purpose is that of "transcending petty differences and establishing an effective coalition."[54]

Liberation movements thus are beginning to find their true meaning in a universal liberation of humankind, a vision much richer and more comprehensive than any that have inspired the actions of the world's privileged classes. In the process, the oppressed peoples of the world offer a new possibility of liberation to oppressors as well.

In conclusion, the demand that our self-development be put in the context of meeting others' needs, if properly understood and applied, remains a legitimate claim. This claim itself stands as an important corrective to our unrelenting self-centeredness and our self-deception, whether we are part of the privileged classes or part of the oppressed. And it represents, I believe, the actual dynamics by which wholeness and integration are gifted to us as persons, and through which reconciliation is gifted to us as communities and relational beings. It frees all of us, oppressors and oppressed, to envision a new future, to open ourselves to the beauty of others and the richness of their perspectives. It allows us to recognize our common humanity and to appreciate and glory in our fundamental differences. In the offering of ourselves, our humanity is gifted to us in a fullness that we could never create in ourselves and so the possibilities for mutual enrichment become unlimited.

7

CHRISTIAN ETHICS
AND HUMAN COMMUNITIES

Throughout this work I have been stressing the view that what is
distinctive about us as humans is that we have the ability, the
inescapable necessity, of defining both the quality and the shape of
our own humanity. Either consciously or unconsciously we must
give an answer to the question: "What shall I be as a person?"
Ethics is simply a response to a fact about human life: some ways of
being are preferable to others. As such, ethics attempts to provide
criteria, a vision of the human, that will help guide us in the
formation of our humanity.

As I have stressed throughout, however, the development of our
humanity is a collective undertaking. We are largely formed by the
communities of which we are a part, and through our actions,
which shape our communities, we influence the development of
ourselves and others. For better or worse we are inescapably tied to
each other and offer each other new possibilities for development,
while placing significant restrictions on each other's development.
Ethics, then, necessarily must respond to the question, "What
kinds of communities should we create?" It must attempt to provide a vision of these communities, a vision that will foster the
fullest possible human development. Further, Christian ethics, if it
is to be consistent with its claim about the unique value of each
person, must attempt to provide a social vision that will allow for
everyone's fullest possible human development.

In this chapter, then, I will attempt to respond to the question,
"What kinds of communities should we create?" In the process, I

hope to develop a vision that can inform us in the structuring of our communities and in the implementation of public policy. Our concepts of community should be consistent with the themes of the last two chapters, for the goal is the creation of communities in which the fundamental humanity of all persons is respected and in which the potential humanity of all persons can flourish. First, however, I want to respond to the lack of vision and the social pessimism that is currently so pervasive and has had such influence on the Western political and religious tradition.[1]

OUR LIMITED SOCIAL VISION

It is always difficult for persons to envision communities different from those in which they were born and live. Our communities, our social structures, appear fixed, given, like weather or geography. We simply adapt ourselves to what seem to be natural fixtures. In part, then, mere habit prevents us from imagining social structures different from our own. In addition, however, we discover that if we adapt ourselves to existing social structures we are rewarded and if we oppose them we are punished. There are strong incentives for accepting existing communities and their ways of functioning. Children who dislike the competitive environment of our educational institutions discover that they can either conform to that environment and so be rewarded with high grades, parental praise, and eventual vocational success; or they can resist the institution, become ostracized from it, and jeopardize their future chances for financial independence. There are throughout society strong incentives for accepting the existing order and strong deterrents against envisioning something better, fuller, and more humanizing.

In addition, Western ideologies, grounded in a concept of radical individualism, consciously repudiate the significance of the question, "What kinds of communities should we create?" In the United States, particularly, we as individuals have come to believe that we can become whatever we care to be; that through sheer will power and persistence we can largely determine the shape of our own humanity. We really do not believe that our communities profoundly shape us or that social structures largely determine the shape of our lives and the quality of our humanity. In addition, we believe that any problems that might arise are individual problems and so should be solved by individualized treatment rather than social reform. Poverty, alcoholism, mental illness, suicide, cancer, heart disease, are all viewed as individual problems that can be solved by individualized therapies. Poverty can be ended if individuals can overcome their laziness and develop good work habits. Alcoholism or mental illness can be cured by joining Alcoholics Anonymous, or getting personal counseling. Heart disease or cancer requires treatment by a "private" physician. We have lost the awareness that our humanity is inescapably tied to the actions and lives of others and is profoundly shaped by the structures of the communities to which we belong.

So, we fail to realize that we create our communities and structure our societies. Social structures are not like the weather or the geography; social structures exist only because we will them to exist, because we commit our energies to maintaining them.[2] Some persons are homeless, malnourished, whereas others own multiple homes and private airplanes, because we, as a society, choose to maintain such forms of inequality. There is warfare, not because it is inevitable, but because we choose to maintain an international order that makes war inevitable.

We do not have to probe very deeply to discover that private problems such as alcoholism, mental illness, or suicide are largely the product of social forces. Changes in community structures can increase or decrease the incidence of all the problems mentioned above.[3] In addition, cancer and heart disease are diseases of modern technological societies. The incidence of both could be dramatically reduced simply by changing the nature of our economic and political communities.[4] And yet, the myth of individualism remains strong in our culture and is a constant impediment to envisioning altered and reformed communities, a fact that should not surprise us once we understand the roots of the ideology. Many agree with Dom Hélder Câmara: "Individualism causes selfishness, the root of all evil."[5]

Individualism, as we know it, is certainly a by-product of the Judeo-Christian religious tradition. The tradition's profound emphasis on the dignity of the individual has been one of history's most humanizing forces. But the Judeo-Christian tradition, at its best, always understood the individual as part of a broader community and as a person who was both nourished by, and responsible to, the other members of that community.[6] The ideology of radical individualism, at the center of our culture,[7] is a product of the late nineteenth-century; it received formal statement in a philosophy called "social Darwinism."[8] Social Darwinism was an emerging ideology whose primary purpose was to apologize for the emerging modern, urban technological culture whose distinguishing characteristics were radical inequalities of both wealth and power, and brutal dehumanization of society's lower classes.[9]

Social Darwinism, then, had a specific ideological purpose. It developed as a counter to both liberal and Marxist criticisms of the emergent culture in order to show that the massive inequalities of wealth and power that had developed were not only necessary, but good. It did so by drawing an analogy between the social world and the natural world that Charles Darwin had supposedly discovered. The social world, too, is portrayed as a jungle, a struggle for survival, in which the fittest acquire wealth and power, and the least fit become poor and powerless. Moving a step beyond Darwin, however, success and failure are now correlated with the *moral worth* of individuals as well. Not only are the fittest successful, they are also morally superior, the ones most fit to control society's power and wealth. The losers are not only poor and powerless, they are morally suspect, not fit to rule or to make proper use of society's wealth.[10]

Such an ideology had an important function. It allowed the wealthy and powerful to enjoy their status free of feelings of guilt about the suffering they had imposed in acquiring their wealth, and the unscrupulous means by which they had acquired their power. In addition, the complaints and suffering of the poor could be ignored, as could the liberal and Marxist criticisms of society. Everyone had gotten what they had deserved. Justice had been done. The best and the brightest governed society. "It was the best of all possible worlds."[11]

In this way, all social criticism was blunted. If modern, urban existence was causing more illness, if technological society meant more crippling industrial accidents, there was no reason to burden industry with environmental restrictions or worker safety laws.[12] Workers should simply be more careful; and, if necessary, a whole new industry could be developed treating the millions of cases of illness that a severely polluted environment would create.[13] Likewise, poverty was a personal matter. If individuals wanted to advance, they needed only to show more initiative, work a little harder. There was no reason to restructure an economic system that regularly plunged millions of persons into a severe economic depression, or paid wages that were below the poverty level, or simply could not create enough jobs for all workers.[14] In this way, our society created an ideology that still prevents us from seeing the real effect of our social structures upon persons, and so diverts our attention away from the task of envisioning reformed communities and restructured social systems.

In a similar, but unintentional way, Christianity has also distorted our culture's view of the relationship of the individual to society. The Christian tradition, as it has developed, has been informed by a profound social pessimism that has led Christianity to focus primarily on matters of personal psychology and spirituality, and on matters of religious doctrine and liturgy, rather than on issues of community reform and social justice. Rather than concerning itself with the question, "What kinds of communities should we create?," Christianity has focused on such issues as: "How can the individual be saved?"; "What is sound doctrine?"; "What forms of liturgy should we adopt?"

This narrowing of concerns is partly a response to a realistic assessment of the enormous difficulties involved in social reform. Social institutions are very resistant to change. Tremendous amounts of time and effort are needed to produce even the smallest changes. It is easy to understand why church leaders would despair of effecting significant social reform and focus on simpler, more manageable matters. In addition, the church's development as an institution has often depended upon the protection of the church by political powers, and its survival certainly depends upon its being tolerated by the political leaders of the day. The church has thus had a strong incentive to concern itself almost exclusively with matters of personal faith, religious doctrine, and liturgical forms, rather than social issues.

Most significant, however, has been Christianity's unhealthy focus on personal salvation. A movement founded upon the symbolization of one person's giving his life for others soon became a religion whose primary concern was a self-centered quest for personal salvation. There is, perhaps, no greater testimony to the power of our self-centeredness than this transformation of a movement founded upon a notion of love for one's neighbors into an introverted religion concerned with the quest for personal immortality and well-being. Again, however, there is strong social incentive for such a focus. This privatized message contributes to institutional growth and success as the church now provides Christians with the message they want to hear: assurance of personal well-being.

Christianity, of course, has never totally ignored social issues and concerns, nor has it ignored the needs of neighbors. Christians in all ages have attempted to formulate their understanding of the relationship of Christian faith to society at large in both theory and practice. Nevertheless, almost all such attempts have ended by placing social concerns on the periphery of the Christian faith and life rather than at its core. Likewise, almost all such attempts have failed to fully appreciate the extent to which both individuals and the institutional church are inescapably tied to the broader society of which they are a part. A brief survey of some of the representative Christian views of society helps to illustrate this point.

Augustine, the first great social theorist of the church, admitted the need for active Christian social involvement. He was aware that persons were greatly affected by the social conditions in which they lived. He understood that all persons benefit from conditions of peace and justice, and all are harmed by situations of injustice and violence. Christians should work to assure peace and to create a just social order. Nevertheless, Augustine wrote in the context of a crumbling social order, a fact reflected in the profound social pessimism that informs his work. Despairing of ever really reforming society, Augustine ends by proclaiming the flawed nature of all human social institutions and the impossibility of real and substantive social reform.

According to Augustine, social institutions are all motivated by the human desire for power, wealth, and domination over others. At best, Christians can buffer the evil tendencies of human institutions. Ultimately, however, the state of our communities is irrelevant, for God has ordained a second form of community, the church, which is a sanctuary from the world and through which we can receive personal salvation. Love for the neighbor requires us to be socially responsible, but ultimately the important issue is our relationship to the church. Augustine could support the burning of heretics in order to preserve the integrity of the "true church."[15]

In this way, Augustine ends by placing issues of community reform and social policy on the periphery of Christian concerns. The central issue is not social reform, but personal salvation and proper doctrine. In addition, Augustine posits a chasm between the condition and destiny of our communities and that of the church and individual believers. Augustine fails to understand that the church in any age is a reflection of the society of which it is a part. He fails to see that our salvation, our ability to gain personal integrity and be reconciled with the whole of creation, is conditioned by the communities of which we are a part. Nevertheless, this dualism between the sacred and the secular, the personal and the public, the church and the state, has become paradigmatic for much of the Christian tradition that followed.

Luther repudiated the notion of an infallible church that provides a haven in a fallen world. Still, he retains Augustine's basic distinction. Now, however, the distinction is between the private and the public self, and receives formulation in Luther's doctrine of the two kingdoms. Again, the Christian must exercise social responsibility as a necessary aspect of neighborly love. It is important to work to maintain peace, to provide social stability, and to meet the needs of one's neighbor. However, Luther recognizes the imperfectability of social institutions and so declares that social relationships stand under a law different from that governing personal relationships. The individual Christian must, in *personal* relationships, live according to the radical demands of Jesus. So, if Christians are mugged, they should not resist; if neighbors are hungry, Christians should share their food with them. The *public* realm, however, is a corrupt realm where force is permitted and often required of Christians. Here a Christian may be an executioner, for the use of violence is necessary to maintain a just social order. And, Luther, at one point, concludes that killing rebellious peasants is a moral obligation in order to maintain social stability.[16]

What we have once again is a situation in which social reform is secondary to the fundamental goal of Christianity—that of providing personal salvation. The real quest is for a right relationship with God, and the presumption is that individuals may achieve such a relationship irrespective of the conditions of the society in which they live. Again the Christian is provided a sanctuary from the world but now it is found in personal piety rather than in the church. Luther, like Augustine, overlooked the fact that the individual cannot escape the influences of society. Likewise, he overlooked the biblical notion that persons are inescapably tied to their communities and are responsible for all its sins and injustices. He also overlooked the biblical view that salvation is a communal, not a personal, event. Luther's social thought, like that of Augustine, was shaped by a profound social pessimism and intense desire for personal salvation that ultimately directs persons away from serious discussion and concern about the types of communities they are creating and supporting through their daily actions.[17]

The Radical Reformation[18] must be credited with having a much more realistic insight into the relationship of persons to their communities. It refused to allow Christians to have one ethic in their private life and another in their public life. It allowed for no church separate from society.

Most representatives of the Radical Reformation were pacifists who refused military service and, according to the biblical injunction, refused to bow before royalty or swear oaths in court. Additionally, they understood the almost impossible task of becoming a just person in an unjust society, or of becoming a loving person in a society whose members sought domination over one another. Like Augustine and Luther, however, they also recognized the corruptness of most human communities and the immensely difficult task of reforming them. These groups responded by withdrawing from society at large to found self-sufficient communities of their own; communities that were, as much as possible, economically, politically, and religiously separated from the broader society. These communities were founded upon the teachings of Jesus and did, indeed, reflect a peacefulness, cooperativeness, and equality of persons that have seldom been matched in human communities.[19]

One problem, however, was that these communities were largely exterminated by political and religious groups. Their histories are ones of bitter persecution.[20] In this respect, withdrawal was, and often is, a very inadequate practical response to a corrupt social order. In another sense, such withdrawal may represent an abdication of social responsibility. Jesus did not align himself with similar sectarian groups in his own age,[21] but rather plunged into the midst of human communities, demanding reform and proclaiming that all human communities prepare themselves for the coming kingdom of God. Jesus went about representing a God who is found in the struggle to reform and renew all our human communities from the family to the international political order.

The Radical Reformation rightly recognized the impossibility of separating a person's life into distinct spheres, religious and secular, private and public. But like the movements spawned by Augustine and Luther, it too ended up making social reform secondary to finding a personal haven and an arena for personal salvation.

In our own society, Christianity is a many-sided phenomenon. Christian theories of social responsibility include all the traditional responses mentioned above as well as newer movements such as Christian realism and liberation theology.[22] In this respect, it is not quite correct to speak of "Christianity today," in the singular. Nevertheless, it does seem that for most Christians, social reform, the building of human communities, remains secondary to what they perceive to be the real task of Christian faith—providing a means for personal salvation. If anything, Christianity in the United States has become more privatized, less socially responsible, than in most earlier historical periods. There is a widespread feeling that the church should stay out of politics and stick to religion—that is, its task is one of preaching a message of personal salvation.

For a variety of reasons, then, we are not predisposed to be social reformers, to dream about new forms of human community, to envision new social structures. Rather, we are more likely to adapt ourselves to existing social structures and to blame our discontent and our social conflicts on personality problems and personal disturbances. But such an approach is inconsistent with what we now know about ourselves and our relationship to our communities. Modern psychology, from Freud to the present, has disclosed the profound impact that our communities have on shaping our basic personality structure and values. Our ability to become something fundamentally different from what we are requires a total restructuring of our lives and relationships. Conversion to a new lifestyle usually entails a break with familiar communities and immersion into new ones. The convert to a religious cult breaks ties with family and old friends, assumes a new name, and becomes part of a new community. Less dramatically, the physician, lawyer, or business person takes on a new identity and set of values when he or she becomes part of a new professional community.[23]

Similarly, our new sociological insights demonstrate quite clearly that even our most personal values, problems, and actions have social roots. Certain social conditions increase our competitiveness, raise crime rates, and destroy family relationships. On the other hand, our most private actions have social effects. Our personal sexual morality contributes to the general sexual mores of our community. Our increased use of credit to buy goods and services contributes to national inflation rates and a general social economic instability. It is increasingly clear that we cannot make many profound changes in our lives, or solve our basic personal problems, without profound changes in our communities and our social structures.

Coincidentally, the knowledge we have gained about our intimate relationship to our communities confirms the basic insights of the biblical understanding of human communities. Both the Old and New Testaments presume the inseparability of individuals from their communities. Only rarely in the Old Testament does God address a particular individual, nor is there any notion of salvation as an escape from communities. Rather, God almost always addresses the people, the community, and salvation is always presented as salvation of the people of Israel. The salvation of the individual and the salvation of communities are intimately tied together. Likewise, God seldom upbraids a person for personal sins, but more often reprimands the entire community for its collective injustices. All will be punished for supporting an unjust economic order, for oppressing the poor, for failing to respect the needs of the powerless. All are responsible, for all members of the community, through their daily activities, support the prevailing community relationships and social structure. There is no salvation without a fundamental reform of the social order.

The New Testament certainly has a more personal orientation. Jesus speaks directly to particular persons and offers salvation to specific individuals. Nevertheless, his message is always placed within the context of the fundamental reform of human communities. Persons are not going to be saved from a corrupt, deteriorating social order. Rather, the kingdom of God is coming; human communities will be remade. Persons must repent so that they are able to live in the kingdom that is coming. They must begin to alter their lives to make them consistent with the demands that will be placed on them in God's kingdom. They must learn to love one another, even the enemy; to turn the other cheek when struck; and be prepared to share all they have with the poor.[24]

Similarly, although Jesus does focus on personal sins, he still holds persons accountable for the actions of their communities; and even his concern over individual sins is a concern primarily about the social effects of their sin. So, Jesus is concerned about the hoarding of wealth, not because greediness is itself evil (which it is), but because of the effect of such greed on the poor. Likewise, our intense concern with our own security is sinful because it makes us defensive, closed to the needs of others, unable to create conditions favoring true reconciliation with others. In Jesus, as well, there is no idea of a radical separation of individuals from their communities. The condition and destiny of both are inextricably linked. Persons will be saved only as human communities are remade in the coming kingdom of God. We can be remade only as our societies and communities are reordered.

Any significant contemporary response to our human dilemma must begin with the awareness that personal destinies are forged with the destinies of our societies. Our personal survival depends upon the ability of our societies to find ways of living together that will avoid a nuclear holocaust; our personal satisfaction depends upon our ability to create economic communities that are just and provide fulfilling human work. From this perspective, the biblical understanding of the relationship of persons to their communities provides a profound understanding of our responsibility for our communities and of the ways in which personal liberation is tied to the need for social reform. If Christianity is to provide a significant ethical response to the modern situation, it must repudiate much of the dominant Christian tradition and return to its biblical roots. Such a recovery is based on the premise that, as Juan Luis Segundo recognizes:

The longstanding stress on individual salvation in the next world represents a distortion of Jesus' message. He was concerned with man's full and integral liberation, a process which is already at work in history and which makes use of historical means.[25]

In addition, this recovery of the biblical tradition requires a repudiation of the dualism that was embraced by Augustine and became a dominant theme of Christian tradition, a dualism that separates the destiny of individuals from that of their historical communities. Again, as Segundo maintains, this change requires that we recognize:

There are not two separate orders—one being a supernatural order outside history and the other being a natural order inside history; that instead one and the same grace raises human beings to a supernatural level and provides them with the means they need to achieve their true destiny within one and the same historical process.[26]

We are, then, tied to our communities. Our personal destiny, the very shape and quality of our humanity, is linked to that of all the other persons who are part of our community. Just as we cannot escape the task of shaping our own humanity, we cannot escape the fate of building our community. We have no choice. Each of our actions either supports our communities and social structures or exerts pressure on them to change.

My conviction is that change is absolutely necessary. Our existing communities exact a tremendous cost in human suffering in the forms of enforced mass poverty, destruction of families, increasing mental illness, alcohol and drug addiction, and violent international conflict. In addition, our social structures now threaten our environment with nuclear and ecological destruction. There is no real choice. We must act to remake our communities and reform our social structures. Concern for our own survival and well-being demands as much. Christian concern for the other, for all others, requires that we act consistently to reshape our communities in such a way as to put an end to the suffering of others.

Before we can act, however, we need a vision of the goals we are trying to reach, of the kind of communities we are trying to create, for to paraphrase the authors of Proverbs and Joel, "Where there is no vision the people perish" (Prov. 29:18). But, as I have tried to indicate, both our cultural and religious traditions discourage "our daughters from prophesying, our old men from dreaming dreams, and our young men from seeing visions" (Joel 2:28).

The task of envisioning a new form of human community has been taken up in the modern era by the Marxist movement.[27] Its vision has been powerful, and now over half the world shares that vision. Nevertheless, many of its dreams have turned into nightmares. Embedded in the West and in the biblical tradition is a more humanistic vision based upon respecting the fundamental human needs of all persons and upon creating conditions in which the human potential of all can be more fully realized. I now want to present a vision of the communities we should be trying to build through our daily actions and our collective social policy.

ENVISIONING THE NEW COMMUNITY

In reality, of course, we live in many different and overlapping communities. We live and interact in families, neighborhoods, regional communities, and nation states. In addition, we live and work in religious and educational institutions and in economic enterprises and structures. Each of these various communities has a profound influence upon us, and we must consider the shape that these communities must have if they are to contribute to our own humanization and that of others. In any given society, all these communities interact with each other and have a general shape that is given to them by the larger cultural ethos of which they are a part. Because of this, the vision I will be presenting will be a broad, general one, directed toward the general cultural ethos. The specific implications of this vision for our multiple communities should be somewhat apparent. Although we need to create visions specific to each of these particular communities, I do not have the space, in this introductory work, or the wisdom to carry out the task, but it is certainly one of the functions of ethics.[28]

In beginning to sketch a vision of the new community, it is important to first stress the legitimacy and integrity of all the multiple communities that compose the larger society. The Catholic social tradition is informed by the "principle of subsidiarity," which argues that society is properly composed of various levels of communities and organizations, and each level has its appropriate role and functions.[29] Emil Durkheim, too, saw the need for "intermediary organizations" between the individual and the gigantic political and economic institutions that were emerging with modern societies.[30] In our own society, likewise, there is a growing reaction against big, impersonal organizations and a demand that more power be returned to local levels.[31]

All these movements share a recognition that persons need to feel they are a part of a coherent, personal community; that our very well-being depends upon having roots in a community, a place to be. In addition, all these traditions recognize that some things are simply done better (i.e., more efficiently or more humanely) when done on a local level. Finally, all recognize that only such smaller, independent communities can act as a safeguard against the totalitarian thrust of large institutional structures. Thus, maintaining smaller, independent communities is a necessary means of assuring persons a degree of control over their own lives.

Simply assuring the existence of smaller, independent communities and centers of power, however, does not guarantee that our communities will be humanizing or that power will be used any more wisely by local communities than by national structures. The history of "states rights" in the United States is a history that involves the suppression of minority rights and the open persecution of blacks.[32] Likewise, small, private businesses are more likely to exploit employees than are highly unionized national corporations.[33] What is needed is a vision to inform the shape and nature of our communities regardless of their size or social function. Such a vision is provided by our notion of the humanity we are trying to create. We will now look at the implications of both our fundamental and potential humanity for the kinds of communities we should be attempting to create.

Our Communities and Our Fundamental Humanity

A truly humanizing society must respect the fundamental needs of human beings. From a Christian perspective, it must respect the fundamental needs of all persons regardless of sex, age, race, religion, or economic status. Such a society is founded on the recognition of the rights of all its citizens to basic economic necessities, access to health care and education, an environment that enhances the development of stable communities of care, and an environment that permits the free exercise of religion and spiritual development. This society, however, must not only *recognize* these rights but take active steps to assure that these rights are met. The meeting of our fundamental human needs is not a social option, it is not an act of charity by the powerful vis-à-vis the less fortunate; as the Judeo-Christian tradition recognizes, persons have a God-given right to the resources and conditions necessary for meeting their fundamental needs.

In important respects, then, the Judeo-Christian tradition stands in stark opposition to the values of modern capitalist societies. As Charles Curran rightly observes:

> The basic Christian attitude is that the goods of creation exist to serve the needs of all. The purpose of the goods of creation is to serve all God's people, and no one has a right to arrogate superfluous goods to oneself at the expense of the neighbor in need.[34]

We are free to use what we need, but God remains the ultimate owner. Consequently, the hoarding of wealth by the rich is perceived as an act of theft that deprives the poor of their basic needs and takes from them the gifts God had intended for them.[35] Another biblical concept is that of the "jubilee year" when wealth and land were to be redistributed, debts were to be canceled, and slaves were to be set free and provided with the resources for financial independence. Such redistribution is just for it is simply a redistribution by God of gifts given to the people.[36] In addition, the Bible is full of condemnations of the wealthy for taking what rightfully belongs to the poor. The Judeo-Christian tradition is quite clear that we have no right to excessive wealth in a world where others are poor.

Similarly, the Judeo-Christian tradition repudiates the notion that persons have a right to excessive property because they have worked for it, and repudiates the notion that persons have a right to dispose of their property as they please. The primary purpose of work is not personal gain, in the narrow sense of increased personal wealth or power, but an attempt to improve the lives of all persons in the community and to mold the community itself into the image of the kingdom of God.[37] Our use of wealth is to be determined by the needs of the neighbor and the needs of the community. It is clearly immoral to use our wealth in a way that benefits ourselves but brings harm to others in the community. Social reform, love of the neighbor, must inform our use of our wealth.

Such a vision of society demands massive reform of our cultural values and of our economic and political structures. E.F. Schumacher has written a book with the provocative title, *Small Is Beautiful: Economics As If People Mattered.*[38] In the Judeo-Christian tradition, all aspects of our life together must be arranged "as if people mattered." Reducing the standard of living of the poor in order to improve the economy, or redesigning a manufacturing plant so that it can produce goods more efficiently even though the jobs of workers become more routinized and dehumanizing, reverses the priorities of the Judeo-Christian faith. It gives more importance to money-making and efficiency than to persons. Our communities must be so designed that human needs take priority over the needs of an abstract economy or the quest for larger corporate profits. This is a vision of a radically reformed society.

The Christian stress on the equality of all persons, and the demand that our communities be measured by their treatment of the least well off, further emphasize the radical vision of the Judeo-Christian faith. This vision requires a strong commitment to the rights and needs of those who have been the victims of our society. All our policies, all our social structures, must first be judged by their effects on the poor, the powerless, and minorities. Such concerns cannot be an afterthought, an addendum to a policy whose primary concern is strengthening national power or increasing economic productivity. The Judeo-Christian tradition affirms that we will be judged by, that the quality of our personal and corporate humanity will be measured by, our treatment of the least well-off. Our communities must be so designed as to ensure that the poor have all the necessary resources for the development of their full humanity. Our institutions must be so structured that the powerless can become full, functioning members of society.

This brief look at the Judeo-Christian tradition presents a vision of human communities much closer to that of the Marxist vision of society than that of the Western capitalist vision. In part this is no coincidence: Marx's vision of society has deep roots in the biblical tradition.[39] Nevertheless, there remain some fundamental differences. In practice, Marxist societies, on the whole, have not done a good job of guaranteeing human political rights or protecting human freedom. Nevertheless, they have far exceeded capitalist states in meeting the basic economic needs of their populations.[40] Still, the Judeo-Christian tradition maintains a vision that demands significant reform of existing Marxist societies, and insists on an important perspective on our relationship to the natural world that neither Marxist nor capitalist societies honor. It is clear that both economic systems are guilty of large-scale abuses of the natural environment, which now threaten us with resource depletion and disastrous levels of environmental pollution. Both systems have proceeded as if human beings have an absolute right to use the environment as they please. Both seem bent on exhausting the planet in the quest for ever-increasing economic growth.[41]

The Judeo-Christian tradition teaches that the world is gifted to us. We are stewards who are to tend and keep the natural world, using what we need, but duty-bound to preserve its beauty and usefulness. We are to pass the beauty and productivity of the world on to future generations; they have as much right to the world's resources as we. In this respect, the Judeo-Christian faith offers a vision that demands significant reform of both Western and Marxist economic systems and offers the hope of a sustainable, ecologically sound form of economic community.[42]

Finally, the Christian claim about the universality of human community and the equality of all persons requires that we view the fundamental needs of persons from a global perspective. The glaring inequality of wealth among nations is a violation of the Christian social vision. Not only is the gap between rich and poor nations immense, it is still growing. Rich nations, despite their foreign aid programs, continue to take more wealth from poor countries than they return to them.[43] The rich nations of the world are continuing to rob poor nations of the very resources the poor nations need to meet the fundamental needs of their own peoples. The imbalances are intolerable. Our food consumption patterns deprive the poor of access to needed nutrition.[44] Our commitment of money and time to the development of arcane and supersophisticated forms of medical technology means that basic medical care is denied to the world's poor.[45] The Christian vision of human community demands a basic reordering of international economic and political structures so that the world's resources can be more equitably shared and all persons have access to the resources necessary for meeting their fundamental needs. Put the other way around, if we were to reorder our communities to assure that they meet the fundamental needs of all humankind, we would be required to dramatically restructure most of our existing human communities.

As noted above in discussing "the human," our fundamental humanity is simply the base, the core out of which our full humanity develops. In constructing our vision of society and developing guidelines for the formation and reformation of our human communities, we must also look at the implications of our potential humanity for the structuring of our human communities.

Our Potential Humanity and Our Communities

If our communities are to foster our human development, then they must be formed in such a way that their structures and values also support and contribute to the development of our potential humanity. Inasmuch as our potential humanity confronts us as a question, a mystery to be explored, our communities must provide an open, tolerant context for the exploration of this mystery. From the perspective of the Judeo-Christian tradition, however, part of the mystery includes a desire for personal wholeness and integrity. Our communities must be structured so as to support this quest. In addition, our community values and structures must contribute to our search for reconciliation with others and with the natural world that supports us.

Such a concept of community requires social structures that allow freedom for the most individualized forms of development and yet do so in such a way that our individual development becomes a means of enriching and contributing to the development of others and to the communities of which we are a part. The implications of such a vision are almost endless and have specific implications for all our particular communities (families, neighborhoods, ethnic groups, nation-states). I will dwell on only a few of the more obvious, necessary, and general implications of such a vision for our human communities.

The quest for wholeness entails the development of communities where persons are encouraged to develop their unique talents and personal skills and interests. This requires an educational environment designed to foster these individual talents. Such an educational system is dramatically different from that existing in our nation, or most nations, today. Most educational programs are designed to breed conformity in values and ideology, and to prepare students to accept work roles that society deems necessary for its prosperity.[46] Persons are shaped to fit preexisting vocational slots. These practices have resulted in widespread alienation of workers from their jobs, and a sense of meaningless routine that spreads into all areas of their lives. Concern for personal development might also require a guaranteed annual income that allowed persons to pursue their interests even if their chosen "vocation" had little immediate market value.[47]

In order to contribute to the individual's sense of integrity, our communities must allow room for pluralism and have a genuine respect for human differences. Persons must be allowed to express their cultural and esthetic differences and to express disagreement with the prevailing values and tastes of a particular culture. Our communities, thus, must incorporate an appreciation of differences as sources of enrichment and growth, seeing in human variety the beauty that we see in the variety of nature—geography, flora, and fauna. These community attitudes will permit persons to develop their own particular identities in a setting where they feel accepted, valued, and respected.

For our culture, social tolerance and support will require a profound shift in our racial and sexual attitudes. Not only must we learn to accept the worth and value of women and persons of color, but we must see them as having a special value. Their unique histories, the history of their oppressions, gives them insights and perspectives that we badly need. Not only is their very existence a thing of beauty, they offer us new perspectives on social, cultural, and international problems that our traditional approaches are unable to solve.

Our sense of wholeness, of integrity, also depends upon having a sense of meaning, a purpose to our existence. A sense of meaningfulness develops only as we feel that our work and our lives are part of an ongoing process that has some purpose and direction. As Jonathan Schell has noted, the nuclear holocaust that haunts us threatens any sense of meaning that we might have, because all that we have lived for and labored for may be gone in a flash: "The possibility that the living can stop future generations from entering into life compels us to ask basic new questions about our existence, the most sweeping of which is what these unborn ones, most of whom we will never meet even if they are born, mean to us."[48] But even apart from the nuclear threat, ours is a culture with no purpose or direction. Persons are condemned to spending their lives doing work that has little personal value or purpose. Their lives become fragmented, disjointed. As Studs Terkel notes, work should be. "a search, too, for daily meaning as well as daily bread, for recognition as well as cash, for astonishment rather than torpor, in short, for a sort of life rather than a Monday through Friday sort of dying."[49]

A life of wholeness and integrity, then, depends upon communities with some purpose and direction. For such purpose and direction to be satisfying, it cannot be imposed from above but must grow out of community dynamics.[50] General agreement on such purposes may be hard to find if goals are explored along utopian lines. But such agreement is relatively easy to find in creating communities where persons are cared for and can care for others; creating a world where persons are free from the threats of violence; creating a world where one is confident that one's children and grandchildren will be able to enjoy and build upon what we have done. This is a vision with almost universal appeal: creating communities, structures, and values that will allow us and our descendants to live out our full humanity.

In the creation of such communities, as Terkel sees, work too is redefined:

Perhaps it is time the "work ethic" was redefined and its idea reclaimed from the banal men who invoke it. In a world of cybernetics, of an almost runaway technology, things are increasingly making things. It is for our species, it would seem, to go on to other matters. Human matters. Freud put it one way. Ralph Helstein puts it another. He is president emeritus of the United Packinghouse Workers of America.

"Learning is work. Caring for children is work. Community action is work. Once we accept the concept of work as something meaningful—not just as the source of a buck— you don't have to worry about finding enough jobs."[51]

The pursuit of a humane world, of human-centered communities, provides our lives and our work with meaning. Work has a purpose and merges once again with the rest of our lives. All we do, whether in our leisure, our work, our parenting, our relationships with others, is done as part of a whole life dedicated to making and keeping our life, and that of others, human, and to enjoying the presence and humanness of one another. In our parenting we teach our children values of peace and justice, show them how to care for and enjoy each other and the world. In our work, we struggle to create a just and peaceable world where all persons are well fed and military ranks are thinned. In our leisure we simply would enjoy each other and the world and the life that is gifted to us. Our life would be of a single piece, we would be whole in what we do; our lives would be a seamless web.[52]

Finally, a sense of integrity requires that we have a degree of control over our own lives, and a share of power in the formation of our communities. Without such control and power we come to feel that we are but cogs in a machine, puppets subjected to others' purposes and bidding. Our communities must be democratic in the fullest sense of the term. There must be room for genuine participation in the decisions and formation of the community. "This principle is grounded in a recognition that people have a human right to participate as peers in the decisions that affect their lives. It also reflects the fact that, given our very different human experiences, we are all learners as well as teachers when it comes to world affairs."[53] The forms of such participation may be different in the family and in the school, but it dare never be absent.

Certainly this requirement would demand total restructuring of the world's many totalitarian societies. But even for American society, such a vision would radically restructure political and economic communities. At the political level, more decisions would be left to the local community, and national representatives would be truly selected by, and accountable to, the constituency they represent. The current practices, which restrict office-holding to persons of wealth and make them accountable to the lobbies of the rich and powerful, are not acceptable.[54] There is something wrong with a system where over fifty percent of the population are women but no president has ever been a woman and less than 2 percent of the Congress is composed of women. Similarly, the majority of Americans—women, persons of color, blue-collar workers, and low-income persons—have no national political representation. Ours is a government of affluent white males who represent the interests of a small, disproportionately advantaged minority.

But the creation of democratic communities would have an even more profound effect upon our economic communities. Although our political structures are at least partially democratic and claim to be based on democratic principles, our economic structures are profoundly antidemocratic. As Francis Fox Piven and Richard Cloward have shown, capitalism and democracy are at war with each other in our society. They represent opposing principles for organizing human communities.[55] Capitalism gives to the few—the wealthy—the right to decide what will be produced, how it will be produced, the conditions to which workers will be subjected and, to a large extent, how goods will be distributed.[56] The majority probably want to see hunger ended in our nation and to see the homeless housed; but a minority dictates that instead we will get new computer games, more sophisticated weaponry, and a greater variety of gourmet frozen foods. At the whim of the few, concerned primarily with increasing personal and corporate wealth and power, we have a system that produces goods and services we do not need, but refuses to produce what we need, destroys the environment, and creates meaningless, hazardous jobs.[57]

Our concern to create an economic community that respects the dignity of persons and gives them a degree of control over the economic system will require the democratization of our economic communities. Strict external controls must be placed on businesses to protect the environment and the safety of workers, and even over the rights of corporate movement and investment.[58] In addition, individual firms must be reorganized as workers' cooperatives where workers can make decisions about the shape and nature of their work environment, the nature and quality of goods produced, and the use and distribution of corporate profits. Only such radical democratization of our economic communities can create an environment in which persons can have a sense of wholeness in their lives, a sense of meaning in their work, and a feeling that they are active, respected participants in the national economy.

As noted in the last chapter, however, our growth in personal wholeness must be united to our desire for reconciliation with others and with the natural environment. Nurturing and encouraging our drive toward reconciliation will also require a basic transformation of our communities. It will require a shift in our values from competitive, self-seeking values, to cooperative, mutually-affirming values; a shift from economic-centered, nation-centered, to global, ecologically sensitive, values. The notion of a society based on principles of Social Darwinism, "survival of the fittest," must be replaced by a vision of a society grounded in an organic understanding of persons and work.

With Paul we must affirm that no individual is more important than another, no work more significant than other work, as long as the work contributes to the fullness and humanness of the community. Running a corporation, being a politician, a doctor, a lawyer, is no more important than caring for children, cleaning bathrooms, or collecting garbage. All these things must be done if society is to function and be a healthy society. As Paul notes:

> But as it is, God arranged the organs in the body, each one of them, as he chose. If all were a single organ, where would the body be? As it is, there are many parts, yet one body. The eye cannot say to the hand, "I have no need of you" nor again the head say to the feet, "I have no need of you" [1 Cor. 12:18–21].

In terms of our communities, such a recognition of the worth of all members would require us to remove the trappings of status that surround certain occupations. It would mean an end to executive washrooms and to a paternalistic attitude toward secretaries, nurses, janitors, and blue-collar workers. In addition, it would require a definite change in salary scales, making salaries more equal and commensurate with the work done. As things stand now, as a general rule, the harder, more dehumanizing the job, the less the pay. Such inequalities in payment are not justified, and they are a barrier to reconciliation.[59] As the Old Testament attests, the formation of social classes leads to alienation of persons from one another and to a growing class hatred and suspicion. The wealthy cannot understand the life situation of the poor, the poor chafe under their oppression by the rich, and so animosity grows. The jubilee year was meant to ensure that the needs of the poor would be met and to eliminate a cause of social division and conflict. Reconciliation requires the elimination of radical class division.

Our change in community values will also force us to adopt a new understanding of the natural environment in which we dwell. We need to understand our inescapable dependence on it and, more profoundly, to see its intrinsic worth and value, and to discover the wisdom and beauty of nature. Our religious traditions and our culture must find and tap once again the spiritual power of the natural world[60] and so develop communities and structures that respect the integrity of nature and provide opportunities for affirming our interconnectedness with it.[61] Our ability to recover ecologically sound values and to build environmentally sensitive communities and methods of production are important keys to the full development of our humanity. We must come to see ourselves and our communities as part of a much larger whole. Our reconciliation with the estranged parts of ourselves, and with each other, certainly depends upon our reconciliation with the very forces of nature that give us life and sustain us.

And reconciliation, like the desire for wholeness and integrity, will require active attempts to combat racist, sexist, and nationalistic attitudes. Education must expose persons to both the inadequacies of their own traditions and heritage, and to the positive insights and accomplishments of other traditions. Included in such education must be cross-cultural exchanges and experiences. Both formal and informal education must stress the need to respect the fundamental human rights of all persons.

This concern for reconciliation must, of course, extend across national boundaries. Certainly reconciliation necessitates a fundamental transformation of our nationalistic values. As Christians we are called to view all persons as children of God, equal in worth and value. But beyond this, global interdependency requires us to understand that our problems—the threat of nuclear annihilation, pollution of the environment, starvation in the Two Thirds

World—can be solved only through the cooperation of all peoples. We must see other nations as resources, not threats, members of a global family who offer great richness to each other. We must work for the surrendering of the competitive nationalist ideologies that are the cause of the current "cold war" between East and West, and of the "hot wars" that have been so numerous in the last several decades.[62] Without such a change, real progress in meeting our collective human needs is impossible.[63]

As in the national sphere, however, a simple change of values is not enough; there must also be significant changes in social structures. This will certainly involve a restructuring of the international economic order. The current order is founded on historical patterns of power and domination, and assures that rich nations will grow richer at the expense of poorer nations.[64] The inequalities that this system perpetuates remain a major cause of human suffering and international conflict.

Structural changes will require a shift toward authentic forms of international negotiation and the establishment of effective international courts of law.[65] Nation-states must surrender much of their autonomy in international affairs and agree to be bound by higher principles of law transcending national self-interests. For such structures to be effective, there will have to be an accompanying reduction in the world's major military powers and a demilitarization of Third World nations, which have become pawns in the cold war between East and West. The demilitarization of the globe must be accompanied by economic restructuring as we shift our economies toward meeting basic human needs and away from producing weapons of death and social destruction.[66]

Finally, reconciliation is possible only if we can create positive forms of conflict-resolution. We will never create communities utterly free of conflict. In fact, conflict is a sign of social vitality and an important means of community development. In communities where pluralism and difference are encouraged, we may find an increase in conflict. To date, much of our conflict—whether in the family, the community, or the international realm—has been resolved through the use of physical and psychological violence. Such violence exacts a heavy price from all of us, both perpetrators and victims. We must begin to learn and teach positive means of conflict-resolution: the use of mediation, bargaining, and forms of nonviolent confrontation. We will need to apply such forms of conflict-resolution at both the personal and local levels as well as at the national and international level. Conflict itself must come to be viewed as an opportunity for growth and enrichment of all parties, not an event in which one party wins and the other loses.

There is, of course, no end to the implications for change in our communities if they are to contribute to the development of the full humanity of all members of the human race. To be sure, the vision of communities so reformed seems utopian, unrealizable. But it is the vision offered by the Old and New Testaments, the vision of the kingdom of God. It is a kingdom of peace and justice where the fundamental needs of all humankind are met. It is a kingdom where persons are liberated into full personhood, into wholeness, and where persons are reconciled to one another and the gift of creation, and become gifts to each other. Both the Old and New Testaments teach that our full humanity can flourish only in such communities—under seemingly utopian social conditions. But how are we to respond to a vision of community life, of social organization, that seems impossible to create, given what we know about ourselves and the history of human communities? We will look at this issue in the next, and last, chapter.

8

EMBODYING OUR VISIONS

As we saw at the end of the last chapter, what we do is not only a function of our character, principles, values, and visions; it is also a product of what we believe is possible, what we hope for, and what we are willing to risk. Our actions, our human and social development, are thus closely linked to our assessment of both the situation in which we find ourselves and of the possibilities for change. Careful study of the real possibilities is especially important for Christians and others whose final moral principle is embedded in concern for the well-being of others. Failing to do what can be done to improve the quality of others' lives constitutes a moral failure on our part; but so does causing harm through rash actions that have no possibility of success and consequently end up causing additional hurt to the neighbor.

The notion of careful calculation to protect the neighbor from unnecessary harm is so strong in the Christian tradition that one of the guidelines for "just war" is that such wars have a chance of success.[1] When no reasonable chance exists, even wars of self-defense are perceived as immoral. They cause additional harm to the neighbor without the possibility of an eventual good end. The idea of "calculating love" has even been applied to reflections on the ethics of revolution. Those attempting to develop a Christian warrant for revolution have returned to the idea that a revolution with no reasonable chance of success is an immoral undertaking.[2]

The assessment of what is possible, however, is related not only to our empirical assessment of particular situations, but also to broad theological presumptions about the nature of the historical process of which we are a part. Theological disagreement over the possibilities for change constitutes a major area of debate in the field of Christian ethics, and is the cause of a fundamental division between Christians in the contemporary world. In this chapter I want to briefly respond to this debate, give my opinion on what we should risk, and finally conclude by applying the approach I have developed in this book to two concrete issues in order to show how the abstract categories and discussions of this work inform concrete decisions. In my response to particular issues, I am not claiming that my positions are the only correct ones, or that they are the only ones that can be developed from the premises of my work.

As should be clear by now, morality is both public and private. To the extent that we are formed by our communities, our morality has a common base and set of assumptions. Nevertheless, to the extent that we are all formed as unique mixtures of experiences and community influences, there will be considerable differences in the way we view moral problems and approach similar situations. Still, I think there is some value in making a position public and stating as clearly as we can the reasons (as best we know them) for the positions we advocate, recognizing that there is an element of the intuitive, the inexpressible, in all our moral decisions. Nevertheless, in making our positions public, we share our experiences with each other and make possible an ongoing moral dialogue that can serve as one of the foundations for an open, pluralistic, humanizing community.

CHRISTIAN REALISM

The term "Christian realism" is normally used to signify a particular approach to Christian ethics associated with the neoorthodoxy movement of the 1930s and 40s, and is particularly identified with the work of Reinhold Niebuhr.[3] The end of the nineteenth century was a period of intense social optimism. There was a prevailing cultural view in the United States that humankind had been gradually evolving in its moral wisdom and activity, and that the world was on the threshold of a new era, an era of worldwide peace, prosperity, and cooperation. The secular realm was dominated by a liberal philosophy that understood education as the key to moral improvement, and there was a national movement to provide universal education with the hope that it would be morally uplifting and so hasten the arrival of a new era in human history. In the religious sphere, there was a general belief that spiritual renewal was the key to the new age. If all persons would simply become "more Christian," the new age would dawn. Even as astute an observer of social ills as Walter Rauschenbusch[4] could write:

> Perhaps these nineteen centuries of Christian influence have been a long preliminary state of growth, and now the flower and fruit are almost here. If at this juncture we can rally sufficient religious faith and moral strength to snap the bonds of evil and turn the present unparalleled economic and intellectual resources of humanity to the harmonious development of a true social life, the generations yet unborn will mark this as that great day of the Lord for which the ages waited, and count us blessed for sharing in the apostolate that proclaimed it.[5]

Certainly the empirical reality of the age seemed to run counter to the notion of a new age in human history. Industrialization had created dirty, unsanitary cities and filled them with armies of the poor and destitute. Strikers protesting unsafe working conditions and eighty-hour work weeks were met with violence as owners sent out private armies and government officials sent out the state and national militia to force workers back to their jobs.[6] Concerned persons made significant attempts to minister to the victims of the emerging industrial world.[7] But most observers viewed these ills as passing phenomena that would soon be cured by the moral education of the populace and its spiritual reawakening. Both religious and cultural missionaries carried their programs for moral reform abroad in the attempt to create a peaceful world. Missing were calls for the restructuring of society, for the redistribution of wealth and power that might have made a more just and peaceful society a reality.[8]

The optimism of the liberal world was, of course, shattered by the brutality of World War I and the suffering caused by the worldwide depression of the 1920s and 30s. Still, vestiges of the old optimism remained as World War I became "the war to end all wars." As international relations deteriorated, however, and the world crept closer and closer to World War II, a serious attempt was made to respond to what seemed to be the inescapable drift toward evil that seemed to dominate social and world events. Both cultural and religious thought attempted to formulate a "new realism" that would take account of the fundamentally "self-interested" motive of persons and societies. In the theological vernacular, religious liberalism could not account for the actual working of human society, because it overlooked the inescapable sinfulness of humans. Politically there was a realization that the relationship between groups is more a function of power balances than moral sentiments, and that there is an inherent tendency on the part of groups to attempt to dominate each other.

One of the lasting outcomes of this new "realism" was a discrediting of utopian dreams and visions of the "liberal way," and a recognition that the negativities of human history can never be fully overcome. In addition, there was a new awareness of the limited effectiveness of educational and religious appeals in bringing about social change.[9] Rather, real change was now understood as requiring a change in power relationships. This meant that little change could be expected without significant political struggle for, as Niebuhr wrote, "There is as yet no evidence that a privileged class, which yields advantage after advantage peacefully, will finally yield the very basis of its special position in society without conflict."[10]

The new realism thus counseled persons and politicians to be very sober in their estimates of the possibilities of social change. It also encouraged them to pay careful attention to the human and social desire for power and domination over others. Basic political and social strategies were to be based upon balancing the various powers against each other so that no group could be assured of easy or certain victory over other groups. In the area of civil rights, this meant that minorities could not expect better treatment simply because they appealed to the moral sentiments of the dominant group. Rather, minorities had to develop strategies for acquiring political power. Such programs might include voter registration, strikes, or economic boycotts. In the international realm, the way to peace was no longer seen to be that of disarmament, but rather peace would be achieved by balancing the military strength of competing political blocs so that no one nation could realistically gain anything by attacking another.[11]

This new realism was an important corrective to the social liberalism it replaced. As it correctly pointed out, all social change requires careful, empirical assessment of existing conditions and the likely effect of various options for change. In addition, it focused upon power relationships and the economic and political factors involved in social change. In important respects it was, initially, much more radical than the social liberalism it sought to replace. Social liberalism was founded on the premise that "men's hearts"[12] could be changed while inequalities of wealth and power could largely be left intact; poverty could be ended without the rich surrendering their luxuries; social justice could be achieved without the powerful giving up their power. The new realism recognized that change required radical social restructuring, the redistribution of both power and wealth. In this respect, Christian realism was quite radical.[13]

Unfortunately, Christian realism was quickly distorted by those with power into a conservative religious and political doctrine that no longer emphasized the need for radical social change, but now emphasized the innate human sinfulness that supposedly made most social change both impossible and undesirable. Christian realism became for many a defense of the status quo, of existing capitalist structures and policies, and of the imperfect democratic political structures of the United States and Western societies. Despite the immense inherent problems of economic and political systems, they were defended as the best possible compromise in a world where persons are perceived as inherently sinful and social groups inescapably motivated by collective self-interest. The radical restructuring envisioned in socialism, purer forms of democracy, or serious commitment to disarmament were, and continue to be, dismissed by many of the contemporary exponents of Christian realism as being unrealistic in a world whose defining characteristic is human sinfulness.[14]

In response to this misuse of Christian realism, a new theological movement, liberation theology, has emerged.[15] It is a response by the world's oppressed, by the powerless, to the social and political world they confront. To the poor, minorities, women, and the politically oppressed, the prevailing political and economic compromises are not acceptable; the suffering caused by our institutions is understood as unjust and dehumanizing. Social change, with all the risks involved, is considered preferable to the existing social order. Liberation theology thus grows out of the sufferings of a people and its discovery of a biblical God who intervenes in history in behalf of the oppressed to create a more just world. Liberation theology begins with a different assessment of the existing situation and different notions of what can be hoped for and what we should risk. Still, it is a realistic view of life, informed and hardened by the historical suffering of the world's oppressed.

Liberation theology, unlike the religious liberalism of the last century, and like Christian realism, believes that change requires more than a change in human hearts and minds; it requires significant restructuring of the social order and redistribution of power. Like Christian realism, it sees the need for careful assessment of the current social situation and the development of careful, informed strategies of social change. In addition, it is aware of human sinfulness and of the need to take account of that sinfulness in developing a new social order. Nevertheless, it is profoundly different from Christian realism in important respects, for it emphasizes human possibilities as well as human sinfulness. A perfect society cannot be achieved, but history shows that some societies are more just than others, and concludes that we are under constraint by our God to make our societies as just as possible. In addition, liberation theologians present a God who acts in history and who links our ultimate destiny with our historical drama. This is an important departure from Christian realism, which feels we need to act in history out of love for the neighbor, but whose God is ultimately not an actor in history and does not tie our ultimate destiny to our historical activity.

This last difference is crucial since it relates to the issue of human hope and action. For the Christian realist, we can hope for very little. Human history is dominated by human sin, God is not an actor in social events, and the best we might hope for is the temporary minimizing of the effects of human evil on our communities and social structures. Rosemary Radford Ruether properly summarizes this theological position:

> The God who is beyond history, who ever transcends our historical processes, is the only God who can save us. Only

the radically transcendent can keep us from being trapped by our works, can revitalize even the boldest of our answers, and thereby keep us constantly open to the future. Does this process move toward any goal? For Niebuhr and the neoorthodox this process itself generally had no goal. It was the permanent situation of man within history. The transcendent stood over against history in a dialectical relationship with it, but, by the very nature of historical reality, there could be no final synthesis of the two.[16]

Liberation theologians, however, have absorbed the "theology of hope," a theology that pictures a God who acts in history to redeem us and our communities, a God who also goes ahead of us, calling us forward. Such a God does not guarantee a perfect future, but such a God allows us to risk more, even risk failure, for we are not the only actors. God may make possible what humans cannot achieve. We are thus called to attempt to stretch the limits of the possible.

As we come to the end of the twentieth century, Christians are fundamentally divided over the question of our responsibility to each other, and to the shaping of the communities that inform our lives. Perhaps most Christians continue to see no relationship between God and our human communities. God is still extrahistorical, working outside the events of our lives and history to prepare a spiritual resting place for our souls. We are called to be socially responsible because love for the neighbor requires it, but still such activity is secondary to our real task of establishing a proper spiritual relationship with God. Earlier I discussed what seems to me to be the inadequacy of both approaches. Now there is a growing awareness on both sides of the religious spectrum that our human destiny is inescapably linked to the nature and shape of our communities.

The religious right, in the name of God, is trying to impose a particular vision of society upon all human communities.[17] In the United States, this is a community founded upon the principles of capitalism, nationalism, patriarchalism, and puritanical sexual morality. The religious right would maintain the uneven power relationships now in place between men and women, whites and persons of color, the rich and the poor. They would maintain a community built on hierarchical relationships, founded on the idea that some should rule and others should be ruled. I have discussed the inadequacy of this vision of human community.

Countering this vision of hierarchical communities, of domination of some by others, of complete social uniformity, are the various Christian liberation movements. As disparate as they are, each movement reflecting the specific concerns of a particular group of persons, they share a common vision of community based upon a fundamental equality of persons, and a sharing of power and resources. All persons are to be given a voice in the development of these communities. The creation of these communities requires fundamental restructuring of the existing society and international order, and is founded on the hope that something more positive, more humanizing, might emerge. Liberationists make their claim, fully aware of the risks, fully aware of the dangers of human sinfulness, but recognizing that the suffering imposed by our existing structures is so great that the only faithful, loving response is to risk change.

In the matter of hope and action, as in all other areas of our lives, we must take a position. Consciously or unconsciously, our actions will reflect one attitude or another; neutrality is impossible. As this book evidences, I have chosen a liberationist perspective. The empirical evidence seems overwhelming that our existing communities and social structures cause immense suffering and pain to hundreds of millions of the world's population. The scope of suffering is both unnecessary and intolerable, and its continued existence directly contradicts the Christian claim that we are required to accept the risks of change out of love for the neighbor.

In addition, I am convinced that the Bible witnesses to a God of the poor and oppressed who demands that we judge our communities by the effects upon the poorest and most powerless. To be faithful to the God of the Bible requires that we put the needs of the poor ahead of the wants of the affluent and try to view society through the eyes of the poor. Such a task is not easy, for as Howard Zinn notes, we have been conditioned to understand history from the perspective of the affluent, the successful, the powerful. The history of the United States is the history of successful heroes. But there is another side to history, one we must learn to see if we are to be faithful to the God of the Bible. With Howard Zinn we must alter our vision so that "my focus is not on the achievement of the heroes of traditional history, but on all those people who were the victims of those achievements, who suffered silently or fought back magnificently."[18]

I am also convinced that the Bible portrays a God who acts to redeem our communities and whose salvation includes our reconciliation to each other. To be faithful to this God requires that our quest for salvation include our struggle to redeem our communities.

Our struggles and our actions must be informed. We must recognize the limitations placed upon us by our particular historical situation and by our own human nature. We must be "as wise as serpents and innocent as doves" (Matt. 10:16). Still, our actions must be viewed against the backdrop of the vision of what it means to be fully human in our relationships and our communities. Each action then becomes an attempt to move the present reality a bit closer to our vision; or, in extreme situations, to prevent the further erosion of our common humanity. In this respect, our lives gain a certain continuity. What becomes important is not each of our actions in isolation, but the general thrust of the lives we live. We can risk action, we can accept our mistaken judgment, knowing that we are forgiven, freed from our mistakes to move toward a richer and fuller future. We become part of an ongoing history of persons who have tried under various circumstances and conditions to create communities in which the fullest possible development of our humanity could take place and in which universal reconciliation becomes a possibility. And, given our belief in a God who works with us, we are empowered to test and stretch the limits of the possible.

Finally, though, we live in a world whose situation has altered so dramatically in the last decades that only a radical, visionary response to our predicament is "realistic." At present, only radicalism is realism. Traditional Christian realism draws much of its power from the belief that "idealistic" responses to problems will cause greater suffering and chaos than that caused by the prevailing compromises. In the words of Sharon Welch, "People are dying now, and our sane lack of caring is an intrinsic part of their deaths. Just as we have become inured to the human costs of our economic system, of our government's support of 'friendly' authoritarian regimes, so we continue to blithely or callously or ignorantly benefit from those systems, failing to demand, in the name of the people, their radical transformation."[19]

It is now evident that our compromises have created conditions that daily dehumanize millions and cause immense suffering. In addition, our industrial consumer culture has brought us face to face with ecological disaster. Despite our unwillingness to face the implications of our technological system, the reality remains: we are marching toward economic, political, and ecological collapse.[20]

Even more apparent is the failure of "power politics" to create a safe, peaceful world. The end product of "political realism" is a world held captive to the ideology of nuclear deterrence where we all become hostages to terrorism.[21] The technological instability of the deterrence system, the proliferation of nuclear weapons, and growing international tensions all make nuclear war a growing probability.[22] In the light of a suffering humanity and the multiple threats to human and global survival, "realism" itself becomes increasingly "unrealistic." Our existing compromises, our business as usual, lock millions into lives of suffering and bring us closer and closer to ultimate catastrophe. We have reached a point in human history where risk-taking offers the only possible hope, the only chance of escape for the world's suffering peoples and for our own survival. The worst possible consequences of radical change are no worse than the effects of the "realism" that presently controls our public policy and behavior.[23] And, alternatively, our radical responses offer the only slight possibility of hope that we still have. Only such change can avoid catastrophe.

We have entered a historical period when Christian radicalism is not only the position most consistent with the biblical worldview; it appears to be the only Christian response that offers any genuine hope to the world's poor and oppressed, or offers any real hope of human survival. There is no guarantee, of course, that even such radical action will save us; nevertheless, it seems to be the only option that offers any real possibilities. So, as we come to the end of the twentieth century, Christians stand caught between a vision of a just, peaceful, reconciled world, and a reality that offers daily witness of our inhumanity and brutality toward each other and our planet. We must live in that tension and respond to the vision of a more humane world in the hope of the possibilities that history still offers. Our actions must be careful, calculating, and well planned.

We must attempt to be thoughtful and consistent as we try to humanize ourselves and our communities through our actions. I now want to show briefly by reference to two specific issues, how the approach to Christian ethics developed in this volume provides guidance in our response to particular moral issues.

TWO ISSUES

As I have indicated throughout, the primary function of ethics is to help us decide what we should become as persons and what kind of communities we should create. In fact, the creation of our personhood and our communities takes place as we respond to particular situations and problems. Ethics, then, must also respond to the question "What should I do, or what policies should we, as communities, adopt?" in response to particular issues. In this section I want to show how the approach to ethics presented in this book helps us to formulate responses to particular issues. I have chosen two issues to demonstrate the applicability of my approach. In each instance, I have treated the issue very briefly, necessarily overlooking some of the important empirical data, and many of the traditional philosophical and ethical problems associated with the issue. Nevertheless, I feel that even a brief treatment given to some practical issues provides some insight into both the strengths and weaknesses of the approach to Christian ethics I have developed.

The two issues I have selected are (1) distribution of medical care and (2) nuclear arms policy. I have chosen them, in part, because they are issues with which I am familiar and which I consider important. Both issues also reflect upon the nature of ourselves and our communities. There are also some other specific reasons for choosing these two issues. First, the distribution of medical care is a serious issue in our society. It affects the lives of millions, but receives almost no attention in either popular or specialized literature. I have decided to focus on nuclear arms policy because I consider it a critical issue, and one for which only a more "radical" approach offers any hope of avoiding nuclear catastrophe. Secondly, I have chosen these two issues because other issues equally important (e.g., affirmative action, environmental policy, economic justice) have been discussed both directly and indirectly throughout this work.

The Right to Medical Care [24]

The issue of the right to medical care is a response to our concern for the fundamental humanity of persons. As Charles Curran observes, "Although health care is not the most fundamental need of the person, it is of great significance. Health is necessary for the proper and full functioning of the life of the person."[25] Good health is certainly a prerequisite for the full development of our potential humanity. Proper health, of course, is a function of more than medical care. It is related to genetics and various environmental factors such as adequate diet, housing, and education. Nevertheless, there are times when medical care is necessary. The failure to provide such care when it is available is fundamentally unjust and a violation of a person's basic human rights.[26] From this perspective I want to focus on the medical care system in the United States.

There is no question that the United States has the resources to meet the basic medical needs of all its citizens. We spend over 10 percent of our national income on medical care, by far the highest in the world,[27] and have one of the world's highest doctor per population ratios.[28] Nevertheless, the United States compares unfavorably with other developed nations in general measurements of health such as longevity and infant mortality. Our infant mortality rates are higher than those of Hong Kong, Singapore, and most of the European nations.[29] Our unfavorable comparisons are largely a result of radical disparities of health patterns among groups in the United States. When the poor and near poor are excluded from the averages, the United States compares favorably with any nation in the world. When we look at the health statistics of only the poor and near poor, the results are shocking. Many poor areas in the United States have infant mortality rates comparable to those of Third World countries, and life expectancy for black males is below that of persons living in China, Cuba, and Mexico, and is on a par with persons living in South Korea, Thailand, and Vietnam.[30] How can we account for these radical disparities?

For many Americans, the claim that our medical care system is arbitrary and unjust, denying necessary medical care to millions, will come as a shock. After decades of agitation, the United States government responded in the 1960s with two programs: Medicare for the elderly and Medicaid for the poor.[31] These programs were an attempt to assure that all persons in our society would have access to necessary medical care. Most Americans have assumed that these programs have guaranteed all persons in society the right to medical care. And there is no doubt that these programs have been of great benefit to millions.

The programs, however, are flawed and leave many with no, or inadequate, medical care. Even with these two programs, there are an estimated 34 million persons who are not eligible for government programs and who cannot afford private insurance. In addition, 70 million more persons can afford only minimal private insurance coverage and so face the possibility of personal bankruptcy and impoverishment if ever faced with a serious illness.[32] Further, despite popular opinion, Medicaid does not guarantee medical care for the poor and the requirements for coverage are themselves often dehumanizing. Medicaid is a state-run program in which individual states set eligibility and benefits standards. In twenty-nine states, two-parent families, no matter how poor, are not eligible for Medicaid.[33] And, throughout the system, car ownership or home ownership can disqualify a person for Medicaid benefits. As Michael Harrington notes, "America is the only nation in the world where home ownership disqualifies people for medical care."[34]

Medicare, a more generous program than Medicaid, similarly does not guarantee the elderly adequate medical care or prevent them from being impoverished because of illness. Despite the Medicare program, elderly households with incomes below $10,000 a year have out-of-pocket medical expenses amounting to 16 percent of their income and this percentage is expected to rise.[35] Even for those persons who qualify for Medicare or Medicaid, and for whom the programs provide adequate levels of care, there may still be problems. Physicians in the United States are not required to accept either Medicare or Medicaid patients. One study in Portland, Oregon, found that only one-third of the city's doctors were willing to treat Medicaid patients.[36] And, in 1984, faced with a possible governmental freeze on the rate of Medicare payments to physicians, the AMA threatened the public with withdrawal of services to the elderly. Those covered by governmental programs thus often receive lower quality medical care and are often subjected to hours and hours of waiting in crowded clinics before receiving any care at all.

We have, then, a medical care system that provides the finest health care in the world for our richest citizens, and provides adequate health care for its middle class. But for millions in the United States the quality of medical care is poor or nonexistent. This multitiered system of medical care is a product of a mixed market system that makes medical care dependent on one's ability to pay, and gives physicians and health care providers tremendous power in determining the cost, quality, and availability of health care. The rewards to health care providers have been tremendous. Physicians in the United States are by far the highest paid in the world. The average physician earns over $100,000 a year and some specialists have annual incomes of $350,000 to $500,000.[37]

The emergence of conglomerates running chains of hospitals will aggravate discrepancies by exaggerating the role of the profit motive in providing medical care. As Paul Starr concludes at the end of his comprehensive study on the emergence of corporate medicine: "A corporate sector in health care is also likely to aggravate inequalities in access to health care. Profit-making enterprises are not interested in treating those who cannot pay."[38]

It is sad that the medical profession itself has been a primary impediment in the attempt to create a more just medical care system. The AMA conducted intense propaganda campaigns against, and lobbied vigorously against, both Medicare and Medicaid. These campaigns put posters in doctors' offices and handed out pamphlets to private patients. The concern for ever-higher salaries for doctors has been so great that on several occasions the AMA has closed medical schools or reduced the number of admissions in order to reduce competition between physicians that was perceived to be a cause of declining income.[39] Coupled with a national ideology of laissez faire, the result is that the United States is the only modern industrialized nation, with the exception of South Africa, that does not guarantee its citizens a right to health care.[40]

The United States, then, by the criteria of the Judeo-Christian ethic—"concern for the least well-off"—has a very inadequate and unjust system of medical care. Despite claims that we have the "finest health care system in the world," we have one of the worst, if measured by its effects on the least well-off. The system also shapes up badly when faced with the question, "What kind of society do we want to be?" The values of our current medical care system suggest we are a society that places the accumulation of private wealth ahead of the needs of society's poor, places the concern for profit ahead of the concern for health and well-being. The Judeo-Christian ethic demands a thorough transformation of such a system.

Whether change can best be handled through a nationally guaranteed health insurance program or through a national health care service will require careful study and dispassionate debate. What is clear is that our current system is unacceptable.

The Christian tradition also provides an important model in Jesus the healer. Jesus heals out of compassion and concern, out of the desire to restore persons to some degree of wholeness. This is a far cry from "practice for profit," and is an important reminder that for the physician, "earning his living can be only a secondary motive for his vocational choice."[41] Encouraging a sense of vocation among medical care personnel will be an important task for, as Charles Curran notes, any adequate and just system of medical care will greatly restrict the freedom of practitioners in comparison with the present system.[42]

In conclusion, the fundamental reform of our health care system is, from the Judeo-Christian perspective, imperative. It is imperative because such reform is essential if the fundamental humanity of all our citizens is to be respected. Reform of the medical care system would also be an important symbolic statement in the reordering of our national values and priorities. In remaking this system, we loudly proclaim the priority of human values over values of profit and self-interest. We as Christians, and as churches, must also address this issue because at the moment it has fallen from public view and debate. Inequality of care is growing. Nevertheless, there is a widespread notion that we, as a nation, cannot afford any new social programs or initiatives. Oddly, there is good evidence that a uniform system of guaranteed medical care would be less costly than what we currently have.[43] More important, until such a transformation occurs, millions will unnecessarily suffer and be stunted in their human development. Many millions more will live with the anxiety of knowing that losing their jobs may deprive their families of medical care, or that a catastrophic illness will literally take the roof from over their heads. The great injustice, of course, is that such suffering and anxiety are unnecessary. We have the resources and personnel to ensure that the basic medical needs of all persons in our country be met.

The Case for Unilateral Disarmament Initiatives

Perhaps no other issue better evidences the bankruptcy of our contemporary political and moral systems than the nuclear arms race. Despite recognition of the dangers involved in the development of nuclear weapons, and the early demands by the very scientists who developed them that the arms race be halted, the arms spiral has continued at an ever-increasing pace. In 1960, the United States had 6,500 strategic[44] nuclear warheads and the Soviet Union 300. By 1980 the numbers had risen to 10,000 (U.S.A.), and 6,000 (U.S.S.R.). Current development plans will make those numbers 18,000 (U.S.A.) and 20,000 (U.S.S.R.) by the year 1990.[45] To put these numbers in context, 200–300 warheads would be enough to destroy either country and possibly put an end to all life in the northern hemisphere and maybe the planet.

Even more frightening, however, are a number of recent developments that make nuclear war more likely and the possibilities for significant arms reduction agreements more remote. First, a number of technical developments have greatly heightened the prospects for war. The computerization of our weapons systems makes war by accident a real possibility. The malfunctioning or misprograming of computer systems has put us on full alert on numerous occasions and in November 1979 brought us close to launching a nuclear attack on the Soviet Union.[46] In addition, the greater accuracy of our weapons makes it possible for us to hit and destroy Soviet missiles before they are launched. The temptation for a first strike grows every day. In order to avoid the loss of weapons in a first strike, both nations are moving to a launch-on-warning system; missiles would be launched from their silos by computer, without human intervention, at the moment that there is warning of an attack from the other side, thus further increasing the likelihood of war by error. Other developments—the cruise missile, which is so small it can be hidden and so is not capable of being verified under an arms agreement treaty, or a stealth bomber that can penetrate detection systems without notice—enhance the climate of nuclear distrust between the superpowers. Finally, the cold war climate between the superpowers and the spread of nuclear weapons to more and more nations[47] make the possibility of a nuclear holocaust increasingly likely.

All persons, of course, should be seriously worried about the nuclear trap we are creating for ourselves and the inability of world leaders to get control of the arms spiral. Simple concern for personal preservation should make all of us concerned. Christians, however, should have additional reasons for their concern. The strong prohibitions against killing others and our respect for the humanity of others should be strong incentives for repudiating the nuclear arms race as a way of maintaining peace through a balance of power. It is quite clear that the use of nuclear weapons is immoral according to traditional Christian "just war" theory because of the indiscriminate nature and the immense scope of their destructive power.[48] In addition, Christian concern for preserving the natural environment that has been gifted to us, and a realization that we have no right to put an end to the experiment that God has begun, are strong reasons for repudiating the arms race.

None of these concerns, of course, not even the last, are exclusively Christian concerns. One need not be formally religious to be concerned about other persons and the environment, or to recognize with Jonathan Schell that morally our power over life is not ours to exercise, for "neither as individuals nor as a species have we created ourselves."[49]

Even if we believe that nuclear war can somehow be avoided, that nuclear deterrence will somehow prevent war, it is clear that the maintenance of this balance of terror is itself immoral and dehumanizing. Simply living under the uncertainty of the nuclear cloud has dehumanizing effects on our lives, relationships, and communities. As Robert Jay Lifton writes on the basis of his extensive study of the effects of the nuclear threat on our psyches:

> It is true that none of our actions, problems, or symptoms is caused by nuclear weapons alone. But it is also true that nothing we do or feel—in working, playing, and loving, and in our private, family, and public lives—is free of their influence. The threat they pose has become the context for our lives, a shadow that persistently intrudes upon our mental ecology.[50]

Just as important, however, is the fact that our nuclear threats to others require of us an intolerable personal and social dehumanization. It requires that we be willing to be mass murderers; that we be willing to slaughter hundreds of millions of persons; that we give our consent to join the ranks of the officials of the Nazi death camps as mass murderers. Such a willingness represents the most fundamental dehumanization of ourselves that is possible; any morally sensitive person recognizes the need to repudiate and resist such a policy.

Beyond the destruction of our own humanity and corruption of our social goals, the arms race is a cause of physical harm to millions of human beings. The diversion of resources into the production and distribution of weapons deprives the poor of resources necessary for their very survival. World military spending has reached $900 billion a year, $1.7 million per minute. One hour of the world's military budget would provide vaccinations for 3.5 million children who will eventually die from preventable childhood diseases.[51] As Dorothee Sölle puts it, "The arms race kills even without war."[52] Our weapons of death are already killing persons and the arms race will continue to kill even if the weapons are never used.

Christian concern for the poor, the suffering, the needy, condemns the diversion of resources that is part of our deterrence policy. As the U.S. Catholic bishops conclude, citing the Pastoral Constitution from Vatican II, "The arms race is one of the greatest curses on the human race and the harm it inflicts upon the poor is more than can be endured."[53]

Like the Catholic bishops of the United States, then, we reach the conclusion that the nuclear arms race and its policy of deterrence are both dangerous and immoral.[54] Our concern for the neighbor, our love of the enemy, demands an end to the arms race and our current deterrence policy. Both the United States and the Soviet Union have given partial support to such a goal in their erratic attempts to negotiate nuclear arms treaties. The history of these negotiations, however, provides little room for optimism. The recently signed INF treaty is the first treaty between the superpowers in over a decade and is the first actual disarmament treaty ever signed. All previous treaties have merely limited the rate of the arms build up; this treaty actually removes some existing weapons. Nevertheless, the INF treaty is very limited in its effects. It bans intermediate nuclear weapons from Europe, but does little to reverse the arms race or end the nuclear danger. The treaty applies to less than five percent of the nuclear arsenals of the two superpowers and leaves in tact the British and French nuclear forces and over four thousand tactical nuclear weapons which belong to the United States. Both the United States and the Soviet Union are also able to overcome any perceived strategic losses through retargeting other parts of their nuclear arsenals. Finally, the INF treaty has had no impact on the military budgets of either country and does nothing to curtail development of new weapons systems.

If the INF treaty has any major impact, it is in terms of its symbolism and its possible effects on improving relations between the superpowers. The treaty is viewed by many as a prelude to additional disarmament treaties. The history of the arms talks, though, show that such follow up, despite the eurphoria that surrounds the signing of any treaty, is far from certain. Still, should the START talks continue and be successful, even the most extreme proposals to date would include a reduction in strategic weapons to about five thousand per side, a dramatic reduction, but still enough warheads to destroy each society more than ten times over. More discouraging is the fact that the new disarmament proposals are being carried on in the context of discussions of developing more mobile missiles that would be less detectable and also less verifiable should a treaty be signed. In other words, the disarmament talks are based on the premise of creating a smaller but more effective deterrent force.

The difficulty, of course, is that the failure to break the deterrence mindset does little to offset the dangers of nuclear war. The only real safety, and the only moral option for Christians who refuse to consent to be potential mass murderers, is to move beyond deterrence thinking as a proper nuclear weapons policy. As Christians we must seriously consider and advocate a program of gradual unilateral nuclear disarmament.

Unilateral action has historically been dismissed as politically unwise and unrealistic, a surrendering of power to an evil enemy. The time for unilateral action has come, however. The nuclear situation has become increasingly volatile and we may no longer have time to pursue a careful, negotiated series of mutual arms reduction agreements. Positively, our immense nuclear capacity means that we can freeze that capacity and even greatly reduce it without risking our security or altering our ability to totally annihilate the Soviet Union should it choose to use its nuclear weapons. Such a change can build on the positive atmosphere created by the

INF treaty and further alter the international climate and open up new possibilities for armament reductions.

A realistic program might begin by unilaterally freezing our military budget, halting our weapons development programs, and stopping further deployment of nuclear weapons. Following that, we might wait for a Soviet response. Whether there is or is not a Soviet response, we might then initiate a reduction of our nuclear arsenal and again await a Soviet response. The Soviet Union might respond in kind and we could enter into a period of nuclear deescalation. Even if there is no Soviet response, however, we must seriously consider the possibility of total unilateral nuclear disarmament. There are a number of practical and moral reasons for such a course of action.

First, it removes from us the stigma of being mass murderers and world executioners. Secondly, it is not clear that even our nuclear disarmament provides the Soviet Union with any real military advantage. The use of nuclear weapons against us would destroy our nation; the Soviet Union would gain little economically or politically. In addition, the effects of fallout would result in considerable damage to the Soviet Union, especially in light of recent information about a "nuclear winter." Thirdly, it seems impossible that the Soviet Union, putting aside nuclear attack, could successfully occupy the United States. The Soviets are having tremendous difficulty simply controlling the Eastern bloc nations. At most, the United States, without the threat of nuclear weapons, would lose some of its ability to force its economic and political policies upon Third World nations, resulting in a partial loss of international prestige and perhaps a slight decline in national prosperity.

We have entered an era that demands risk-taking; playing it safe will lead to absolute disaster. And, morally, we must search for better, more humane ways of defending ourselves and our values. As Bernard Häring recognizes, "It is a worldwide growing conviction that, in our day, the option between violence and nonviolence is an option between the extreme danger of extinction and the chance for a dignifying survival."[55] India gained its freedom from Great Britain without ever firing a shot. Norway, by carefully planned acts of corporate resistance, retained its values and humanity in spite of Nazi occupation.[56] We can no longer rely on military might and the balance of power as means for solving conflict or preserving our cultural values. Our physical survival and the survival of our humanity require a fundamental shift in our nuclear policy.

Clearly, then, the Christian vision presents multiple reasons for risking unilateral actions in the realm of nuclear disarmament. Our current policy destroys our very humanity, turning us into potential mass murderers and risking the destruction of the gift of life that has been entrusted to us. In addition, the God who goes ahead of us gives us reason to hope, demands that, like Abraham, Moses, Ruth, and Jesus, we leave our past securities behind, for they are destructive securities, and walk hopefully into a new future. The Christian view of persons, however, also reminds us of a shared humanity; we can be certain that, like us, the enemy loves and hates, feels joy and sorrow, laughs and cries, and so may indeed respond positively to the initiatives we offer. On the other hand, our vision of a shared humanity reminds us that, like our enemy, we too love and hate, are altruistic and self-centered, and are not really to be trusted with the destructive power we now hold. The only guarantee we have against becoming mass murderers is to divest ourselves of that power.

CONCLUDING REMARKS

It should be clear by now that ethics is not a method for arriving at clear, simple answers to our moral problems. At best, ethics allows us to be reflective and self-conscious about the effect of our choices on our individual and corporate humanity. Likewise, Christian ethics does not provide ready-made answers, but rather provides a vision of the humanity we seek and of the communities we should attempt to build. The vision, along with its guiding principles and stories, gives our life a general direction, provides our actions with a fundamental consistency, but certainly does not give certain answers to many specific moral problems, or assure us that we will always make the best decisions.

Still, Christian ethics, at its best, provides some critical insights for life in the contemporary era. It reminds us that our individual lives are inescapably tied to the lives of all the others who inhabit our planet or will do so in the future. In addition, our lives are tied to the very life of the planet itself. If we choose to live an egocentric, self-defensive existence, we will contribute to the destruction of the lives of others and ultimately to our own lives as well. Or we may choose to commit ourselves to life together and seek to enhance the quality of life for all, and, in the process, find that our own humanity is enhanced. In the most basic sense, our age has made our interdependency inescapable, and we shall literally perish or flourish together.

Finally, Christian ethics should not divide persons from each other, but rather create an attitude of openness toward, and cooperation with, all who are working for similar goals and values regardless of their worldview. There is no room in the world for Christian arrogance or the assumption by any group that it, and it alone, is in full possession of the truths of existence. Life remains a mystery whose origins and purposes remain hidden. Christians do have some glimpses into these mysteries, insights they must share with others. But, the history of Christian peoples, marked by brutality and insensitivity to others, shows that there is much we do not understand. We must be open to the insights that others bring and collectively probe the mystery of our existence.

We live, to paraphrase Charles Dickens, "in the best of times and the worst of times." Millions suffer daily from hunger, poverty, and political oppression. The world stands on the edge of a nuclear holocaust and each day the possibilities of ecological disaster move closer. Yet never before in history have the resources to combat these evils been so great. We have the resources to eliminate hunger, to put an end to poverty. We have the scientific knowledge to rearrange our standards of living to avoid ecological disaster. We know in detail the tragic results of a nuclear exchange and know what steps to take to avoid it.[57] What is needed is a new ethical awareness, a willingness to honestly face the consequences of our personal and collective decisions for our humanity and that of others. It remains to be seen whether or not, in the clarity of such self-awareness, we are capable of the personal and social reform necessary to eliminate the suffering that is part of our current life together, or to avoid the catastrophes that stand before us. As Christians, however, inspired by the vision of the kingdom of God, by Abraham's journey into an unknown future,[58] we can do nothing else but proclaim the necessity for change, and point out a direction. Finally, like Ruth,[59] we must leave behind our familiar world and journey into the future with those now struggling to free themselves and others from oppression, whose struggle may liberate all from the holocaust that now awaits us.

NOTES

INTRODUCTION

1. This theme in liberationist thought is a sharp departure from the traditional Western emphasis on the role of autonomy in ethical reflection. There is a good discussion of this shift in *The Ethics of Liberation—The Liberation of Ethics*, Dietmar Meth and Jacques Pohier, eds. (Edinburgh and New York: *Concilium*, 1984).

2. Beverly Wildung Harrison, "Theological Reflection in the Struggle for Liberation: A Feminist Perspective," in *Making the Connections: Essays in Feminist Social Ethics*, Carol Robb, ed. (Boston: Beacon, 1985), pp. 235–266.

3. The concept of "historical projects" is central to liberationist thought. For a good discussion of its meaning and role, see José Míguez Bonino, *Toward a Christian Political Ethics* (Philadelphia: Fortress, 1983), chap. 8; and Gustavo Gutiérrez, *A Theology of Liberation* (Maryknoll, N.Y.: Orbis Books,1973), chap.11.

4. This is not true of feminist thought, which has regularly addressed the issue of nuclear disarmament and has self-consciously attempted to build an ecological consciousness and ethic. For examples of the latter, see Rosemary Radford Ruether, *New Woman/New Earth: Sexist Ideologies and Human Liberation* (New York: Seabury, 1975) and Susan Griffin, *Woman and Nature: The Roaring Inside Her* (New York: Harper and Row, 1978).

1. ETHICS AS A HUMAN ENTERPRISE

1. William E. May, *Becoming Human: An Invitation to Christian Ethics* (Dayton, Ohio: Pflaum, 1975), p. 2.

2. Peter L. Berger, *The Sacred Canopy: Elements of a Sociological Theory of Religion* (Garden City, N.Y.: Doubleday, 1969), p. 5.

3. Daniel C. Maguire, *The Moral Choice* (Garden City, N.Y.: Doubleday, 1978), p. 3.

4. Harmon L. Smith and Louis W. Hodges, *The Christian and His*

Decisions: An Introduction to Christian Ethics (Nashville: Abingdon, 1969), p. 13.

5. Maguire, *Moral Choice,* p. 71.

6. Richard McCormick, "Scripture, Liturgy, Character, and Morality," in *Readings in Moral Theology, No. 4: The Use of Scripture in Moral Theology*, Charles Curran and Richard McCormick, eds. (New York: Paulist, 1984), p. 289.

7. Stanley Hauerwas's emphasis on the role of character in ethical decision-making has directed attention toward the social nature of our moral life. He has continued to stress the need for nurturing communities for the development of Christian character. Unfortunately, he has yet to fully incorporate the awareness of the social nature of morality into his views. He continues to presume that the church, as a community, can largely separate itself from society and create a fundamentally new type of society. As such, he believes that personal renewal can occur without the renewal of the larger, secular society. See especially his work, *The Peaceable Kingdom: A Primer in Christian Ethics* (University of Notre Dame Press, 1983).

8. Hauerwas, *Peaceable Kingdom,* p. 21.

9. Arthur J. Dyck, *On Human Care: An Introduction to Ethics* (Nashville: Abingdon, 1977), p. 22.

10. For a good account of the effects of the social turmoil of the 1960s on our society's moral vision and character, see Steven M. Tipton, *Getting Saved from the Sixties: Moral Meaning in Conversion and Cultural Change* (Berkeley: University of California Press, 1982).

11. For a significant interpretation of the effects of the Vietnam tragedy on individuals and on our society, see Walter H. Capps, *The Unfinished War: Vietnam and the American Conscience* (Boston: Beacon, 1982).

12. The term is from Michael Harrington's classic work, *The Other America: Poverty in the United States* (New York: Penguin, 1962). It focused the attention of the nation on the plight of the poor.

13. This criticism applies to naturalistic understandings of natural law, which attempted to find eternal laws to govern human conduct. There are other, more dynamic understandings of natural law that do not come under this criticism and are quite compatible with the style of ethics I am discussing in this volume. For examples of such uses of natural law, see Charles Curran, "Natural Law," in *Themes in Fundamental Moral Theology* (University of Notre Dame Press, 1977), pp. 27–80; or Bernard Häring, *Morality Is for Persons: The Ethics of Christian Personalism* (New York: Farrar, Straus, and Giroux, 1971), esp. chap. 14, 15, and 16.

14. This particular statement of the Kantian maxim comes from George F. Thomas, *Christian Ethics and Moral Philosophy* (New York: Scribner's,

1955), p. 424. Thomas (pp. 421–47) offers a good discussion of the Kantian maxims and their relationship to the Judeo-Christian tradition.

15. Matthew 7:12. This is, of course, the biblical form of the golden rule. As Matthew indicates, this rule is not something new to Christianity but is invoked by Jesus as a reminder of one of the fundamental rules of behavior for the Jewish community. Matthew concludes, ". . . for this is the law and the prophets."

16. This is a much too simplistic description of what is both an important method of ethical decision-making and an important formulation of the concept of justice. Readers of this book are encouraged to read more widely in the text itself: John Rawls, *A Theory of Justice* (Cambridge, Mass.: The Belknap Press of Harvard University, 1971). In the introduction to the book, Rawls offers a helpful guide to reading his work, especially for those who wish to understand the basic concepts and methodology but who do not care to read the entire work.

17. Thomas Merton, *No Man Is an Island* (New York: Harcourt, Brace, Jovanovich, 1955), p. 126.

18. I am indebted to Edward Langerak of the Saint Olaf Department of Philosophy for this helpful analogy for understanding the role of ethical reflection in moral decision-making.

19. Dyck, *Human Care,* p. 28.

20. Here I appeal to Garth L. Hallett, *Christian Moral Reasoning: An Analytical Guide* (University of Notre Dame Press, 1983). On pp. 46–47, he makes the case for using moral terms in their broadest, most common-sense meaning.

21. This insight is basic to Augustine's work, as Waldo Beach and H. Richard Niebuhr note in their *Christian Ethics*, 2nd edition (New York: Ronald Press, 1973). On p. 108, they present a quote from Augustine's *Enchiridion,* which summarizes this insight. Augustine writes: "For when there is a question as to whether a man is good, one does not ask what he believes, or what he hopes, but what he loves."

In many respects, Luther simply recovers the Augustinian insight into the centrality of our love for determining our character. In his explanation of the first of the Ten Commandments, Luther declares: "Now I say whatever your heart clings to and confides in, that is really your God" (*Dr. Martin Luther's Large Catechism* [Minneapolis: Augsburg, 1935], p. 44).

22. The term "moralscape" is used by Daniel Maguire in *The Moral Choice,* chap. 1. Charles Curran uses the concept of "stance" in a similar fashion. See, e.g., "The Stance of Moral Theology" in *New Perspectives in Moral Theology* (University of Notre Dame Press, 1976), pp. 47–86.

23. Ralph B. Potter, *War and Moral Discourse* (Richmond: John Knox Press, 1973).

24. Ibid., pp. 23-24.

25. Ibid.

26. The Holocaust has had a profound influence upon the worldview of millions of individuals, and in some respects upon the global worldview of the post-Holocaust world. For two examples of the influence of the Holocaust experience on worldviews, see Richard L. Rubenstein, *After Auschwitz: Radical Theology and Contemporary Judaism* (Indianapolis: Bobbs-Merrill, 1966), and Tom F. Driver, *Christ in a Changing World: Toward an Ethical Christology* (New York: Crossroad, 1981).

27. Dyck, *Human Care*, pp. 20-21.

28. For some brief examples, we need only compare our way of interpreting disease or natural disasters with biblical views. Our scientific worldview causes us to understand these events differently. For a discussion in this change in interpretive framework, see Rudolf Bultmann's classic work, *Jesus Christ and Mythology* (New York: Scribner's, 1958).

In a different area, Edward S. Herman's *The Real Terror Network: Terrorism in Fact and Propaganda* (Boston: South End Press, 1982) is a frightening account of the distorted view that citizens of the United States have of international affairs because of the selective treatment of issues by the news media. Chapter 4 is especially helpful in documenting the ways in which news and information are controlled and managed in the United States.

29. H. Richard Niebuhr, *The Responsible Self: An Essay in Christian Moral Philosophy* (New York: Harper and Row, 1963), p. 62.

30. See Thomas S. Kuhn, *The Structure of Scientific Revolutions*, 2nd edition (University of Chicago Press, 1970). In an article, "Toward a Feminist Biblical Hermeneutics: Biblical Interpretation and Liberation Theology," in *Readings in Moral Theology, No. 4* (pp. 354-82), Elisabeth Schüssler Fiorenza uses this idea from Kuhn to show the importance of paradigm shifts in understanding the Bible. She understands the movement to a feminist and liberationist hermeneutic as representing such a paradigm shift.

31. Lawrence Kohlberg and Carol Gilligan have offered two alternative modes of moral development that seem to indicate a difference in the way in which men and women in our society view moral problems. According to Kohlberg (who has studied, almost exclusively, white males), moral issues are perceived primarily as problems about which rules or principles should be obeyed. Gilligan (who has principally studied white females) finds that moral problems are viewed in terms of their effects on persons and relationships. Nevertheless, in both theories it is the problems that cannot be solved within existing moral frameworks that prompt persons to adopt

new frameworks. Kohlberg's writings are significant and include two large volumes: *Essays on Moral Development, Volume One: The Philosophy of Moral Development* (San Francisco: Harper and Row, 1981), and *Essays on Moral Development, Volume Two: The Psychology of Moral Development* (San Francisco: Harper and Row, 1983).

Carol Gilligan's work is nicely summarized in her book, *In Different Voice: Psychological Theory and Women's Development* (Harvard University Press, 1982).

32. Stanley Hauerwas has done an excellent job of showing how narrative and stories enrich our moral lives and sharpen our ethical reflection. See especially his essays, "From System to Story: An Alternative Pattern for Rationality in Ethics" (pp. 15–39), and "Story and Theology" (pp. 71–81), both in *Truthfulness and Tragedy: Further Investigations into Christian Ethics* (University of Notre Dame Press, 1977).

However, his exclusive focus on narrative actually diminishes the richness of the moral life by failing to see the significance of other components of our humanity, which contribute to our moral lives and ethical reflection.

Oliver F. Williams and John W. Houck, in *Full Value: Cases in Christian Business Ethics* (New York: Harper and Row, 1978), show the practical insights generated by the narrative approach by focusing on the way in which our stories (images of ourselves and our social roles) influence decisions in the world of business.

33. This, of course, is the classic statement of hedonistic ethics. In all fairness, such an ethic may be a very responsible reaction to the human situation. See, for example, "The Epicureans" by Bertrand Russell, in *A History of Western Philosophy* (New York: Simon and Schuster, 1945), pp. 240–51. Russell shows the close connections between this classic position and modern utilitarianism, especially the work of Jeremy Bentham.

34. In responding to our ability to analyze and criticize particular worldviews, Langdon Gilkey concludes: "Even the skeptical, questioning, critical 'tradition' . . . requires a certain vision of reality, history, truth, society, human being, and of procedures for inquiry into these realities which must be presupposed, participated in, and believed if creative criticism is to be possible" (*Message and Existence: An Introduction to Christian Theology* [New York: Seabury, 1980], p. 31).

35. This traditional historical dualism accounts in large measure for the social inactivity of Christians. It is, of course, the root of Marx's charge that religion is the opiate of the people. For an example of this approach, see a short article by Gilbert C. Meilander, Jr., "Christians and the Nuclear Dilemma: An Unfashionable View," *The Cresset* (Nov. 1982), pp. 7–10. He argues that our obsessive concern over a nuclear holocaust comes from our having made human survival into an idol. For Christians, he believes

that such concerns must be secondary to the concern for salvation. Despite the claim that this view is "unfashionable," it is actually characteristic of the larger part of the Christian tradition both in the past and in the contemporary setting.

Rosemary Radford Ruether has reversed Meilander's claim, arguing that our excessive concern for personal immortality has made the ego into an idol and seriously distorts the theocentric, neighbor-centered nature of the Christian faith. In *New Woman/New Earth: Sexist Ideologies and Human Liberation* (New York: Seabury, 1975), she writes:

> Perhaps this also demands a letting go of the self-infinitizing view of the self that culminates in the wish for personal immortality. One accepts the fact that it is the whole, not the individual, which is that "infinite" out of whose womb we arise at birth and into whose womb we are content to return at death, using the human capacity for consciousness, not to alienate ourselves from nature, but rather, to nurture, perfect, and renew her natural harmonies, so that earth might be fair, not only for us and our children, but for all generations of living things still to come [p. 211].

36. Augustine, *City of God*, David Knowles, ed. (London: Penguin, 1972), p. 593 (book XIV, chap. 28).

37. This summary of Augustine's position is from Beach and Niebuhr, *Christian Ethics*, p. 108.

38. The masculine form is intentionally used here, because what is described seems to be a peculiarly male phenomenon.

39. This is a pervasive theme in Marx's writings. See Robert L. Heilbroner, *Marxism: For and Against* (New York: Norton, 1980), chap. 4.

For an early but significant statement of this thesis by Marx, see "Estranged Labor," in *The Economic and Philosophic Manuscripts of 1844* (New York: International Publishers, 1969), pp. 106–19.

40. The reference here is to Thomas Hobbes and his classic work in political philosophy, *Leviathan*.

41. As Alan Geyer, *The Idea of Disarmament: Rethinking the Unthinkable* (Elgin, Ill.: Brethren Press, 1985), indicates, the decision to use atomic weapons on Hiroshima and Nagasaki was more an attempt to intimidate the Soviet Union than a necessary action to end the war (p. 18).

Similarly, Michael Walzer, *Just and Unjust Wars: A Moral Argument with Historical Illustrations* (New York: Basic Books, 1977), pp. 263–68, concludes that the use of atomic weapons on these two Japanese cities was both immoral and unnecessary.

42. This traditional definition of justice is a summary of Aristotle's

treatment of justice in book 5 of the *Nicomachean Ethics*. It is not immediately clear, however, what is each person's due. Aristotle provides numerous examples in his treatment of justice in order to develop a perception of what is due to particular persons. From our perspective it is clear that "what is due" is very much determined by cultural traditions.

43. See Jenny Pearce, *Under the Eagle: U.S. Intervention in Central America and the Caribbean* (Boston: South End Press, 1982).

44. In a pluralistic society, shared values tend to decrease, whereas rules, in the form of laws, tend to increase. In the United States, the result has been the reduction of almost all values to monetary values. Milton Friedman in his *Free to Choose: A Personal Statement* (New York: Harcourt, Brace, Jovanovich, 1980) understands freedom as the freedom to invest and to consume.

On the other hand, as the laws that bind us together become more complex, the use of courts becomes our primary way of resolving personal and social disputes. This method of resolving disputes, as the primary means, is a social and historical aberration. See Jethro K. Lieberman, *The Litigious Society* (New York: Basic Books, 1981).

45. William K. Frankena, *Ethics*, 2nd edition (Englewood Cliffs, N. J.: Prentice-Hall, 1973).

46. For a summary of this debate, see Harvey Cox, ed., *The Situation Ethics Debate* (Philadelphia: Westminster, 1968).

47. Immanuel Kant makes the strongest possible claim for always telling the truth regardless of consequences in his tract from 1797, *On the Supposed Right to Lie from Altruistic Motives*. He states: "To be truthful (honest) in all declarations, therefore, is a sacred and absolutely commanding decree of reason, limited by no expediency" (quote taken from Robert M. Veatch, *Death, Dying, and the Biological Revolution: Our Last Quest for Responsibility* [Yale University Press, 1978], p. 210).

48. Joseph Fletcher, *Situation Ethics: The New Morality* (Philadelphia: Westminster, 1966), p. 120.

49. See Thomas Merton, ed., *Gandhi on Non-Violence* (New York: New Directions, 1965). This theme is at the heart of Gandhi's philosophy and teaching, and is evident in his claim: "In 'satyagraha' the cause has to be just and clear as well as the means" (p. 28).

50. Alvin Toffler documents the effects of rapid and continuous social change on persons and societies in his book, *Future Shock* (Toronto: Bantam, 1974).

A similar view is presented by Robert Jay Lifton in his essay, "Protean Man," in *History and Human Survival: Essays on the Young and Old, Survivors and the Dead, Peace and War, and on Contemporary Psychohistory* (New York: Vintage, 1971), pp. 311–30. Here he relates the disturbing effects of transcience, a product of social change to our awareness of our newly created capacity to destroy life on this planet.

51. As Paul Ramsey indicates, such processes as artificial insemination or in vitro fertilization are not really cures for infertility. The condition of infertility remains after the treatment. In his own words, "By contrast, in vitro fertilization is arguably 'not a medical' procedure. It concentrates on the 'product,' not on a medical condition which itself can be cured, if at all, only in the actual patient there is." As Ramsey argues, such procedures are altering our notion of the practice and function of medicine ("Shall We 'Reproduce'?: Rejoinders and Future Forecast," *Journal of the American Medical Association*, 220 [1972]: 1481). Charles Curran offers a good overview of the moral issues surrounding in vitro fertilization and offers a thoughtful response to Paul Ramsey in "In Vitro Fertilization and Embryo Transfer," in *Moral Theology: A Continuing Journey* (University of Notre Dame Press, 1982), pp. 112–40.

52. There has been a great deal of discussion over whether our conceptions of "human rights" are universal or simply a product of Western thought. I will not address this issue but merely indicate that the two United Nations' Covenants—*The United Nations' Covenant on Civil and Political Rights*, and *The United Nations' Covenant on Economic, Social and Cultural Rights*—have been ratified by almost all member nations (the United States being a notable exception). The detailed covenants (the first has twenty-seven articles and the second, fifteen) suggest a general agreement on the basic human rights that persons should have to ensure human development.

For the full texts of these covenants and the earlier *Universal Declaration of Human Rights*, see Walter Laqueur and Barry Rubin, eds., *The Human Rights Reader: A Unique Sourcebook and Documentary History on the Issue of Human Rights* (New York: New American Library, 1979), pp. 197–233.

53. This issue is emphasized by all the liberation theologians. Liberation is understood as entailing a right to be involved in the shaping of the processes and structures that shape our humanity. Gustavo Gutiérrez sees this increased demand for participation as the beginning of a new era in human history. He writes of his own culture:

Large numbers of Latin Americans suffer from a fixation which leads them to overvalue the past. This problem has been correctly interpreted by Paulo Freire. It is one of the elements of what he has called a precritical consciousness of a man who has not taken hold of the reins of his own destiny [*A Theology of Liberation* (Maryknoll, N.Y.: Orbis, 1973)].

54. For a discussion of this particular controversy, which received national attention and even enshrined itself on posters and T-shirts, see Loretta Schwartz-Nobel, *Starving in the Shadow of Plenty* (New York: Putnam's, 1981), pp. 157–80. My point is, of course, that there seems to be a fundamental moral discrepancy between attaching great value to an endangered, but insignificant species of fish, and at the same time dismissing a human fetus as an insignificant piece of tissue. Schwartz-Nobel makes a similar point in showing that concern over these fish exceeded that over farmers who were being displaced from their farmlands, often being forced to leave homesteads that had been in the family for generations.

55. Our moral confusion has brought us to the brink of environmental and nuclear disaster, and has left us uncertain about how to proceed. We are now aware that the extreme value we have placed on national power and the control of the environment is a primary cause of the disasters that threaten us. Nevertheless, we remain paralyzed, unable to give up either of these values in order to replace them with ones that are life-affirming.

56. Max Weber saw no way out of the "iron cage" that modern capitalism and rationalism have constructed without some form of visionary renewal of society. At the end of *The Protestant Ethic and the Spirit of Capitalism* (New York: Scribner's, 1958), he writes:

> No one knows who will live in this cage in the future, or whether at the end of this tremendous development entirely new prophets will arise, or whether there will be a great rebirth of old ideas and ideals, or, if neither, mechanized petrification, embellished with a sense of convulsive self-importance [p. 182].

57. The term "kairos" is used by Paul Tillich to refer to that moment "at which history, in terms of concrete situation, had matured to the point of being able to receive the breakthrough of the central manifestation of the Kingdom of God" (*Systematic Theology* [New York: University of Chicago Press, Harper and Row, 1967], vol. 3, p. 369). As Tillich indicates, such moments restore a sense of coherence, meaning, and direction to history.

The "kairos" concept is also important to the work of Bernard Häring. In *Morality Is for Persons*, he clearly points to both the personal and social implications of the concept: "Thus the situation—the kairos—is not looked upon chiefly as an occasion for self-perfection but rather as a personal call for service and for receptivity to the dignity and needs of person. It is this alertness for the 'kairos' that makes human life rich and fulfilled according to the degree of openness and dedication" (p. 110).

2. THE SOURCES OF CHRISTIAN ETHICS

1. Waldo Beach and H. Richard Niebuhr, *Christian Ethics*, 2nd edition (New York: Ronald Press, 1973), p. 4.

2. See E. Clinton Gardner, *Christocentrism in Christian Social Ethics: A Depth Study of Eight Modern Protestants* (Washington, D.C.: University Press of America, 1983), for an excellent account of contemporary ethicists who hold this position. Gardner defines this position as "christocentric ethics" and discusses the difficulties of developing a viable social ethic for a pluralistic society from this starting point.

3. Emil Brunner, *The Divine Imperative* (Philadelphia: Westminster, 1973), p. 43.

4. Ibid., p. 51.

5. H. Richard Niebuhr, *The Responsible Self: An Essay in Christian Moral Philosophy* (New York: Harper and Row, 1963), p. 43.

6. Many introductions to ethics provide such a typology. William K. Frankena, in *Ethics*, 2nd edition (Englewood Cliffs, N.J.: Prentice-Hall, 1973), presents a widely used account of types of ethics.

7. See esp. Kant's *Theory of Ethics*. The relevant portions can be found in *Kant Selections,* Theodore M. Greene, ed. (New York: Scribner's, 1957).

8. For an account of this position, see E. O. Wilson, *Sociobiology: The New Synthesis* (Harvard University Press, 1975), or David P. Barash, *Sociobiology and Behavior* (New York: Elsevier, 1977). For a study of religious ethics from this perspective, see Wolfgang Wickler, *The Biology of the Ten Commandments* (New York: McGraw-Hill, 1972).

9. This is a central theme in all of Fromm's work, but is most forcefully presented in *The Art of Loving* (New York: Bantam, 1970).

10. See Friedrich Nietzsche, *Beyond Good and Evil* (New York: Random House, 1966).

11. See Albert Camus, *The Rebel* (New York: Knopf, 1954).

12. For a discussion of secularization, see Bryan Wilson, *Religion in Secular Society* (Baltimore: Penguin, 1966); Robert E. Bellah, *Beyond Belief: Essays on Religion in a Post-Traditional World* (New York: Harper and Row, 1970), esp. his essays, "Religious Evolution" and "Meaning and Modernization"; Michael Harrington, *The Politics at God's Funeral: The Spiritual Crisis in Western Civilization* (New York: Harper and Row, 1984); or Gregory Baum, *Religion and Alienation: A Theological Reading of Sociology* (New York: Paulist, 1975), esp. chap. 7.

13. For a discussion of these changes and their effects on theology and ethics, see Langdon Gilkey, *Message and Existence: An Introduction to Christian Theology* (New York: Seabury, 1980) and Gardner, *Christocen-*

trism. An excellent overview of the forces that have shaped modern culture and the challenge they pose for theology and religious ethics is found in "Section A: The Horizon," of Hans Küng's monumental work, *On Being a Christian* (Garden City, N.Y.: Doubleday, 1976).

14. For a discussion of this enterprise, see Langdon Gilkey, *Religion and the Scientific Enterprise* (New York: Harper and Row, 1970).

15. Religious opposition to the theories of Copernicus and Darwin *et al.* provides, historical examples of the religious resistance to the expansion of human knowledge. Others, like Freud and Marx, documented the opposition of religion to social progress through its infantilization of the human psyche and the legitimation of unjust social structures. See Sigmund Freud, *Civilization and Its Discontents* (New York: Norton, 1962), and *The Essential Marx: The Non-Economic Writings*, Saul Padover, ed. (New York: Mentor, 1978), section IX.

16. The first atomic bomb to be exploded (July 16, 1945, at Los Alamos, New Mexico) was named Trinity. More recently the United States government outraged many persons by naming one of the new Trident nuclear submarines Corpus Christi (the Body of Christ).

17. I am reminded of an exchange with a student from India who explained to a class I was teaching on Christian ethics and economics that he was taking the class in hopes of resolving a great puzzle. He admitted that he was unable to understand why the rich world is the Christian world when Christianity claims to be a religion of love, which counsels its adherents to share their wealth with the poor. Why was it, he wondered, that the rich Christian nations seemed so concerned with increasing their already excessive wealth and so little concerned with helping the poor nations overcome their poverty.

18. Liberation theology, as a religious movement, is attempting to reverse this alliance and realign the church with the concerns of the poor. Where liberation has begun to effect such a realignment, the church has become the subject of intense persecution. See Penny Lernoux, *The Cry of the People* (Garden City, N.Y.: Doubleday, 1980) for a documentary history of this in Latin America.

19. For a good summary of studies linking religious belief with racism and sexism, see Keith A. Roberts, *Religion in Sociological Perspective* (Homewood, Ill.: Dorsey Press, 1984), pp. 325–72. For ties to anti-Semitism, see Charles Y. Glock and Rodney Stark, *Christian Beliefs and Anti-Semitism* (New York: Harper and Row, 1969).

20. Michael Harrington, *The Vast Majority: A Journey to the World's Poor* (New York: Simon and Schuster, 1977), p. 95.

21. Beach and Niebuhr, *Christian Ethics*, p. 11.

22. See Bruce C. Birch and Larry L. Rasmussen, *Bible and Ethics in the*

Christian Life (Minneapolis: Augsburg, 1976), and a collection of important essays on the role of scripture in Christian ethics in Charles E. Curran and Richard A. McCormick, eds., *Readings in Moral Theology, No. 4: The Use of Scripture in Moral Theology* (New York: Paulist, 1984).

23. Charles Curran, "The Role and Function of the Scriptures in Moral Theology," in *Readings in Moral Theology, No. 4*, p. 187.

24. See Gerhard Ebeling, *Luther: An Introduction to His Thought* (Philadelphia: Fortress, 1972), chap. 6: "The Letter and the Spirit."

25. For a further development of a use of scripture in ethics quite similar to mine, see James M. Gustafson, *Theology and Christian Ethics* (Philadelphia: Pilgrim, 1974), chap. 6: "The Place of Scripture in Christian Ethics: A Methodological Study." Another good discussion of the complex ways in which scripture informs Christian ethics is found in John Gallagher, *The Basis for Christian Ethics* (New York: Paulist, 1985), chap. 8, 9, and 10.

26. Paul Tillich, *Biblical Religion and the Search for Ultimate Reality* (University of Chicago Press, 1955), p. 3.

27. For a classic account of the role of the Bible in questioning us, see Karl Barth, *The Word of God and the Word of Man* (New York: Harper and Row, 1957). An excellent recent exercise in our examination by scripture is Frederick Herzog's *Liberation Theology: Liberation in the Light of the Fourth Gospel* (New York: Seabury, 1972). This notion of a dialogue with scripture stands at the center of Ernesto Cardenal's work with Nicaraguan campesinos. The powerful results of such scriptural dialogue are contained in four volumes of material collected by Cardenal under the title, *The Gospel of Solentiname* (Maryknoll, N.Y.: Orbis, 1976–1982).

28. Gustafson, "Place of Scripture," p. 145.

29. This is one of the conclusions reached by Norman K. Gottwald in his monumental study, *The Tribes of Yahweh: A Sociology of the Religion of Liberated Israel, 1250–1050 B.C.E.* (Maryknoll, N.Y.: Orbis, 1979). See esp. chap. 55: "Socioeconomic Demythologization of Israelite Yahwism."

30. See the article by Phyllis A. Bird, "Images of Women in the Old Testament," in *The Bible and Liberation: Political and Social Hermeneutics*, Norman K. Gottwald, ed. (Maryknoll, N.Y.: Orbis, 1983), pp. 252–88. Bird concludes:

> Israel's best statements about women recognize her as equal with men, and with him jointly responsible to God and to cohumanity. That Israel rarely lived up to this vision is all too apparent, but the vision should not be denied [p. 279].

31. In *A Theology of Liberation* (Maryknoll, N.Y.: Orbis, 1973), Gustavo Gutiérrez provides an all-encompassing view of the biblical notion of liberation, which includes both personal and social liberation from all the factors and structures that constrict human development. This includes liberation from the power of sin as well as political and economic liberation.

From a different perspective, this broader concept of liberation as being the key to understanding the Christian faith and also the person and work of Jesus is shown in two works by Schubert Ogden: *Faith and Freedom: Toward a Theology of Liberation* (Belfast, Christian Journals Limited, 1979), and *The Point of Christology* (San Francisco: Harper and Row, 1982).

32. Paul Lehmann, *Ethics in a Christian Context* (New York: Harper and Row, 1963), p. 85.

33. For a discussion of the biblical understanding of the relationship of human redemption to the redemption of the whole of nature, see Eric C. Rust, *Nature—Garden or Desert?: An Essay in Environmental Theology* (Waco, Texas: Word Books, 1971). A discussion of this ecological sensitivity is also found in Bernard Häring, *Free and Faithful in Christ, Vol. 3: Light to the World* (New York: Crossroad, 1981), chap. 5.

34. The centrality of Jesus, the Christ, to Christian ethics has marked the work of Christian ethicist Bernard Häring, despite some significant changes in his understanding of ethics. See his earlier work, *The Law of Christ*, and his more recent *Free and Faithful in Christ*.

35. The reference here is to Paul Tillich's understanding of the transformative power of Jesus as the Christ. See his *Systematic Theology* (New York: University of Chicago, Harper and Row, 1967), esp. vol. 2, pp. 78–96.

36. For the effects of these varying conceptions of Jesus on the shape of Christian ethics, the classic works are: H. Richard Niebuhr, *Christ and Culture* (New York: Harper and Row, 1951), and James M. Gustafson, *Christ and the Moral Life* (New York: Harper and Row, 1968).

37. Despite the addition of birth stories in Matthew and Luke, the baptism of Jesus marks the significant event in the synoptic Gospels, at which time Jesus' special relationship to God is recognized. Clearly the birth stories do represent a movement from the simpler account of Mark toward the high christology of the Gospel of John. For a discussion of the varying christological understandings of the New Testament, including a discussion of "adoptionist christology," see Morton Scott Enslin, *Christian Beginnings, Part I and Part II* (New York: Harper and Row, 1956), chap. 12.

38. The various understandings of Jesus in the four Gospels are evident

in the careful reading of the Gospels themselves. Scholarly summaries of these views can be found in any good New Testament introduction. See, e.g., Paul Feine, Johannes Behm, and Werner Georg Kümmel, *Introduction to the New Testament* (Nashville: Abingdon, 1966); W. D. Davies, *Invitation to the New Testament: A Guide to Its Main Witnesses* (Garden City, N.Y.: Doubleday, 1969); or D. Moody Smith and Robert A. Spivey, *Anatomy of the New Testament: A Guide to Its Structure and Meaning* (New York: Macmillan, 1969).

For a discussion of the different ethical emphases of each of these Gospels related to their various understandings of the person of Jesus, see Thomas W. Ogletree, *The Use of the Bible in Christian Ethics: A Constructive Essay* (Philadelphia: Fortress, 1983), chap. 4.

39. For a summary of the findings of the attempt to locate a "historical Jesus," see Günther Bornkamm, *Jesus of Nazareth* (New York: Harper and Row, 1960); Hans Conzelmann, *Jesus* (Philadelphia: Fortress, 1973); or Joachim Jeremias, *The Problem of the Historical Jesus* (Philadelphia: Fortress, 1964). These three works form the basis for the summary of the "historical Jesus" that follows.

40. This claim by liberation theologians is now being widely recognized as one of the distinctive marks of Christian ethics. See, e.g., the widely disparate works: Ogletree, *Use of the Bible*, pp. 68–69, 128, 196; Robert McAfee Brown, *Making Peace in the Global Village* (Philadelphia: Westminster, 1981); and Garth L. Hallett, *Christian Moral Reasoning: An Analytic Guide* (University of Notre Dame Press, 1983), pp. 138–55. The concept of a "preferential option for the poor," of course, stands at the center of the U.S. Catholic Bishops' pastoral, "Economic Justice for All: Catholic Social Teaching and the U. S. Economy, the Third Draft," *Origins*, vol. 16, no. 3 (June 5, 1986). The document is an excellent example of the challenge that a "preferential option for the poor" offers to existing social policies and structures.

41. In developing my understanding of Jesus I follow the method of Tom E. Driver, *Christ in a Changing World: Toward an Ethical Christology* (New York: Crossroad, 1981). In this book he indicates that "the proposed Christology shall be subjected, while it is formulated, to ethical judgment" (p. 21).

This is basically the method for doing theology proposed by liberation theologians like Gustavo Gutiérrez (*Theology of Liberation*, pp. 10–11), and José Míguez Bonino (*Doing Theology in a Revolutionary Situation* [Philadelphia: Fortress, 1975], chap. 5: "Hermeneutics, Truth, and Praxis").

42. Near the end of the musical by Andrew Lloyd Webber and Tim Rice, Judas reflects on his role in Jesus' death and agonizingly concludes, quite correctly according to the theology of John's Gospel:

My God I am sick. I've been used
And you knew all the time God!
I'll never know why you chose me for your crime
For your foul bloody crime
You have murdered me! You have murdered me!

Judas has been reduced to a puppet in God's play.

43. For a discussion of this problem and the formulation of a more inclusive christology, see Patricia Wilson-Kastner, *Faith, Feminism, and the Christ* (Philadelphia, Fortress, 1983). An excellent response to the issue as it pertains to the Catholic Church is found in Daniel Maguire's *The Moral Revolution: A Christian Humanist Vision* (San Francisco: Harper and Row, 1986), chap. 11.

44. See Albert B. Cleage, Jr., *The Black Messiah* (New York: Sheed and Ward, 1969).

45. Tom E. Driver, *Christ in a Changing World*, sees this "compound of universalism and exclusivism [producing] a latent doctrine of nonpersons [which] has been the plague of Christianity throughout its history." As he indicates, it is especially women, nonwhites, and non-Christians who have suffered under the doctrine of nonpersons.

46. Thomas Merton, *Raids on the Unspeakable* (New York: New Directions, 1966), p. 33.

3. A FRAMEWORK FOR CHRISTIAN ETHICS

1. Throughout this work, the use of "God-language" should be understood in a symbolic rather than a literal sense. For a discussion of the symbolic use of religious language, see Paul Tillich, *Dynamics of Faith* (New York: Harper and Row, 1958). A similar discussion about the use of "God-language" can be found in David Tracy, "Analogy and Dialectic: God Language," in David Tracy and John B. Cobb, Jr., *Talking About God: Doing Theology in the Context of Modern Pluralism* (New York: Seabury, 1983), pp. 29–38.

2. Fyodor Dostoyevsky, *The Brothers Karamazov* (New York: New American Library, 1957), pp. 216–18.

3. Plato, *Euthyphro, Apology, Crito, Phaedo: The Death Scene* (Indianapolis: Bobbs-Merrill, 1956), p. 11.

4. As Ian Barbour shows, *Myths, Models, and Paradigms: A Comparative Study in Science and Religion* (New York: Harper and Row, 1976), scientific investigation and observation are controlled by the existing, dominant, paradigms. The mechanistic paradigm has been very successful in generating large bodies of knowledge about ourselves and our world,

and has been remarkable in the new technologies it has developed. Such a paradigm, however, has not been without its costs. Some of the developed technologies (e.g., nuclear technologies, chemical pesticides) threaten us with health hazards and environmental destruction. The shift to a more ecologically informed paradigm is viewed by many as a necessity if science is to continue to serve a constructive role in human and natural development. See the collection of essays edited by Rita Arditti, Pat Brennan, and Steve Cavrak, *Science and Liberation* (Boston: South End Press, 1980).

5. See book 12 of Aristotle's *Metaphysics*.

6. Beverly Wildung Harrison, *Making the Connections: Essays in Feminist Social Ethics* (Boston: Beacon, 1985), p. 17.

7. See John B. Cobb and David Ray Griffin, *Process Theology: An Introductory Exposition* (Philadelphia: Westminster, 1976), chap. 3. This is also a primary thesis of Hegel's *The Philosophy of the Spirit*. See also the discussion of the role of the doctrine of creation in Christian ethics by Charles Curran, *New Perspectives in Moral Theology* (University of Notre Dame Press, 1976), pp. 57–65.

8. The idea of God's continuous activity is a central theme of modern theology, informing a number of different "types" of theology. It is a central theme in many of the liberation theologies (Gutiérrez, *Theology of Liberation*), in theologies of hope (Jürgen Moltmann, *Theology of Hope: On the Ground and Implications of a Christian Eschatology* [New York: Harper and Row, 1967]), in process theologies (Cobb and Griffin, *Process Theology*), and in the mystical theology of Teilhard de Chardin (*The Divine Milieu* [New York: Harper and Row, 1965]).

9. See Paul Tillich's essay, "The Struggle Between Time and Space," in *Theology of Culture* (London: Oxford University Press, 1969), pp. 30–39.

10. This contrasts with the view of time that is part of the Greek tradition and predominant in the traditions of most Eastern religions and philosophies. In these traditions history is events. History itself has no meaning and salvation requires escape from the meaningless cycle of change and repetition. For a discussion of these contrasting views of history, see Thorlief Boman, *Hebrew Thought Compared with Greek* (New York: Norton, 1970), part 3: "Time and Space."

11. As recent scholarship has shown, the male-dominated Christian tradition has overlooked numerous portrayals of the maternal nature of God. For a discussion of the motherly side of God the parent, see Virginia Ramey Mollenkott, *The Biblical Imagery of God as Female* (New York: Crossroad, 1983).

12. See, for example, James Limburg, *The Prophets and the Powerless* (Atlanta: John Knox, 1977), or Donald Kraybill, *The Upside-Down Kingdom* (Scottdale, Pa.: Herald Press, 1978). This theme is also fundamental

to much liberation theology. It informs the theology of James H. Cone in *God of the Oppressed* (New York: Seabury, 1975), and is the organizing theme for a collection of essays by Gustavo Gutiérrez, *The Power of the Poor in History, Selected Writings* (Maryknoll, N.Y.: Orbis, 1983).

13. Gustavo Gutiérrez warns that we should not glorify or spiritualize the state of poverty. Poverty is a harsh, demeaning condition and the poor suffer cruelly under the imposed conditions of deprivation. It is their great need that solicits God's care (*Theology of Liberation*, pp. 287–306).

In an updated version of his classic work on poverty, Michael Harrington shows that counter to our guilt-relieving myth, the poor are not happier or more anxiety-free than the well-to-do who have to bear such heavy social responsibilities. In fact, the poor are subjected to considerably more stress and live lives of intense psychological, as well as physical, suffering (*The Other America: Poverty in the United States* [New York: Pelican, 1981], pp. 128–46).

14. For a good summary of some traditional formulations of the problem of "theodicy" (the relationship of God to evil), see the essays by Stephen T. Davis, "Free Will and Evil" (pp. 69–83), and David R. Griffin, "Creation Out of Chaos and the Problem of Evil" (pp. 101–19), in *Encountering Evil: Live Options in Theodicy*, Stephen T. Davis, ed. (Atlanta: John Knox, 1981).

15. For a development of this idea, see John B. Cobb, Jr., *God and the World* (Philadelphia: Westminster, 1974).

16. Dietrich Bonhoeffer, *Letters and Papers from Prison* (New York: Macmillan, 1966), p. 220.

17. Hans Küng, *On Being a Christian* (Garden City, N.Y.: Doubleday, 1976), p. 75.

18. The prophet Hosea presents the relationship of God to the people of Israel as that of a faithful lover to an unfaithful spouse.

19. This theme influences Jürgen Moltmann's theology of hope and John Cobb's process theology. In *God and the World*, Cobb describes God's influence on history as that of "a call" to become something more than we are (see esp. chap. 2).

20. The idea of God's absence as a call to human maturity is a theme in Bonhoeffer's *Letters and Papers from Prison* (see esp. pp. 219–20). This theme also appears in Jacques Ellul's *Hope in Time of Abandonment* (New York: Seabury, 1977).

21. This traditional understanding of evil is articulated by Augustine in *City of God* (New York: Pelican Books, 1972), in the following words: "There is no such entity in nature as 'evil'; 'evil' is merely a name for the privation of good" (p. 454). A similar understanding of evil informs the work of Paul Tillich (e.g., in *Systematic Theology*, vol. 2, pp. 59–78). The

classic treatment of the topic remains John Hick's *Evil and the God of Love* (Great Britain: Fontana, 1975).

22. For an outstanding reformulation of theology that recaptures the biblical insight, see James B. Nelson, *Embodiment: An Approach to Sexuality and Christian Theology* (Minneapolis: Augsburg, 1978).

23. Reinhold Niebuhr, *The Nature and Destiny of Man*, vol. 1 (New York: Scribner's, 1964), chap. 6 and 7.

24. Enrique Dussel, *Ethics and the Theology of Liberation* (Maryknoll: Orbis, 1978), p. 17. Paul Tillich, *Love, Power, and Justice: Ontological Analyses and Ethical Applications* (New York: Oxford University Press, 1974), discusses the effects of these dynamics on personal and social relationships. Anne Wilson Schaef in her excellent book, *Women's Reality: An Emerging Female System in the White Male Society* (Minneapolis: Winston, 1981), sees this notion of "power over others" as a predominantly male notion and offers an alternative notion of power as "shared power" (pp. 124–29).

25. Curran, *New Perspectives*, p. 66.

26. Thomas Merton, *The Seven Storey Mountain* (New York: Harcourt, Brace, 1948), p. 128.

27. Nelson, *Embodiment,* pp. 17–18; 97–103, 135.

28. For an excellent account of the Christian understanding of history and human responsibility for history, see Langdon Gilkey, *Reaping the Whirlwind: A Christian Interpretation of History* (New York: Seabury, 1981).

29. One of the most significant changes brought about by modern culture is our ability to control, and possibly plan, the future of natural evolution. Our understanding of genetics and nuclear physics, along with the corresponding technologies of control, gives us the ability to create new elements and life forms. We have the power to shape the future. The question, of course, is whether we have the wisdom. See, for example, June Goodfield, *Playing God: Genetic Engineering and the Manipulation of Life* (New York: Random House, 1977); and Horace Freeland Judson, *The Eighth Day of Creation: The Makers of the Revolution in Biology* (New York: Simon and Schuster, 1979).

30. For a brief discussion of the effects of Christian symbolism on the treatment of the environment, see Lynn White, Jr., "The Historical Roots of Our Ecologic Crisis," *Science*, 155 (1967): 1203–7; and "The Biblical Interpretation of Nature and Human Dominion," in *Faith, Science and the Future: Preparatory Readings for the 1979 Conference of the World Council of Churches* (Philadelphia: Fortress, 1979), pp. 34–43.

31. The idea of fulfillment is not necessarily linked to the idea of an

infinite existence. The early parts of the Old Testament presume that life has temporal limits and can and should be lived within those limits. Likewise the work of psychologists such as Erich Fromm and Erik Erikson relates fulfillment to our ability to accept our human limitations. See Erich Fromm, *To Have or To Be?* (New York: Bantam, 1981), esp. pp. 69–70; and Erik H. Erikson, *The Life Cycle Completed: A Review* (New York:Norton, 1982).

32. For a good discussion of the traditional Christian claim that the basis of sin is our desire to "become God," see Reinhold Niebuhr, *The Nature and Destiny of Man*, vol. 1, pp. 186–203.

33. Paul Tillich shows the destructiveness of this anxiety for ourselves and others in *The Courage to Be* (Yale University Press, 1965); and on our social institutions in *Love, Power and Justice*.

34. The perspective of Amerindians on our attitudes and relationships to the environment provides a badly needed corrective for our traditional Western views. A number of books have dealt with this theme. Vine Deloria's *God Is Red* (New York: Dell, 1973), and Carl Starkloff's *The People of the Center: American Indian Religion and Christianity* (New York: Seabury, 1974), provide good comparisons between the attitudes toward nature in the dominant Christian tradition and those of Amerindian religious traditions.

A brief quote by Heinmot Tooyalaket (Chief Joseph) of the Nez Perce provides an insight into the Amerindian reverence for creation: "The earth and myself are of one mind. The measure of the land and the measure of our bodies are the same. . . . Do not misunderstand, but understand me fully with reference to my affection for the land. I never said the land was mine to do with as I chose. The one who has the right to dispose of it is the one who has created it" (from Dee Brown, *Bury My Heart at Wounded Knee: An Indian History of the American West* [New York: Bantam, 1970], p. 300).

35. Charles Birch and John B. Cobb, Jr., *The Liberation of Life: From the Cell to the Community* (New York: Cambridge University Press, 1981), presents a theologico-philosophical model, grounded in an ecological perspective, for understanding existence.

James Gustafson's work, *Ethics from a Theocentric Perspective* (University of Chicago Press, 1981), is not as explicitly concerned about using an ecological model. Nevertheless, it represents a fundamental shift away from the anthropocentric model that has dominated Western culture since the Enlightenment. The fundamental relationship of ecological sensitivity to the Christian faith is even surfacing in the liberation theology of the Two-Thirds World. This represents a new and distinctive change in perspective. See the documents from the Puebla Conference of the Latin American Catholic Bishops, *Puebla and Beyond*, John Eagleson and Philip Scharper, eds. (Maryknoll, N.Y.: Orbis, 1979), esp. pp. 140, 169, 193, and 275.

36. The responsible use of our scientific knowledge and technology was the subject of a world conference, "Faith, Science, and the Future," sponsored by the World Council of Churches at the Massachusetts Institute of Technology in 1979. The documents of the conference are recorded in *Faith and Science in an Unjust World,* vol. 1: *Plenary Presentations*, Roger Shinn, ed. (Philadelphia: Fortress, 1981), and *Faith and Science in an Unjust World,* vol. 2: *Reports and Recommendations*, Paul Albrecht, ed. (Philadelphia: Fortress, 1981).

37. For a further discussion of the corporate nature of salvation, see Charles L. Kammer, III, *The Kingdom Revisited: An Essay on Christian Social Ethics* (Washington, D.C.: University Press of America, 1981), pp. 115–25. The work includes a more developed statement of my understanding of the relationship of the individual to society.

38. Works documenting this phenomenon are more and more numerous. Two classic treatments of these dynamics are by Betty Friedan, *The Feminine Mystique* (New York: Dell, 1963), and Dorothy Dinnerstein, *The Mermaid and the Minotaur: Sexual Arrangements and Human Malaise* (New York: Harper and Row, 1977). An excellent work that documents the male reaction to the loss of control of family and sexual relationships is Barbara Ehrenreich's *The Hearts of Men: American Dreams and the Flight from Commitment* (Garden City, N.Y.: Anchor/ Doubleday, 1983).

39. For a discussion of the effects of "pro-family" politics on persons and the family, see Ruth Sidel, "The Family: A Dream Defused," in *What Reagan Is Doing to Us*, Alan Gastner, Colin Greer, and Frank Riessman, eds. (New York: Harper and Row, 1982), pp. 54–70.

40. This, of course, is a description of the program for economic recovery that has been variously labeled "supply side economics" and "Reaganomics." For a discussion of the effects of this economic policy on the poor, see Frank Ackerman, *Reaganomics: Rhetoric vs. Reality* (Boston: South End Press, 1982), pp. 77–118.

41. Bernard Häring, *Free and Faithful in Christ,* vol. 3: *Light to the World* (New York: Crossroad, 1981), p. 326.

42. For a discussion of both the possibilities and limits of historical transformation, see José Míguez Bonino, *Doing Theology in a Revolutionary Situation* (Philadelphia: Fortress, 1975), pp. 132–53; and his more recent work, *Toward a Christian Political Ethics* (Philadelphia: Fortress, 1983).

43. For a discussion of the Socratic position, see W. K. C. Guthrie,

Socrates (Cambridge University Press, 1971), pp. 130–41. For a discussion of the difference between the Socratic understanding of sin and that of the Christian tradition, see Søren Kierkegaard, *Philosophical Fragments* (Princeton University Press, 1969), esp. pp. 11–60.

44. The difficulty of willing to be the particular person that we are called to be is treated by Søren Kierkegaard in *The Sickness Unto Death*, under the heading, "In Despair at Not Willing to Be Oneself," and "In Despair at Willing to Be Oneself." The treatment provides an important insight into the anxiety that drives us to deny our particularity.

45. Erich Fromm, *To Have or To Be?*, provides an important discussion of two alternative forms of relationships: those that are accepted as gifts, and those that we attempt to dominate and control. See esp. chap. 2, 5, and 6.

46. The Constitution of the United States (1787), in Article I, Section 2, counted three-fifths of the slave (black) population of a state in determining its number of congressional representatives. This was superseded by Amendment 14 in 1868.

47. The immigration policies of the United States have consistently discriminated against persons of color. Our immigration policies have, however, reached a new level of viciousness in our refusal to provide asylum for refugees from Haiti, El Salvador, and Honduras who are fleeing the right-wing terrorism of governments that the United States supports. Because we officially support these governments, we have refused to admit that refugees fleeing these countries are political refugees. This has led to the regular deportation of persons to their homelands where many of them are then subject to arrest, torture, or execution. The Lutheran Council in the U.S.A., 360 Park Avenue South, New York, New York 10010, provides a newsletter that is an excellent source on current U.S. immigration policies and the plight of refugees.

48. For a good discussion of the effects of national self-interest on policy deliberations, see John C. Bennett and Harvey Seifert, *U.S. Foreign Policy and Christian Ethics* (Philadelphia: Westminster, 1977), esp. pp. 28–34 and 51–96; and, the U. S. Catholic Bishops' Pastoral, *Economic Justice for All: Catholic Social Teaching and the U. S. Economy* (third draft), section D.

49. Paul Tillich, *Systematic Theology*, vol. 1, offers the following definition: "Idolatry is the elevation of a preliminary concern to ultimacy. Something essentially conditioned is taken as unconditional, something essentially partial is boosted into universality, and something essentially finite is given infinite significance (the best example is the contemporary idolatry of religious nationalism)" (p. 13).

50. Charles Curran, *Moral Theology: A Continuing Journey* (University of Notre Dame Press, 1981), p. 46.

51. H. Richard Niebuhr, *The Responsible Self: An Essay in Christian Moral Philosophy* (New York: Harper and Row, 1963), p. 112.

4. THE CHRISTIAN MORALSCAPE

1. A distinction is usually made between a principle and a rule. Principles are usually understood to be more general, such as, "We should respect the humanity of others." Rules provide more specific guidelines for our behavior; for example, "The abortion of a fetus during the last trimester of pregnancy is not acceptable unless the life of the mother is in danger" (the Supreme Court in 1973 in the Roe vs. Wade decision made this guideline into law). For a traditional presentation of this distinction, see Paul Ramsey, "The Case of the Curious Exception," in *Norm and Context in Christian Ethics*, Gene H. Outka and Paul Ramsey, eds. (New York: Scribner's, 1968), pp. 67-138.

A similar distinction is made, although different terminology is employed, by John C. Bennett in his discussion of "middle axioms." See *Christian Ethics and Social Policy* (New York: Scribner's, 1946), pp. 76-85. Although I readily admit the usefulness of the distinction, it is not particularly important for an introduction of this kind. In addition, my approach to ethics does not allow for the neat division that Ramsey presumes. Rules may be derived from principles, but in actual experience principles may be a later development to provide a rational grounding for a rule that has an intuitive base. Because ethics involves the application of an entire moralscape, the exact relationship of principles to rules is not as important as in some other ethical systems, like those of Ramsey and natural law theorists.

2. For some uses of this important ethical insight, see Bruce C. Birch and Larry L. Rasmussen, *The Predicament of the Prosperous* (Philadelphia: Westminster, 1978), chap. 7: "Shalom and Christ." See also Letty M. Russell, *Human Liberation in a Feminist Perspective: A Theology* (Philadelphia: Westminster, 1977), pp. 106-9: " 'Shalom': Liberation and Blessing."

3. For a discussion of Old Testament attitudes toward war and peace, see John Howard Yoder, *The Politics of Jesus* (Grand Rapids: Eerdmans, 1975), esp. chap. 1-4. See also Vernard Eller, *War and Peace from Genesis to Revelation* (Scottdale, Pa.: Herald Press, 1981).

4. For important discussions of the idea of peace as something active and positive, see Edward LeRoy Long, Jr., *Peace Thinking in a Warring World* (Philadelphia: Westminster, 1983), and Gray Cox, *The Ways of Peace: A Philosophy of Peace As Action* (New York: Paulist, 1986).

5. For an elaboration of this vision and its biblical development, see John Bright, *The Kingdom of God: The Biblical Concept and Its Meaning*

for the Church (New York: Abingdon, 1963). For a discussion of its role in contemporary Christian social ethics, see José Míguez Bonino, *Toward a Christian Political Ethics* (Philadelphia: Fortress, 1983), chap. 7, and Charles L. Kammer, III, *The Kingdom Revisited: An Essay on Christian Social Ethics* (Washington, D.C.: University Press of America, 1981).

6. The revival of science in the Christian West was marked by a concern to gain a fuller understanding of God's glory and to use this knowledge for the improvement of human life and to the further glory of God. Although this put some limits on the early development of science, it nevertheless provided an important context of responsibility within which to carry out scientific study and technological innovation. See, for example, R. Hooykaas, *Religion and the Rise of Modern Science* (Grand Rapids: Eerdmans, 1972).

7. A number of theologians and ethicists are so impressed with our tendency to misuse our knowledge and power that they advocate a very conservative (in the best sense of conserving what is good and human about that which currently exists) application of our knowledge. For thoughtful applications of this position, see Paul Ramsey, *Fabricated Man: The Ethics of Genetic Control* (Yale University Press, 1970), Jacques Ellul, *The Technological Society* (New York: Vintage, 1964); and Edna McDonagh, *Doing the Truth: The Quest for Moral Theology* (University of Notre Dame Press, 1979), esp. chap. 8.

8. In his book, *On Human Care: An Introduction* (Nashville: Abingdon, 1977), Arthur J. Dyck shows that the Ten Commandments act as "constraints against evil" and provide the necessary "moral requisites of community" (pp. 92–113). Walter Harrelson, *The Ten Commandments and Human Rights* (Philadelphia: Fortress, 1980), finds the basis for our modern understanding of human rights in the Ten Commandments.

The concern for the well-being of all is so prominent in the Old Testament that the commandment "Observe the sabbath day, to keep it holy" protects servants and even beasts of burden (oxen) from abuse by commanding that they, too, be given a day of rest (Deut. 5:12–14).

9. For a discussion of the importance of the concept of the equality of persons, see J. Philip Wogaman, *A Christian Method of Moral Judgment* (Philadelphia: Westminster, 1976), pp. 94–104.

10. Antoine Vergote, "God Our Father," in *Moral Formation and Christianity*, Franz Böckle and Jacques-Marie Pohier, eds. (New York: Seabury, 1978), p. 9.

11. Beverly Wildung Harrison, *Making the Connections: Essays in Feminist Social Ethics* (Boston: Beacon, 1985). This important distinction is also used by Waldo Beach in his book, *The Wheel and the Cross: A Christian Response to the Technological Revolution* (Atlanta: John Knox, 1979), as an important tool for distributing goods and making policy decisions.

12. For an often cited example of this position, see William K. Frankena, *Ethics*, 2nd edition (Englewood Cliffs, N.J.: Prentice-Hall, 1973), p. 47.

13. A similar claim is made by Reinhold Niebuhr, *Moral Man and Immoral Society* (New York: Scribner's, 1960), pp. 253-55.

14. On the relationship of the life and death of Jesus to Christian nonviolence, see Yoder, *Politics of Jesus*, and James W. Douglas, *The Non-Violent Cross: A Theology of Revolution and Peace* (New York: Macmillan, 1968).

15. For a discussion of the use of "moral presumptions" in Christian ethics, see Wogaman, *Christian Method*, chap. 2: "The Concept of Methodological Presumption." Richard McCormick's discussion of exceptions to moral norms, "Norms and Consequences," in *Notes on Moral Theology, 1965 through 1980* [Washington, D.C.: University Press of America, 1981], pp. 349-67), presents a very similar view.

16. For an important discussion of the effect of our embodiedness on our thoughts and actions, see Juan Luis Segundo, *The Liberation of Theology* (Maryknoll, N.Y.: Orbis, 1976), esp. chap. 1: "The Hermeneutic Circle." As Segundo states: "Now a liberation theologian is one who starts from the opposite end. His suspicion is that anything and everything involving ideas, including theology, is intimately bound up with the existing social situation in at least an unconscious way" (pp. 7-8).

17. Albert Camus, *The Rebel: An Essay on Man in Revolt* (New York: Vintage, 1956), esp. pp. 105-11. As Camus recognizes, religion has often been a prime contributor to the fanaticism that leads to the massacre and enslavement of others.

18. The "principle of the double effect" is an important methodological acknowledgment of the unavoidable ambiguity of many of our actions and an attempt to provide a way of making moral decisions in the face of unavoidable harm. A good discussion of recent understandings and uses of the principle is found in Peter Knauer, "The Hermeneutic Function of the Principle of Double Effect," in *Readings in Moral Theology, No. 1: Moral Norms and Catholic Tradition*, Charles Curran and Richard McCormick, eds. (New York: Paulist, 1979), pp. 1-39.

19. The emphasis on "doing the truth" as the primary focus of Christian life and theology is one of the primary distinguishing marks of liberation theology. For a good summary of the distinctiveness of this approach as compared with traditional academic theology, see Gustavo Gutiérrez, "Liberation Praxis and Christian Faith," in *The Power of the Poor in History* (Maryknoll, N.Y.: Orbis, 1983), pp. 36-74. Gutiérrez writes, "For theology is an attempt to do a reading of the faith from a point of departure in a determined situation, from an insertion and involvement in

history, from a particular manner of living our encounter with the Lord in our encounter with others" (p. 370).

20. Daniel Maguire, *The Moral Revolution: A Christian Humanist Vision* (San Francisco: Harper and Row, 1986), p. 226.

21. For a traditional depiction of the function of the commands of the Christian faith, see Calvin's "first use of the law," in *Calvin: Institutes of the Christian Religion*, John T. McNeill, ed. (Philadelphia: Westminster, 1975), pp. 351-55. This inability to fulfill the law is the basis for the doctrine of "justification by grace through faith."

Luther holds a similar view on the function of the law. See Gerhard Ebeling, *Luther: An Introduction to His Thought* (Philadelphia: Fortress, 1972), chap. 8: "The Twofold Use of the Law." Charles Curran shows the continued relevance of this function of the radical commands of the Christian faith in "The Relevancy of the Gospel Ethic," in *Themes in Fundamental Moral Theology* (University of Notre Dame Press, 1977), pp. 5-26.

22. This, of course, is what all liberation theologies attempt to do, to provide a perspective from those on the bottom, those who are oppressed by, and excluded from, society. This is also the reason why Marxist social analysis is an indispensable, though not the only, tool for Christians to use for understanding the context of their actions. Only Marxism has a built-in methodological presumption that ensures that the needs and views of the lowest classes and oppressed groups of society will be acknowledged. See José Míguez Bonino, *Christians and Marxists: The Mutual Challenge to Revolution* (Grand Rapids: Eerdmans, 1976).

23. The history of Christian mission is very ambivalent. Missionaries participated in the subjugation and extermination of Amerindian populations in the Americas. On the other hand, some missionaries, like Bartolomé de Las Casas, were the Amerindians' staunchest defenders. See Enrique Dussel, *History and the Theology of Liberation* (Maryknoll, N.Y.: Orbis, 1976), esp. chap. 3, and his *A History of the Church in Latin America: Colonialism to Liberation* (Grand Rapids: Eerdmans, 1981), esp. parts 1 and 2.

The development of indigenous Third World theologies is doing a great deal to change the basic understanding of mission. For an example of some of these changes, see *Mission Trends No. 3: Third World Theologies*, Gerald H. Anderson and Thomas F. Stransky, eds. (New York: Paulist, 1976).

24. For a concrete model to use in doing this analysis, see Joe Holland and Peter Henriot, *Social Analysis: Linking Faith and Justice* (Maryknoll, N.Y.: Orbis, 1983).

25. Letting the worst-off starve is one solution to the problem of world hunger proposed by advocates of "life boat ethics." For an elaboration of the "life boat" argument, see Garrett Hardin, "Lifeboat Ethics: Food and Population," in *Finite Resources and the Human Future*, Ian G. Barbour, ed. (Minneapolis: Augsburg, 1976), pp. 32–47. Christian ethicists have consistently found this to be an unacceptable approach to the problem. See, for example, Roger Lincoln Shinn, *Forced Options: Social Decisions for the 21st Century* (New York: Harper and Row, 1982), chap. 4.

26. See H. Richard Niebuhr's discussion of the various types of Christian ethics in *The Responsible Self: An Essay in Christian Moral Philosophy* (New York: Harper and Row, 1963), chap. 1, and a similar discussion by Charles Curran in *Moral Theology: A Continuing Journey* (University of Notre Dame Press, 1982), pp. 35–61.

27. For a discussion of the tragedy of corporate policy in the United States, see Robert Goodman, *The Last Entrepreneurs: America's Regional Wars for Jobs and Dollars* (Boston: South End Press, 1979).

28. Niebuhr, *Responsible Self*, chap. 1.

29. Ibid., p. 145.

30. Joseph Fletcher, *Moral Responsibility: Situation Ethics at Work* (Philadelphia: Westminster, 1975), p. 14. In his *Situation Ethics: The New Morality* (Philadelphia: Westminster, 1966), Fletcher responds specifically to the issue of abortion in showing how his approach to ethics and its stress on understanding the particular situation differs from other approaches (pp. 37–39).

31. James B. Nelson, *Embodiment: An Approach to Sexuality and Christian Theology* (Minneapolis: Augsburg, 1978), p. 127.

32. This is the basic position of a tradition that flows through Luther. Luther is quite blunt in his proclamation that the sole criterion that determines the goodness of an act is the character of the actor (whether the actor is in right relationship to God or not). He states ("Freedom of a Christian," in *Martin Luther: Selections From His Writings*, John Dillenberger, ed. [Garden City, N.Y.: Doubleday, 1961], p. 60): "As the man is, whether believer or unbeliever, so also is his work—good if it was done in faith, wicked if it was done in unbelief."

This tradition has gained new popularity under the rubric "ethics of character." For some contemporary statements of this position, see Stanley Hauerwas, *Vision and Virtue: Essays in Christian Ethical Reflection* (University of Notre Dame Press, 1981); idem, *A Community of Character: Toward a Constructive Christian Social Ethic* (University of Notre Dame Press, 1981); Alasdair MacIntyre, *After Virtue* (University of Notre Dame Press, 1981).

The problem with this approach is that it distorts the Christian imperative of love for the other by focusing moral concern on the self. I will return to this problem in chap. 6, below.

33. One can hardly do ethics today without being acutely aware of the insights of Freud and Marx. Freud disclosed the power of the subconscious on our behavior (see, e.g., Philip Rieff, *Freud: The Mind of the Moralist* [Garden City, N.Y.: Doubleday, 1961], chap. 3: "The Hidden Self").

Marx demonstrated the degree to which a prevailing social morality reflects the interests of society's affluent and controlling class (see, e.g., Isaiah Berlin, *Karl Marx: His Life and Environment* [London: Oxford University Press, 1968], chap. 6: "Historical Materialism," or José Miranda, *Marx Against the Marxists: The Christian Humanism of Karl Marx* [Maryknoll, N.Y.: Orbis, 1978], chap. 4: "Determination in Marx's Thought").

34. The inability to know fully the consequences of any action is one of the classic criticisms against utilitarian theory and any attempt to locate the goodness of an act solely in its consequences. For a good summary of the problems with utilitarian theory, see Charles E. Curran, "Utilitarianism and Contemporary Moral Theology: Situating the Debate," in *Readings in Moral Theology, No. 1.*

35. Dyck, *Human Care*, p. 28.

36. The dynamic, prodding quality of love is central to Reinhold Niebuhr's understanding of the interaction of love and justice in Christian ethics. See his *The Nature and Destiny of Man,* vol. 2: *Human Destiny* (New York: Scribner's, 1964), chap. 9: "The Kingdom of God and the Struggle for Justice." See as well E. Clinton Gardner, "Justice and Love," in *Social Ethics: Issues in Ethics and Society*, Gibson Winter, ed. (New York: Harper and Row, 1968), pp. 66–77.

37. Paul Ramsey, in *Basic Christian Ethics* (New York: Scribner's, 1950), views this covenantal loyalty as the distinguishing characteristic of Christian ethics; see esp. chap. 10.

38. For a theoretical discussion of the grounds for such an alliance of protest against the dehumanization of persons by modern culture, see Paul Tillich, "The Theological Significance of Existentialism and Psychoanalysis," in *Theology of Culture* (London: Oxford University Press, 1959), pp. 76–111.

39. There has been an ongoing debate about whether there is anything unique about Christian ethics. The contemporary debate was stimulated by James M. Gustafson's *Can Ethics Be Christian?* (University of Chicago Press, 1975), and is carried on in the volume, *Readings in Moral Theology No. 2: The Distinctiveness of Christian Ethics*, Charles E. Curran and Richard A. McCormick, eds. (New York: Paulist, 1980).

My position is that no single element, except its symbolism, is unique to

Christian ethics. All its specific elements are combined into a moralscape that is, however, quite distinctive.

5. SHAPING OUR HUMANITY

1. For a development of this theme, see William C. May, *Becoming Human: An Invitation to Christian Ethics* (Dayton, Ohio: Pflaum, 1975), chap. 4.

2. Charles Curran, *Themes in Fundamental Moral Theology* (University of Notre Dame Press, 1977), p. 208.

3. Spencer Klaw, *The Great American Medicine Show: The Unhealthy State of U.S. Medical Care, and What Can Be Done About It* (New York: Penguin, 1976), pp. 4-9.

4. See ibid., p. 4.

5. For good discussions of the natural law tradition, see George M. Regan, *New Trends in Moral Theology: A Survey of Fundamental Moral Themes* (New York: Newman Press, 1971); James M. Gustafson, *Protestant and Roman Catholic Ethics* (University of Chicago Press, 1978), esp. chap. 1 and 3; and Charles Curran, "Natural Law," *Themes in Fundamental Moral Theology*, pp. 27-80.

6. Aquinas describes synderesis as an innate habit that makes us responsive to the first principle of the moral law, "Good is to be done and sought after, evil is to be avoided." For Aquinas's discussion of this concept, see *The Pocket Aquinas*, Vernon J. Bourke, ed. (New York: Washington Square Press, 1960), pp. 196-203. For a summary of contemporary theological understandings of conscience, see Edward LeRoy Long, Jr., *A Survey of Recent Christian Ethics* (New York: Oxford University Press, 1982), chap. 8.

7. For the influence of Kantian thought on Protestant ethics and its notion of law, see Gustafson, *Protestant and Roman Catholic Ethics*, chap. 3.

8. This concept is used throughout Tillich's work. For a brief discussion of its significance, see *Systematic Theology* (New York and Evanston: Harper and Row, University of Chicago Press, 1963), vol. 1, pp. 83-86.

9. Leonardo Boff, *The Lord's Prayer: The Prayer of Integral Liberation* (Maryknoll, N.Y.: Orbis, 1983), p. 54.

10. For an account of Aquinas's own discussion of the virtues, see Waldo Beach and H. Richard Niebuhr, *Christian Ethics*, 2nd edition (New York: Ronald Press, 1973), pp. 210, 226.

For a discussion of the "two-storied" ethic it generates, see H. Richard Niebuhr, *Christ and Culture* (New York: Harper and Row, 1951), chap. 4.

11. For an account of ethics that uses the concept of intentionality as the key to understanding our moral experience, see Howard L. Harrod, *The Human Center: Moral Agency in the Social World* (Philadelphia: Fortress, 1981).

12. This category is used extensively in his work. For a brief account of it, see his *Systematic Theology*, vol. I, pp. 83–86.

13. The reference is to Thomas Hobbes and his classic work, *Leviathan*. A good summary of Hobbes's political philosophy is to be found in Erwin A. Gaede, *Politics and Ethics: Machiavelli to Niebuhr* (Washington, D.C.: University Press of America, 1983), chap. 3.

14. The quote is from Paul Ramsey, *Nine Modern Moralists* (Englewood Cliffs, N.J.: Prentice-Hall, 1962), p. 13. In his chapter on Dostoevsky, Ramsey gives an important analysis of the psychological portrayal rendered in Dostoevsky's novels of characters for whom God has ceased to be the guarantor of human justice and morality.

15. This is the position taken by Jean Jacques Rousseau and is expressed in his two classic works, *Discourse* and *The Social Contract*. See Gaede, *Politics and Ethics*, chap. 5, for a summary of Rousseau's political thought.

This position of essential human goodness is also affirmed by classic Marxism. The need to assert our freedom as a way of recovering our essential humanity is likewise an important element in modern existentialism. See the selection from Sartre's *Being and Nothingness* in Walter Kaufmann, ed., *Existentialism from Dostoevsky to Sartre* (New York: New American Library, 1956), pp. 241–70.

16. See Abraham H. Maslow, *Motivation and Personality* (New York: Harper and Row, 1954), and William Temple, *Christus Veritas* (London: MacMillan, 1964).

For a discussion of the implications of such a view of the human for medical ethics, see Harmon L. Smith, *Ethics and the New Medicine* (Nashville: Abingdon, 1970), pp. 51–54.

17. It is now generally acknowledged that improved sanitation and diet rather than the development of modern medicine is the primary cause of the dramatic increase in life expectancy in modern societies. See Rick J. Carlson, *The End of Medicine* (New York: John Wiley, 1975).

18. The need for medical care is very unevenly distributed. Premature infants and the elderly are the two groups that make the greatest demand on medical services. In addition, the need for intensified medical care is usually related to some medical crisis, an injury or the onset of a serious illness. Some estimates suggest that over 60% of all medical care goes to persons who are terminally ill. The implications of these patterns of use for a just health care system are elaborated by Gene Outka, "Social Justice and

Equal Access to Health Care," in *Bioethics*, revised edition, Thomas A. Shannon, ed. (Ramsey, N.J.: Paulist, 1981), pp. 477–99.

19. Philip R. Kunz and Eric M. Jaehne, *A Sociological Approach to Morality* (Washington, D.C.: University Press of America, 1983), p. 26.

20. The human need for meaningful work has been recently articulated by E. F. Schumacher, *Good Work* (New York: Harper and Row, 1979), and by Pope John Paul II in his encyclical, *Laborem Exercens*. For the text of the encyclical and a good discussion of it, see Gregory Baum, *The Priority of Labor* (New York: Paulist, 1982).

21. This difference in quality does not necessarily imply a relationship of superiority-inferiority. Although it is true that the qualitative difference between human life and that of the rest of the created order gives humans an unparalleled creativity, it also gives them a greater capacity for destructiveness. Of all beings on this planet, only humans threaten it with absolute destruction.

22. Both Cuba and Nicaragua quickly instituted literacy campaigns after their respective revolutions. The results are impressive. Cuba and Nicaragua have literacy rates exceeding 90% of their population. This compares with rates near 60% for El Salvador, Guatemala, and Honduras. See Jenny Pearce, *Under the Eagle: U.S. Intervention in Central America and the Caribbean* (Boston: South End Press, 1982), pp. x–xi.

Paulo Freire's history of expulsions from Latin American countries points out the fear of an educated populace that prevails in Latin American right-wing, totalitarian regimes. For a brief account of Freire's involvement in Latin American literacy campaigns, see Denis Collins, *Paulo Freire: His Life, Works and Thought* (New York: Paulist, 1977).

For an account of Freire's own thought, see his work, *Pedagogy of the Oppressed* (New York: Seabury, 1970).

23. See J. Eugene Wright, Jr., *Erikson: Identity and Religion* (New York: Seabury, 1982), chap. 4 and 5.

24. See Paul Tillich, *Biblical Religion and the Search for Ultimate Reality* (University of Chicago Press, 1972), chap. 2.

25. For a discussion of this basic human experience, see Rudolf Otto, *The Idea of the Holy* (London: Oxford University Press, 1971). For a powerful, poetic statement of this theme, see Ernesto Cardenal, *Love* (Maryknoll, N.Y.: Orbis, 1981).

26. Robert McAfee Brown sees human rights as having a pretheological base and so providing a common ethical core that can be supported by all people. See his book, *Making Peace in the Global Village* (Philadelphia: Westminster, 1981), chap. 5.

27. See David Hollenbach, *Claims in Conflict: Retrieving and Renewing the Catholic Human Rights Tradition* (New York: Paulist, 1979), chap. 3.

28. Robert L. Heilbroner, *An Inquiry into the Human Prospect: Updated and Reconsidered for the 1980s* (New York: Norton, 1980), p. 19.

29. Tillich, *Systematic Theology*, vol. 3, p. 38.

30. For a discussion of the Jungian concept of personality development and personality disturbance, see Jolande Jacobi, *The Psychology of C. G. Jung*, new revised edition (New Haven: Yale University Press, 1962).

A similar discussion but from a Freudian perspective is provided by Karen Horney, *Our Inner Conflicts: A Constructive Theory of Neurosis* (New York: Norton, 1966).

31. The confinement of minorities to prisons and ghettos is actually intensifying in the United States. Blacks make up less than 12% of the overall population, but they comprise almost 50% of the prison population and over 50% of the persons executed since 1930. See *U.S.: A Statistical Portrait of the American People*, Andrew Hacker, ed. (New York: Viking, 1983), pp. 228–32.

Likewise, more than 50% of the American Black population lives in inner-city areas. A mid-1970s study by Karl E. Taeuber ("Racial Segregation: The Persisting Dilemma," in *City Scenes: Problems and Prospects*, 2nd edition, J. John Palen, ed. [Boston: Little, Brown, 1981], pp. 159–67) shows that residential segregation is still primarily a product of racial discrimination, not economics.

32. For a discussion of the effects of this dualism in creating a destructive culture, see Donna Warnock, "Patriarchy Is a Killer: What People Concerned about Peace and Justice Should Know," in *Reweaving the Web: Feminism and Nonviolence*, Pam McAllister, ed. (Philadelphia: New Society Publishers, 1982), pp. 20–29, and Leslie Cagan, "Feminism and Militarism," in *Beyond Survival: New Directions for the Disarmament Movement*, Michael Albert and David Dillinger, eds. (Boston: South End Press, 1983), pp. 81–118.

33. Søren Kierkegaard, in his *The Sickness Unto Death*, provides a compelling notion of the self as being a relationship rather than a particular component or function of our humanity: *Fear and Trembling and Sickness Unto Death* (Princeton University Press, 1968), esp. pp. 146–54. Bernard Häring holds a similar notion of the self; see his *Free and Faithful in Christ*, vol. 1: *General Moral Theology* (New York: Seabury, 1978), esp. pp. 234–43.

34. This description of the life cycle is drawn from Erik H. Erikson's, *The Life Cycle Completed: A Review* (New York: Norton, 1982), esp. chap. 3. Bernard Häring makes use of Erikson's notion of the life cycles in his own discussion of moral development; see *Free and Faithful*, vol. 1, pp. 168–77 and 243–44.

35. Tillich, *Systematic Theology*, vol. 3, p. 34.

36. Ibid, p. 33.

37. Bernard Häring, *Free and Faithful*, vol. 1, p. 234.

38. For an elaboration of the idea of God's enrichment through relationship to the world, see John B. Cobb, Jr., *God and the World* (Philadelphia: Westminster, 1974).

39. Augustine, *City of God*, David Knowles, ed. (Baltimore: Pelican, 1972), p. 502.

40. See Stephen Sapp, *Sexuality, the Bible, and Science* (Philadelphia: Fortress, 1977), pp. 32–34.

41. See Barbara Ehrenreich and Frances Fox Piven, "The Feminization of Poverty," *Dissent*, vol. 31, no. 2 (1984) 162–70, and Gertrude Goldberg and Eleanor Kremen, "The Feminization of Poverty: Only in America?," *Social Policy* (Spring 1987) 3–14.

42. For a discussion of the importance of this equalitarian view of the persons of the Trinity, see Harold Ditmanson, *Grace in Experience and Theology* (Minneapolis: Augsburg, 1977), pp. 82–94.

43. I am adopting Walter Kaufmann's use of "I/You" as being more consistent with the meaning intended by Martin Buber than is his "I/Thou." See Martin Buber, *I and Thou* with Prologue and Note by Walter Kaufmann (New York: Scribner's, 1970), pp. 14–18.

44. Buber, *I and Thou*, p. 60.

45. This line is from Holly Near's song, "Unity," *Speed of Light* (Oakland: Redwood Records).

46. The work and spirit of Saint Francis of Assisi represent the affirmation of the need to be in positive relationship with all that is. See, e.g., *Brother Francis: An Anthology of Writings By and About St. Francis of Assisi*, Lawrence Cunningham, ed. (New York: Harper and Row, 1972).

47. H. Richard Niebuhr, *The Responsible Self: An Essay in Christian Moral Philosophy* (New York: Harper and Row, 1963), p. 124.

48. Beverly Harrison, *Making the Connections: Essays in Feminist Social Ethics* (Boston: Beacon, 1986), p. 263.

49. On the role of psychotherapy in contributing to our wholeness, see Paul Tillich, *The Courage to Be* (New Haven: Yale University Press, 1965), chap. 3, and "The Theological Significance of Existentialism and Psychoanalysis," in *Theology of Culture* (London: Oxford University Press, 1969), pp. 112–26.

See also David E. Roberts, *Psychotherapy and a Christian View of Man* (New York: Scribner's, 1950), and Charles Curran, "Moral Theology, Psychiatry, and Homosexuality," *Transition and Tradition in Moral Theology* (University of Notre Dame Press, 1979), pp. 59–81.

50. For a good analysis of Niebuhr's position in comparison with liberation theology, see Dennis P. McCann, *Christian Realism and Liberation*

Theology: Practical Theologies in Creative Conflict (Maryknoll, N.Y.: Orbis, 1981).

51. A very helpful book in this area is that by Kathleen and James McGinnis, *Parenting for Peace and Justice* (Maryknoll, N.Y.: Orbis, 1981).

52. For a good discussion on regulating industry from inside, see Christopher D. Stone, *Where the Law Ends: The Social Control of Corporate Behavior* (New York: Harper and Row, 1976).

53. The idea of developing a "sustainable" world order has been at the center of the World Council of Churches' discussion for the last decade. See, e.g., *Faith, Science, and the Future*, Paul Abrecht, ed. (Philadelphia: Fortress, 1979). Lester Brown has also developed this theme in his book, *Building a Sustainable Society* (New York: Norton, 1981).

54. Paul Tillich, *The Eternal Now* (New York: Scribner's, 1963), p. 32.

55. Letty Russell has written a number of volumes that use the theme of partnership as the key to understanding authentic human development. She does an excellent job of relating this concept to its biblical and theological roots. In the process she articulates a rich notion of what it means to be human. See her *The Future of Partnership* (Philadelphia: Westminster, 1979), and *Growth in Partnership* (Philadelphia: Westminster, 1981).

56. For a discussion of alternative views of money, knowledge, and power, see Anne Wilson Schaef, *Women's Reality: An Emerging Female System in the White Male Society* (Minneapolis: Winston, 1981), pp. 99–146.

6. MORAL DEVELOPMENT AND RESPONSIBLE EXISTENCE

1. See Lewis Thomas, "How to Fix the Premedical Curriculum," in *The Medusa and the Snail: More Notes of a Biology Watcher* (Toronto: Bantam, 1979), pp. 113–17.

2. For a very graphic account of poverty in Brazil, see Peter L. Berger, *Pyramids of Sacrifice: Political Ethics and Social Change* (Garden City, N.Y.: Anchor Doubleday, 1976), chap. 5.

3. *World View 1982: An Economic and Geopolitical Yearbook* (Boston: South End Press, 1982), pp. 88–91.

4. The concept of "theonomy" is used throughout Tillich's work. For a good summary of the concept, see his *Systematic Theology* (New York and Evanston: Harper and Row, University of Chicago Press, 1967), vol. 3, pp. 249–66.

5. Paul Tillich, *The Protestant Era* (University of Chicago Press, 1957), pp. 56–57.

6. Ibid., p. 46.

7. Ibid.

8. Tillich, *Systematic Theology*, vol. 1, p. 86.

9. Charles Curran, *Themes in Fundamental Moral Theology* (University of Notre Dame Press, 1977), p. 58.

10. H. Richard Niebuhr, *The Responsible Self: An Essay in Christian Moral Philosophy* (New York: Harper and Row, 1963), p. 49.

11. Ibid., p. 52.

12. Charles Curran, *Moral Theology: A Continuing Journey* (University of Notre Dame Press, 1982), p. 45.

13. Niebuhr, *The Responsible Self*, pp. 60–61.

14. See Erik H. Erikson, *The Life Cycle Completed: A Review* (New York: Norton, 1982). In addition, pp. 105–6 contain a good bibliography of Erikson's works.

15. Gail Sheehy, *Passages: Predictable Crises of Adult Life* (New York: Bantam, 1977).

16. For a good summary of the views of Piaget and Kohlberg and a bibliography of their works, see Ronald Duska and Mariellen Whelan, *Moral Development: A Guide to Piaget and Kohlberg* (New York: Paulist, 1975).

17. Carol Gilligan, *In a Different Voice: Psychological Theory and Women's Development* (Harvard University Press, 1982).

18. James Fowler, *Stages of Faith: The Psychology of Human Development and the Quest for Meaning* (New York: Harper and Row, 1981).

19. Alasdair MacIntyre's influential work, *After Virtue: A Study in Moral Theory* (University of Notre Dame Press, 1981), has stimulated renewed interest in the virtues as the basis of morality. Stanley Hauerwas's early work, *Vision and Virtue: Essays in Christian Ethical Reflection* (University of Notre Dame Press, 1981), has reintroduced the concept of virtues into the discussion about the shape of Christian ethics.

20. For a survey of the important documents of monasticism, see Ray C. Petry, *A History of Christianity* (Englewood Cliffs, N.J.: Prentice Hall, 1962), chap. 7. For a broader discussion of the significance of religious movements for moral reform, see Ernst Troeltsch, *The Social Teachings of the Christian Churches*, vol. 1 (New York: Harper and Brothers, 1960), chap. 2, sec. 9.

21. For a brief summary of Wesley's movement, see John Dillenberger and Claude Welch, *Protestant Christianity Interpreted through Its Development* (New York: Scribner's, 1954), pp. 127–36. For a representative selection of his thought, see Waldo Beach and H. Richard Niebuhr, *Christian Ethics* (New York: Ronald Press, 1973), chap. 12.

22. In important respects, much of the conservative religious revival,

and its radical counterpart in the religious liberation movements, are primarily movements of moral reform. For the conservative movement, reform is associated with personal issues such as sexuality, alcohol and drug use. For the radical movement, it is associated with concerns for the reform of economic and political structures. For a good discussion of these related movements, see Harvey Cox, *Religion in the Secular City: Toward a Postmodern Theology* (New York: Simon and Schuster, 1984).

23. This is clearly evident in the temptation stories, where Jesus considers the possibility of being a successful messianic leader, but repudiates this role as being inconsistent with doing God's will. See, e.g., Donald B. Kraybill, *The Upside-Down Kingdom* (Scottdale, Pa.: Herald Press, 1978), pp. 41–94. The notion of a "servant" church is also central to the theologies of liberation that are emerging in the Two-Thirds World. The reconceptualization of the role of the church is, in part, an attempt to free the church from its historical role as a representative of colonial powers to that of a church responsive to the needs of the majority of the people. For a good account of this change, see Phillip Berryman, *Liberation Theology* (New York: Pantheon, 1987). Ronaldo Muñoz offers a good summary of this view of the church in "The Historical Vocation of the Church," in *Frontiers of Theology in Latin America*, Rosino Gibellini, ed. (Maryknoll, N.Y.: Orbis, 1979), pp. 151–62.

24. As if to reinforce the notion that the quest for personal goodness is secondary to his concern for doing God's will, Jesus repudiates the notion that he is "good." In the story of the rich young man who addresses Jesus as "Good Teacher," Jesus responds (Mark 10:18): "Why do you call me good? No one is good but God alone."

25. Leonardo Boff, *The Lord's Prayer: The Prayer of Integral Liberation* (Maryknoll, N.Y.: Orbis, 1983), p. 93.

26. Stanley Hauerwas is now representative of a movement whose major concern is that of creating a perfected Christian community that will elevate the rest of society through the power of its moral example. This is especially evident in his book *The Peaceable Kingdom: A Primer in Christian Ethics* (University of Notre Dame Press, 1983), esp. the last chapter.

27. On Luther's notion that our righteousness is merely imparted to us by God and that we remain sinners, see Gerhard Ebeling, *Luther: An Introduction to His Thought* (Philadelphia: Fortress, 1972), esp. chap. 7. In summarizing Luther's position, Ebeling states, "Thus the Christian is in himself and on the basis of his own powers a sinner; but at the same time, outside himself, on the basis of what God does, and in the sight of God in Christ, he is one who is righteous" (p. 122).

28. See "The Freedom of a Christian," in *Martin Luther: Selections*

from His Writings, John Dillenberger, ed. (Garden City, N.Y.: Doubleday, 1961), pp. 42–85.

29. Berryman, *Liberation Theology,* p. 78.

30. The aristocratic nature of the "ethics of virtue" is evident even in MacIntyre's work, *After Virtue,* which is an attempt to make the ethics of virtue compatible with the important values of modern culture. This is evident in both his repudiation of Marxism and his listing of "heroic societies," which include Greek, medieval, and Renaissance (p. 114). All three societies were very hierarchical in structure and produced cultures that placed little value on women or the common people, and made little reference to the lives or accomplishments of either. Rather, all three cultures were dominated by white males of the leisure class who viewed themselves as the models for human development.

31. See Jolande Jacobi, *The Psychology of C. G. Jung,* new revised edition (New Haven: Yale University Press, 1966), for a similar notion of self-development.

32. Bernard Häring draws on Karl Rahner's concept of the "fundamental option" as a means of describing the basic conversion and reorientation that must occur in our lives if we are to live according to God's purposes for us. This concept is found throughout Häring's work but receives its most systematic treatment in *Free and Faithful in Christ,* vol. 1: *General Moral Theology* (New York: Seabury, 1978), chap. 5.

33. Donald Evans' volume, *Struggle and Fulfillment: The Inner Dynamics of Religion and Morality* (Philadelphia: Fortress, 1981), is an excellent discussion of the importance of "basic trust" to the moral life. His work sees religious and moral development as informed by basic moral attitudes.

34. Ibid., p. 2.

35. Niebuhr, *Responsible Self,* p. 99. Bernard Häring views this conversion in a similar manner: "A fundamental option for God and good is a response to God's good creation and to his order of redemption which is everywhere present" (*Free and Faithful,* vol. 1, p. 195).

36. This principle is the foundational principle for all systems of ethics based on Reformation thought. For a good example of this principle at work, see Joseph Sittler, *The Structure of Christian Ethics* (Baton Rouge: Louisiana State University Press, 1958).

37. Saint John of the Cross, *Dark Night of the Soul* (Garden City, N.Y.: Image Books, 1959).

38. The work of Nietzsche is characterized by a heroic despair. His account of the "death of God" in *The Gay Science* carries overtones of fear. Similarly the works of Albert Camus, *The Rebel* and *The Myth of Sisyphus,* and that of Samuel Beckett, *Waiting for Godot,* carry much of the same despairing courage at living in a world without God.

On the other hand, much of the tenacity of belief evidenced in the revival of contemporary religious fundamentalism may be a subconscious effort to suppress the overwhelming feeling of living in a universe without God or meaning. The dynamics of such belief are presented in Eric Hoffer's *The True Believer* (New York: Harper and Row, 1951).

39. For Luther's brutal attack on the peasants, "Against the Robbing and Murdering Hordes of Peasants," see *Luther: Selected Political Writings*, J. M. Porter, ed. (Philadelphia: Fortress, 1974), pp. 85–88.

Robert McAfee Brown discusses this use of a double standard, especially as it applies to the use of violence in securing one's aims or protecting one's position, in *Religion and Violence: A Primer for White Americans* (Philadelphia: Westminster, 1973).

40. James H. Cone, *Black Theology and Black Power* (New York: Seabury, 1969), p. 139.

41. See Howard Zinn, *A People's History of the United States* (New York: Harper and Row, 1980), esp. chap. 11: "Robber Barons and Rebels." The chapter provides documentation on the mistreatment, and even murder, of workers on which the fortunes of families like the Carnegies and Rockefellers were built.

42. For a discussion of love as the drive toward reconciliation, see Paul Tillich, *Love, Power and Justice: Ontological Analyses and Applications* (London: Oxford University Press, 1974).

43. From *Black Theology: A Documentary History, 1966–1979*, Gayraud S. Wilmore and James H. Cone, eds. (Maryknoll, N.Y.: Orbis, 1979), p. 27.

44. For a sad and disturbing account of the self-hatred generated by our society's racism, see the study by William H. Grier and Price M. Cobbs, *Black Rage* (New York: Bantam, 1969).

45. Cone, *Black Theology*, p. 8.

46. Dorothee Sölle, *Revolutionary Patience* (Maryknoll, N.Y.: Orbis, 1977), p. 53.

47. Ibid., p. 54.

48. Major J. Jones, *Black Awareness: A Theology of Hope* (Nashville: Abingdon, 1971), p. 139.

49. See, e.g., Martin Luther King, Jr., *Why We Can't Wait* (New York: New American Library, 1964), esp. chap. 2 and 8. See also his sermon, "Loving Your Enemies," in *Strength to Love* (Philadelphia: Fortress, 1981), pp. 47–55.

50. Letty M. Russell, *The Future of Partnership* (Philadelphia: Westminster, 1979), p. 162.

51. Patricia Wilson-Kastner, *Faith, Feminism, and the Christ* (Philadelphia: Fortress, 1983), pp. 61–62.

52. The quote is from James Cone, in Wilmore and Cone, *Black Theology*, p. 363.

53. Cone, ibid., p. 445.

54. Cone, ibid.

7. CHRISTIAN ETHICS AND HUMAN COMMUNITIES

1. Clearly the West has experienced periods of social and political optimism. The Renaissance marks such a period, as do the late eighteenth and nineteenth centuries. Such periods, however, are set against a backdrop of pessimism. These more positive periods are always later criticized for their excessive optimism. This is evident in one use of the word "realism" in the West, where it is understood to mean that there is little real hope for significant social and political progress.

2. As Gene Sharp points out, *The Politics of Nonviolent Action, Volume 1: Power and Struggle* (Boston: Porter Sargent, 1973) this is the real power of nonviolent resistance. In the long run, no state or community can continue to function without the acquiescence of a large proportion of its members.

3. This was the inescapable conclusion reached by Emile Durkheim in his classic work, *Suicide: A Study in Sociology* (New York: Free Press, 1951), originally published in the early 1900s. Since then the social roots of "personal" problems have become an accepted sociological fact. See, e.g., Marshall B. Clinard, *Sociology of Deviant Behavior* (New York: Holt, Rinehart and Winston, 1963), or any basic sociology text.

4. For the effect of environment on disease, see Rick J. Carlson, *The End of Medicine* (New York: John Wiley, 1975), pp. 97–111, and André Gorz, *Ecology as Politics* (Boston: South End Press, 1980), chap. 4.

5. Dom Hélder Câmara, *The Desert Is Fertile* (Maryknoll, N.Y.: Orbis, 1982), p. 41.

6. See Robert N. Bellah, *The Broken Covenant: American Civil Religion in Time of Trial* (New York: Seabury, 1975), for a good account of the erosion of the concept of "social responsibility" in American culture.

7. This heavy emphasis on individualism was important in freeing persons from excessive institutional domination. However, it has become linked to a repressive political conservatism now used to protect the wealth and power of the privileged. See Philip Green's study, *The Pursuit of Inequality* (New York: Pantheon, 1981), for a discussion of the ways in which the ideology of "individualism" has now become a repressive force that hinders social reform.

8. See, e.g., Richard Hofstadter, *Social Darwinism in the United States, 1860–1915* (Philadelphia: University of Pennsylvania Press, 1945).

In her book, *The Just Demands of the Poor: Essays in Socio-Theology* (New York: Paulist, 1987), Marie Augusta Neal recognizes the continued power of Social Darwinist ideology in our culture. She sees the developing sociobiology movement as a refinement of this more basic ideology. See esp. chap. 3 and 4.

9. See Frances Fox Piven and Richard A. Cloward, *The New Class War* (New York: Pantheon, 1982), chap. 2, for a discussion of the "new poverty" that occurs with the rise of the modern industrial state. The authors trace the disappearance of the ordinary persons' "subsistence rights" and the emergence of a more stark, brutal form of poverty than had existed in feudal and agrarian societies.

10. The stigmatization of the poor begins in Calvinist England and is continued in the punitive, suspicious attitude we have toward the poor. A good discussion of these attitudes is found in Mariellen Procopio and Frederick J. Perella, *Poverty Profile U.S.A.* (New York: Paulist, 1976), chap. 3. Bellah's *The Broken Covenant* provides a good account of our society's equation of success and virtuousness.

11. The concept is from the seventeenth-century philosopher Leibniz, and is based on the presumption that good and evil are intermingled in such a way that the best world necessarily includes some evil. In a more popular form it connotes the belief that existing evils represent the best possible compromise that can be made.

12. This is precisely the policy that has been reinstituted by the Reagan administration. It has severely curbed worker safety laws and environmental protection laws in order to create a "better business climate." See Robert Lekachman, *Greed Is Not Enough* (New York: Pantheon, 1982), chap. 4, and Victor W. Sidel, "Health Care: Privatization, Privilege, Pollution, and Profit," in *What Reagan Is Doing to Us*, Alan Gartner, Colin Greer, and Frank Riessman, eds. (New York: Harper and Row, 1982). The Reagan policy here, as in so many other areas, is based upon a return to a philosophy grounded in the premises of Social Darwinism.

13. In *Rockefeller Medicine Men: Medicine and Capitalism in America* (Berkeley: University of California Press, 1979) Richard Brown demonstrates that corporate support for modern medicine begins as a response to criticisms that modern industry, through unsafe working conditions and pollution of the environment, has become a major cause of illness. The building of a medical infrastructure is intended to diffuse some of this criticism.

14. Economic instability, low wages, and the failure of our economy to generate enough jobs for all remain the major causes of poverty in the United States. Two and a half million poor families are headed by workers who are employed year round but whose income falls below the poverty

line. Most of the poor in our nation move in and out of poverty depending on the growth or decline of the economy. Our government now recognizes the inability of our economy to generate sufficient jobs, as is evident by its adoption of a "full employment unemployment rate"—that is, a rate of unemployment that is the best our nation can achieve. In 1979, this rate was set at 7%; when operating at its capacity our economic system can no longer provide jobs for 1 of every 14 workers. See Michael Harrington, *Decade of Decision: The Crisis of the American System* (New York: Simon and Schuster, 1980), pp. 89–96 and 225–31.

15. On Augustine's role in the persecution of the Donatists, see Frederick A. Norwood, *Strangers and Exiles: A History of Religious Refugees* (Nashville: Abingdon, 1969), vol. 1, pp. 123–29. For Augustine's own views on the necessity for maintaining the purity and universality of the church, see his *Commonitorium.*

16. See J. M. Porter, ed., *Luther: Selected Political Writings* (Philadelphia: Fortress, 1974), pp. 85–88: "Against the Robbing and Murdering Hordes of Peasants."

17. There is little doubt that the profound split between the public and the personal, which is part of Lutheran heritage, was a contributing factor in the acceptance of the Nazi state in Germany. See José Míguez Bonino, *Toward a Christian Political Ethic* (Philadelphia: Fortress, 1983), chap. 2.

18. For an account of the Radical Reformation, which gave rise to such groups as the Quakers and Mennonites, see Franklin H. Littell, *The Origins of Sectarian Protestantism* (New York: Macmillan, 1972).

19. Women were accorded higher status in these sectarian communities, and most of the communities made no distinction between clergy and laity, leaders and led, or rich and poor. In addition, these communities were early leaders of the antislavery movement and proclaimed a doctrine of the equality of all persons. See Rosemary Radford Ruether, *The Radical Kingdom: The Western Experience of Messianic Hope* (New York: Paulist, 1970), chap. 2.

20. For an extensive treatment of this tragic history, see Norwood's *Strangers and Exiles*, vol. 1 and 2.

21. An important religious group in Jesus' time was that of the Essenes. They withdrew into "pure" communities in order to live a more strict and perfect form of the Jewish faith. John the Baptist is generally regarded to have been a member of this movement and many of Jesus' teachings show the influences of this tradition. Nevertheless, Jesus chose to live among the people, advocating a change in personal and social relationships among the general population rather than withdrawing into a "pure" community.

22. I will treat both Christian realism and liberation theology in greater detail in chap. 8.

23. The effects of professional training programs and peer group pressures on altering persons' lifestyles and values is dramatic. Several good studies of the effects of such socialization on professionals are those by Rosabeth Moss Kanter, *Men and Women of the Corporation* (New York: Basic Books, 1977), and Magoli Sarfatti Larson, *The Rise of Professionalism: A Sociological Analysis* (Berkeley: University of California Press, 1977).

24. For a good discussion of the scope of the transformation required, see Donald B. Kraybill's account of the Zacchaeus story in the Gospel of Luke; *The Upside Down Kingdom* (Scottdale, Pa.: Herald Press, 1978), pp. 131–33.

25. Juan Luis Segundo, *The Liberation of Theology* (Maryknoll, N.Y.: Orbis, 1976), p. 3.

26. Ibid.

27. See John C. Bennett, *Christianity and Communism Today* (New York: Association Press, 1962), esp. chap. 2; and José Míguez Bonino, *Doing Theology in a Revolutionary Situation* (Philadelphia: Fortress, 1975), esp. chap. 1.

28. This is the task of applied ethics and requires the extensive use of historical and social scientific data. The challenge is relating the vision and principles of Christianity to the forms of our community life. Numerous works have been done in this area. A few examples include: James B. Nelson, *Embodiment: An Approach to Sexuality and Christian Theology* (Minneapolis: Augsburg, 1978), which discusses the form of our sexual communities; Robert L. Stivers, *The Sustainable Society: Ethics and Economic Growth* (Philadelphia: Westminster, 1976); J. Philip Wogaman, *The Great Economic Debate: An Ethical Analysis* (Philadelphia: Westminster, 1977), which attempts to give shape to our economic communities; Gerald and Patricia Mische, *Toward a Human World Order: Beyond the National Security Straitjacket* (New York: Paulist, 1977), which attempts to provide a pattern for our world community. Papal encyclicals, such as *Pacem in Terris, Populorum Progressio,* and *Laborem Exercens,* as well as the two pastoral letters by the U. S. Catholic bishops, *The Challenge of Peace* and *Economic Justice for All,* are important attempts to provide guidance from a Christian perspective for the restructuring of our economic and political orders.

29. For a discussion of this principle and its importance as an ethical concept, see John A. Coleman, *An American Strategic Theology* (New York: Paulist, 1982), esp. pp. 224–33, and J. Philip Wogaman, *A Christian Method of Moral Judgment* (Philadelphia: Westminster, 1976), pp. 142–44.

30. See his *Professional Ethics and Civic Morals* (Glencoe, Ill.: Free Press, 1958).

31. See, e.g., Peter L. Berger and Richard John Neuhaus, *To Empower People: The Role of Mediating Structures in Public Policy* (Washington, D.C.: American Enterprise Institute, 1977), and Fritjof Capra and Catherine Spretnak, *Green Politics* (New York: Dutton, 1984). The similarity of the positions advocated is striking in view of the fact that Berger and Neuhaus have been generally aligned with the "new conservatism" in the United States, whereas Capra and Spretnak view themselves as part of a movement for the "radical" transformation of Western societies.

32. "States rights" became part of a movement for local autonomy in order to allow states to avoid compliance with federal civil rights laws. More recently, under the label of "the new federalism," it is part of a strategy for a conservative political realignment and a tool for allowing localities to escape federal environmental, welfare, and educational regulation. See Gartner *et al.*, *What Reagan Is Doing to Us*, esp. pp. 1-23, 71-86, 109-24, and 230-48.

33. See John Kenneth Galbraith, *Economics and the Public Purpose* (New York: New American Library, 1973), esp. chap. 8.

34. Charles Curran, *Moral Theology: A Continuing Journey* (University of Notre Dame Press, 1982), p. 50.

35. See, e.g., Aquinas and the *Summa Theologica*, II-II, question 66; or Calvin and Luther's treatment of the Seventh Commandment, "Thou shalt not steal." See also Robert McAfee Brown, *Making Peace in the Global Village* (Philadelphia: Westminster, 1981), esp. chap. 5, and Larry L. Rasmussen, *Economic Anxiety and Christian Faith* (Minneapolis: Augsburg, 1981), esp. chap. 8.

36. For an excellent discussion of the biblical concept of property and its implications for the relationship of the rich and poor, see Walter E. Pilgrim, *Good News to the Poor: Wealth and Poverty in Luke-Acts* (Minneapolis: Augsburg, 1981); Conrad Boerma, *The Rich, the Poor and the Bible* (Philadelphia: Westminster, 1979); Robert Gnuse, *You Shall Not Steal: Community and Property in the Biblical Tradition* (Maryknoll, N.Y.: Orbis, 1985).

37. The parable of the workers in the vineyard (Matt. 20:1-16) is a classic example of the right of God to distribute resources for the good of persons rather than according to our usual notions of justice. The papal encyclical *Laborem Exercens* by John Paul II, continues this tradition with its recognition that work and the distribution of resources are to be based upon principles that assure the good of all persons and not simply the enrichment of a few.

38. E. F. Schumacher, *Small Is Beautiful: Economics As If People Mattered* (New York: Harper and Row, 1973).

39. See José Miranda, *Marx Against the Marxists* (Maryknoll, N.Y.:

Orbis, 1980). Beverly Harrison is right that Marxist analysis is a necessary tool for understanding and criticizing the contemporary capitalist economic order. As she indicates of Marxism, "We need to appreciate the superiority of the radical paradigm on this point as well as other points identified here. Concern for the basic material well-being that is at the heart of an adequate economic ethic can become a matter of moral urgency as we escape a mood of economic determinism" (*Making the Connections: Essays in Feminist Social Ethics* [Boston: Beacon, 1986], p. 77).

40. Jack Nelson in *Hunger for Justice* (Maryknoll, N.Y.: Orbis, 1980), writes: "Generally, the countries most seriously affected by the world food crises have three things in common. First, their economies are firmly integrated into the international free-enterprise system. Second, their economic production is geared to international markets and is based on the principle of comparative advantage. And third, their domestic economies are free-enterprise economies" (p. 10).

Certainly most Marxist countries remain poor by our standards, but the more equitable distribution of resources means that hunger and malnutrition are less serious problems in some Marxist countries. Cuba is one of the few Latin American countries, and China is one of the few Asian countries, without a serious hunger problem.

41. See Wogaman, *Great Economic Debate*, chap. 8.

42. See ibid. and Stivers, *Sustainable Society.*

43. Nelson, *Hunger for Justice*, chap. 2, and Arthur Simon, *Bread for the World* (New York: Paulist, 1975), pp. 39–46.

44. See Frances Moore Lappe and Joseph Collins, *Food First* (New York: Ballantine, 1979).

45. See Rick J. Carlson, *The End of Medicine* (New York: John Wiley, 1975), pp. 47–62. He writes: "Thirty million people die of starvation alone every year—one every second. Schistosomiasis, cholera, malaria, and diarrhea can be curbed and in many cases eliminated. The technology to control the disease is known. Nonetheless, millions of people suffer and die from them. In the United States, thousands of dollars are spent to install one cardiovascular care unit for treatment of myocardial infarction—a disease more common in highly developed countries—with less than spectacular results" (p. 54).

The disparity is even more apparent in the realm of research. Ten million persons a year suffer from cancer and over \$1 billion are spent in the United States alone each year on research, with moderate result to date. On the other hand, over two billion persons are affected by schistosomiasis, malaria, filariosis, amebiosis, and ascariosis, all fatal or crippling illnesses. Worldwide research funding for all these diseases is less than \$10 million (*Medical Tribune*, March 12, 1980).

46. Jonathan Kozol, *The Night Is Dark and I Am Far from Home: A Political Indictment of the U.S. Public Schools* (New York: Continuum, 1980).

47. In traditional societies, life is more of a whole, with work being an integral part of one's daily activity. It is only in modern societies that work becomes a separate component often unrelated to a person's interests or concerns. However, we are moving into a period when we simply do not need everyone to be involved in so-called productive work, and where, in fact, there is a growing shortage of jobs. We may be facing a future where there is more "leisure" time and also the necessary resources to allow persons to pursue their own interests once again and to reintegrate their work back into their lives. See, e.g., the collection of essays, *Technology, Human Values and Leisure*, Max Kaplan and Phillip Bosserman, eds. (Nashville: Abingdon, 1971).

48. Jonathan Schell, *The Fate of the Earth* (New York: Knopf, 1982), p. 116.

49. Studs Terkel, *Working* (New York: Avon, 1975), p. xiii.

50. Such an approach draws upon the work of Paulo Freire, whose basic philosophy is developed in *Pedagogy of the Oppressed* (New York: Seabury, 1968). The concept of "conscientization" (gaining a critical awareness of one's situation) is central to his approach.

51. Terkel, *Working*, p. xxviii.

52. The collection of essays by Pam McAllister, *Reweaving the Web of Life: Feminism and Nonviolence* (Philadelphia: New Society Publishers, 1982), provides a wonderful insight into the ways in which our lives can be made "all of a piece," a coherent whole that expresses our fundamental beliefs and values.

53. Neal, *Just Demands*, p. 108.

54. Common Cause, a citizens' lobby group, has worked for many years to limit the influence of special interest groups. Its report, *Common Cause Magazine*, is an excellent source of information on the money spent by these various lobbies to influence the governmental process. It also provides information on donations to particular politicians and a review of their voting records. Many of the correlations are striking.

55. This is the central thesis of Piven and Cloward's work, *The New Class War*.

56. See Galbraith, *Economics and the Public Purpose*, or Michael Harrington's *Decade of Decision*.

57. Piven and Cloward, *New Class War*, view much of the legislation in the areas of welfare, job safety, and environmental regulation as democratic (popular) responses to the corporate abuse of power. According to them, the Reagan administration represents the attempt by corpo-

rate powers to reassert their total control over the workings of the economy. See also Frank Ackerman, *Reaganomics: Rhetoric or Reality* (Boston: South End Press, 1982).

58. See Piven and Cloward, *New Class War*, esp. chap. 5.

59. See Lester Thurow, *The Zero-Sum Society: Distribution and the Possibilities for Economic Change* (New York: Penguin, 1981), chap. 1, 7, and 8. Thurow shows convincingly that the level of economic inequality in our society is totally unnecessary even if one presumes a need for unequal rewards in order to motivate persons. As he shows, many nations in the world exceed the productivity rates of the United States, but have a much more equal distribution of salaries and wealth.

60. This is one of the insights of the Amerindian tradition, which our culture needs badly to recover. It is also a fundamental theme in J. R. R. Tolkien's trilogy, *The Lord of the Rings*. Loss of contact with the elemental forces of nature is viewed by him as one of the main reasons why our society is becoming spiritually impoverished and destructive. John Hart, in his *The Spirit of the Earth: A Theology of the Land* (New York: Paulist, 1984), intertwines the insight and sensitivity of Amerindian traditions with the Judeo-Christian tradition. The result provides a significant framework for developing an ecological ethic toward the land.

61. Lewis Mumford, *The City in History: Its Origins, Its Transformations, and Its Prospects* (New York: Harcourt, Brace, and World, 1961), sees the need to reestablish contact with the natural rhythms of life. He feels that the artificial rhythms of the urban environment are destroying our humanity. He draws on a rich tradition of urban planners, including Peter Kropotkin and Ebenezer Howard and their "garden cities," and Patrick Geddes and his idea of "greenbelts."

62. Nuclear deterrence is often hailed as successful because there have been no "major" wars in over forty years. Such a view, however, shows our cultural egocentricity: in fact, there have, been numerous "major" wars, but none that have pitted Western nations against one another. In addition, such a view overlooks the way in which Third World nations have been used as pawns in numerous local conflicts as the two superpowers have fought to gain global domination. Since 1945, over sixty wars have been fought and over 16 million persons have been killed in them; see Ruth Leger Sivard, *World Military and Social Expenditures* (Washington, D.C.: World Priorities, 1986). Such statistics hardly support the claim that nuclear deterrence has brought an era of peace and stability to world affairs.

63. Sivard's *World Military and Social Expenditures* provides overwhelming documentation on the waste of resources on weapons and the resulting unnecessary suffering because of our continued investment in

"things of death" rather than life. For example (pp. 32–33), the world in 1983 spent almost one-third more on military expenses ($728 billion) than on health care ($545 billion) and over fifteen times as much on military expenses as on foreign economic aid to helping developing countries ($37.4 billion). In 1986 world military expenditures reached nearly $900 billion (p. 8).

64. Acknowledgment of this fact has been the source of numerous United Nations sessions and conferences and, in 1973, led to a call for a New International Economic Order. For a good summary of the discussion of changes needed in the international economic system, see the articles in section 5 of *Toward a Just World Order*, vol. 1, Richard Falk, Samuel S. Kim, and Saul H. Mendlovitz, eds. (Boulder, Colo.: Westview Press, 1982).

65. There is an obvious need for a growing reliance on existing institutions like the World Court and the United Nations. A good collection of essays on the need for, possibilities of, and shortcomings of our international system of law is found in *International Law and a Just World Order*, vol. 2, Richard Falk, Friedrich V. Kratchowil, and Saul H. Mendlovitz, eds. (Boulder, Colo.: Westview Press, 1984).

66. Certainly there will be strains on our economic systems as we shift to a "peaceful" economy. However, careful planning can prevent major economic disruption. Ackerman, *Reaganomics*, chap. 4, discusses the effects of excessive military spending on our economy, and, in chap. 8, discusses some strategies for conversion to a "peace" economy.

The classic treatment of this theme remains Seymour Melmam's *The Permanent War Economy: American Capitalism in Decline* (New York: Simon and Schuster, revised edition, 1985).

8. EMBODYING OUR VISIONS

1. For a listing, see James F. Childress, "Just-War Criteria," in *War or Peace?: The Search for New Answers*, Thomas A. Shannon, ed. (Maryknoll, N.Y.: Orbis, 1980), pp. 40–58. As Childress points out, only very limited conditions make war "just" according to this moral theory for there is a "moral presumption against force and war."

2. See, e.g., Robert McAfee Brown, *Religion and Violence: A Primer for White Americans* (Philadelphia: Westminster, 1973), pp. 60–61.

3. Reinhold Niebuhr's most important work in this area is *Moral Man and Immoral Society* (New York: Scribner's, 1932).

4. It is quite clear from his sermons and writing that Rauschenbusch understood many of the social causes of war, poverty, and dehumanization that were operative in early modern industrial society. Likewise, he under-

stood the difficulty of social reform and was not certain that such reform could ever be achieved. It is unfortunate that he is often dismissed along with other more naive figures of the Social Gospel movement as being too simplistic in his analyses and too optimistic in his predictions for the future. See, e.g., chap.1 of *A Theology for the Social Gospel* (Nashville: Abingdon, 1945), where he writes: "We are told that the environment has no saving power; regeneration is what men need; we can not have a regenerate society without regenerate individuals, . . . These half-truths are the proper product of a half-way system of theology in which there is no room for social redemption"(p. 8).

5. Walter Rauschenbusch, "The New Apostolate," in *The Social Gospel in America, 1870–1920*, Robert T. Handy, ed. (New York: Oxford University Press, 1966), p. 337.

6. See Howard Zinn, *A People's History of the United States* (New York: Harper and Row, 1980), chap. 11.

7. This is also the era when settlement houses began and organizations like the Salvation Army and the YMCA were founded, all with the purpose of aiding those caught in the crush of urban industrial life. Such organizations were, however, for the purpose of rendering aid, not for the purpose of reforming society.

8. There was a small socialist movement in the United States at the time, but it never became as influential as it did in Europe and was rejected by the mainstream of reformers at the time. See Michael Harrington, *Socialism* (New York: Bantam, 1972), chap. 6.

9. This is the central thesis of chaps. 2 and 3 of Niebuhr's *Moral Man and Immoral Society.*

10. Ibid., p. 210.

11. This "realistic" approach to world affairs is, of course, the cornerstone on which the modern strategy of nuclear deterrence is built. Hence, the plausibility of nuclear deterrence stands or falls with one's belief concerning the adequacy of "realism" as an ideology.

12. Again, the masculine is used intentionally. Running throughout the era was a general belief that women were innately more peaceful and compassionate, and so had a special role in helping to transform the "hearts of men."

13. *Moral Man and Immoral Society* was quite a radical book, advocating the need for significant political and economic restructuring as well as suggesting that violence might be a morally acceptable method for accomplishing such change.

14. Recent works that use "realism" in this way include: Robert Benne, *The Ethic of Democratic Capitalism* (Philadelphia: Fortress, 1981); Ernest W. Lefever, *Amsterdam to Nairobi: The World Council of Churches and*

the Third World (Washington, D.C.: Ethics and Public Policy Center, 1979); Michael Novak, *The Spirit of Democratic Capitalism* (New York: Simon and Schuster, 1982); idem, *Liberation South, Liberation North* (Washington, D.C.: American Enterprise Institute, 1981); Richard J. Neuhaus, *The Naked Public Square: Religion and Democracy in America* (Grand Rapids: Eerdmans, 1984).

15. Liberation theology is actually a number of movements that share a common concern for the liberation of the whole person. It first came to prominence in the United States with the emergence of black and feminist theologies and with the publication of the work of several Latin American theologians, most notably Gustavo Gutiérrez and Juan Luis Segundo. Variations on the liberationist perspective, however, have appeared among many groups of oppressed peoples. Orbis Books is an excellent source for the works of the many liberation movements.

16. Rosemary Radford Ruether, *The Radical Kingdom: The Western Experience of Messianic Hope* (New York: Paulist, 1970), p. 129.

17. See, e.g., Erling Jorstad, *The Politics of Moralism: The New Christian Right in America* (Minneapolis: Augsburg, 1981), or Harvey Cox, *Religion in the Secular City: Toward a Postmodern Theology* (New York: Simon and Schuster, 1984), part 1.

18. Howard Zinn, *The Twentieth Century: A People's History* (New York: Harper and Row, 1984).

19. Sharon D. Welch, *Communities of Resistance and Solidarity: A Feminist Theology of Liberation* (Maryknoll, N.Y.: Orbis, 1985), p. 89.

20. Robert Heilbroner's *An Inquiry Into the Human Prospect, Updated and Reconsidered for the 1980s* (New York: Norton, 1980) provides a stark reminder that the "crises" of the 1960s and 70s remain very much with us even though our consciousness of them has diminished. In fact, our failure to really face these problems has made our prospects of solving or surviving them even less certain.

21. For a discussion of this ultimate, international form of terrorism, see Richard Barnet, "Ultimate Terrorism: The Real Meaning of Nuclear Strategies," in *Waging Peace: A Handbook for the Struggle to Abolish Nuclear Weapons*, Jim Wallis, ed. (San Francisco: Harper and Row, 1982), pp. 25–31.

22. The collection of essays by George F. Kennan, *The Nuclear Delusion: Soviet-American Relations in the Atomic Age* (New York: Pantheon, 1983), begins with essays from 1950 and ends with those from 1982. The essays, by one of the most knowledgeable persons in the field, present the vision of a slow, inevitable march toward nuclear annihilation, a march made inevitable by wasted opportunities for disarmament and unnecessarily belligerent confrontations between the two superpowers.

23. See Bernard Häring, *The Healing Power of Peace and Nonviolence* (New York: Paulist, 1986), p. 47, for a similar reversal of the understanding of the term "realism." Here he claims that only those who practice the radical nonviolence of Jesus are truly realists.

24. The debate concerning the right to medical care is a complicated one that must address the relative importance of this right in comparison with other rights such as the right to food or to education. Attention must also be given to the fact that medical needs and wants seem to expand with advancing medical knowledge and consumer expectations. These are important issues, but ones I am excluding from consideration in this section because they are not relevant to the discussion here. I am making the case for the right to basic, adequate medical care in a society that has abundant resources for meeting these needs. For a good overview of this spectrum of issues, see Charles Curran, "The Right to Health Care and Distributive Justice," in *Transition and Tradition in Moral Theology* (University of Notre Dame Press, 1979), pp. 139-70.

25. Ibid., p. 153.

26. Health care is one of the rights recognized in the United Nations' Declaration on Human Rights. Charles Curran grounds this right in the person's relationship to God. See his *Transition and Tradition*, p. 150.

27. Frank Ackerman, *Hazardous to Our Wealth: Economic Policies in the 1980s* (Boston: South End Press, 1984), p. 122.

28. Paul Starr, *The Social Transformation of American Medicine* (New York: Basic Books, 1982), p. 422.

29. Ackerman, *Hazardous to Our Wealth*, p. 122.

30. See Andrew Hacker, ed., *U.S.: A Statistical Portrait of the American People* (New York: Viking, 1983), and *World View 1982: An Economic and Geopolitical Yearbook* (Boston: South End Press, 1982).

31. For an account of the history preceding and including the implementation of these programs, see Starr, *Social Transformation*, esp. book 2.

32. See Mark Green, *Winning Back America* (Toronto: Bantam, 1982), p. 191; Spencer Klaw, *The Great American Medicine Show* (New York: Penguin, 1976), pp. 1-2; and Michael Harrington, *The New American Poverty* (New York: Penguin, 1984), p. 50.

33. See Harrington, *New American Poverty*, p. 198.

34. Ibid., p. 50.

35. See E. Richard Brown, "Medicare and Medicaid: Band-Aid for the Old and Poor," in *Reforming Medicine: Lessons of the Last Quarter Century*, Victor W. and Ruth Sidel, eds. (New York: Pantheon, 1984), p. 65.

36. See Klaw, *The Great American Medicine Show*, pp. 52-53. In addition, Brown, "Medicare and Medicaid" (p. 64), reports that nation-

ally, 20% of all physicians treat no Medicaid patients at all, and that 6% of all physicians treat one-third of all Medicaid patients.

37. See Starr, *Social Transformation*, p. 386.

38. Ibid, p. 448.

39. See Klaw, *Great American Medicine Show*, pp. 19–23. See also, Rocio Huet-Cox, "Medical Education: New Wine in Old Wine Skins," in Sidd, eds., *Reforming Medicine*, pp. 129–49, and Starr, *Social Transformation*, pp. 271–89, 333–78, and 421–25.

40. See Ackerman, *Hazardous to Our Wealth*, p. 123. South Africa does, however, guarantee medical care to all its white citizens.

41. Bernard Häring, *Free and Faithful in Christ,* vol. 3: *Light to the World* (New York: Crossroad, 1981), p. 50.

42. See Curran, *Transition and Tradition*, p. 160.

43. See Harrington, *New American Poverty*, p. 51, and Ackerman, *Hazardous to Our Wealth*, p. 123.

44. Strategic weapons are long-range delivery systems such as intercontinental ballistic missiles and long-range bombers, which can deliver nuclear warheads directly from one superpower to the other. In addition, each of the superpowers has between 20,000 and 30,000 short-range (tactical) nuclear weapons, most of which are larger than the warheads dropped on Hiroshima and Nagasaki. A good source of data, definitions, and historical background is available in *Nuclear War: What's in It for You*, compiled by Ground Zero, a nonpartisan educational organization (New York: Pocket Books, 1982).

45. Ibid, Appendix C, Table C–1.

46. See Jonathan Schell, *The Fate of the Earth* (New York: Knopf, 1982), pp. 26–28, and Nigel Calder, *Nuclear Nightmares: An Investigation into Possible Wars* (New York: Penguin, 1981), pp. 140–41.

47. Currently six nations—the United States, Great Britain, France, China, the Soviet Union, and India—are known to have nuclear weapons. Israel and South Africa are suspected of having nuclear weapons and Pakistan is openly trying to develop them. In addition, twenty-five other nations have a nuclear potential and could probably develop nuclear weapons if they chose to do so. Such proliferation of nuclear weapons will create an incredibly volatile, almost uncontrollable, international political climate. See Ground Zero, *Nuclear War*, chap. 17, and Calder, *Nuclear Nightmares*, chap. 3.

48. This is the conclusion of Fr. Robert F. Drinan, *Beyond the Nuclear Freeze* (New York: Seabury, 1983), and is supported by the conclusions of the United States' Catholic bishops' pastoral, *The Challenge of Peace*.

49. Schell, *Fate of the Earth*, p. 178.

50. Robert Jay Lifton and Richard Falk, *Indefensible Weapons: The*

Political and Psychological Case Against Nuclearism (New York: Basic Books, 1982), p. 3.

51. See Ruth Leger Sivard, *World Military and Social Expenditures*, (Washington, D.C.: World Priorities, 1986).

52. This quote provides the title for Dorothee Sölle's book, *The Arms Race Kills Even Without War* (Philadelphia: Fortress, 1983).

53. *The Challenge of Peace: God's Promise and Our Response* (Washington, D.C.: United States Catholic Conference, 1983), pp. 82–83.

54. The United States' Catholic bishops' pastoral, *The Challenge of Peace* (1983), concludes that deterrence as a policy is moral only if it is coupled with a serious pursuit of and program for disarmament. Since the United States has entered a period of record military expenditures, our national policy clearly violates the norm of the bishops' pastoral. For the text of the letter and a report on its history, politics, and significance, see Jim Castelli, *The Bishops and the Bomb* (Garden City, N.Y.: Doubleday, 1983).

55. Bernard Häring, *Healing Power*, p. 81.

56. Ibid., chap. 6 and 7, offers a good discussion and bibliography on strategies of nonviolent civilian defense. A similar discussion is found in Phillips Moulton, *Ammunition for Peacemakers: Answers for Activists* (New York: Pilgrim, 1986), chap. 5.

57. There is now an established body of study and literature labeled "peace studies." An excellent example with a very comprehensive bibliography is Samuel S. Kim's, *The Quest for a Just World Order* (Boulder, Colo.: Westview Press, 1984).

58. Abraham, the founder of the Jewish faith, was called by God to forsake his home and security, and to follow God into an unknown future. This leave-taking seems to be a common feature of the critical moments in the development of Judaism and the emergence of Christianity. Moses and the people of Israel must leave the security of Egypt. Jesus must leave his family and homeland on a journey whose end is uncertain. For the Abraham story, see Genesis, chap.11–25.

59. Ruth, a legendary figure in the Bible, leaves her people and her religion, after the death of her husband, to return with her mother-in-law to her mother-in-law's people. It is a moving example of a person's willingness to surrender her own precious beliefs and culture because of her love for another person. See the book of Ruth in the Old Testament.

Index